WHERE GARDEN MEETS WILDERNESS

Where Garden Meets Wilderness

Evangelical Entry
into the Environmental Debate

E. Calvin Beisner

Introduction by Rev. John Michael Beers

ACTON INSTITUTE FOR THE STUDY OF RELIGION AND LIBERTY
WILLIAM B. EERDMANS PUBLISHING COMPANY

Published jointly 1997 by the
Acton Institute for the Study of Religion and Liberty
161 Ottawa Avenue, NW, Suite 301
Grand Rapids, Michigan 49503
Phone: (616) 454-3080   Fax: (616) 454-9454
and by
Wm. B. Eerdmans Publishing Co.
255 Jefferson Ave. S.E., Grand Rapids, Michigan 49503 /
P.O. Box 163, Cambridge CB3 9PU U.K.

Printed in the United States of America

01 00 99 98 97   5 4 3 2 1

Library of Congress Cataloging-in-Publication Data

Eerdmans ISBN 0-8028-4434-0 (alk. paper)
Acton Institute ISBN 1-880595-09-5 (alk. paper)

To Grace Andrea Bronwyn

"Blessed are the meek,
for they shall inherit the earth."
Matthew 5:5

"To the mineral wealth of the planet, the torrent of energy which bathes it, and the rich diversity of organic life in which our bodies are enmeshed, we must add the fourth and (apart from our knowledge of God) greatest kind of wealth we have: that is, our ability to stand apart (in our consciousness) from the planet—to know it, to name it, to use it, and to see it whole. . . . Ultimately, then, it is that human capability to *know* and to create new things and methods with that knowledge, which is our greatest resource. Without it, none of the planet's other wealth—its mineral capital, its stored and incoming solar energy, its blooming and beautiful life—is wealth at all. The greatest resource is humanity itself, and the capabilities to know, structure, create, and accomplish which seem to distinguish humanity from the rest of creation.

". . . though the planet's wealth is undeniably great, its greatest wealth—the human capacity to know, change, and manipulate—is also the planet's greatest danger. . . . the values that guide our humanity and that inform our structures of use and exploitation need redeeming. And such redemption comes not from the earth, for all its wealth and beauty; it comes from beyond it, from its Creator."

—*Earthkeeping in the Nineties:*
Stewardship of Creation, 106

CONTENTS

❧ ❧

vii

ACKNOWLEDGMENTS

MANY PEOPLE HAVE ACTED AS IRON SHARPENING IRON WITH ME DUR-
ing the past ten years of the development of my understanding of environmental world view, theology, ethics, and science—far too many to name
them all. Special thanks, however, are due to:

• P. J. Hill, Jr., of Wheaton College, who not only has interacted with me
about these and other subjects through the years but patiently read the first
draft of this book and provided invaluable advice for improvement.

• Michael Cromartie, of the Ethics and Public Policy Center, who also
read the first draft and advised me how to improve it, and who generously
involved me in two Ethics and Public Policy Center conferences on environmental and population issues.

• Edwin Olson, of Whitworth College, who has discussed many of the
topics and ideas covered in this book with me by phone and correspondence,
and who strongly encouraged me to write the book.

• Julian L. Simon, of the University of Maryland, both for his many
insightful and provocative writings in the field and for his personal encouragement and instruction while we worked together on *The State of Humanity*.

• George K. Brushaber and other organizers of the Christianity Today
Institute on Population and Global Stewardship, who courageously invited
me to present a contrarian view at its conference in April 1994; the many
participants in that conference also sharpened my thinking through thoughtful questions.

• David Melvin and the National Association of Evangelicals, for including me among lecturers for two seminars on environment and population it

ix

held in the fall of 1994, where again I not only had the opportunity to present my views but also benefited from critical interaction with other lecturers and participants.

• Jerry Wenger, of Covenant College's biology department, for sitting in on a course I taught on population, economy, resources, and the environment and for helping me to improve my thinking through insightful questions and comments.

• Dean Ohlman, previously of Cornerstone College, now of Radio Bible Class, who despite strong disagreements corresponded graciously and thoughtfully with me over several issues discussed in this book.

• Ronald J. Sider, of Evangelicals for Social Action, who also, despite our disagreements, discussed some of these issues with me in a helpful way.

• Calvin DeWitt, of the Au Sable Institute and the University of Wisconsin, who through both his writings and our discussions and correspondence has stimulated my thinking, particularly about the cosmic effects of Christ's redeeming work.

• Edward C. Krug, who gave me many special insights into the mental habits of some environmentalists.

• Victor Porlier, conversations with whom sparked the initial idea for the book, and who assisted in acquiring the grant support necessary to make it happen.

• Howard Ahmanson and the Fieldstead Institute for generous financial support not only in this but also in other research and writing.

As always, I must express special thanks to my wife, Deborah, and to our children—David, Susan, Kilby, Rebekah, Peter, Arthur John, and Grace—for their patience during the many times when I have focused on this work at their expense. On this book as on every other, Debby has given me much wise counsel. Needless to say, I alone am responsible for the book's shortcomings.

E. Calvin Beisner
June 28, 1997

PREFACE

     🐦   🐦

N<small>O ONE IN</small> A<small>MERICA TODAY CAN IGNORE ENVIRONMENTALISM AS A</small> public issue. It permeates public discussion in the media, the schools, the political arena, and even our churches. It is entirely appropriate that evangelicals should join this discussion. We have special insights—theological, historical, and cultural—that enable us to contribute positively to environmental debate and understanding. It is reason for thanksgiving, therefore, to see the founding of organizations like the Evangelical Environmental Network, the Christian Environmental Association, and the Christian Society of the Green Cross.

At the same time that we should be thankful for this strong entrance of evangelicals into environmental discussion, we should also want good intentions to be coupled with sound thinking. *Caring* about the environment provides motivation, but to make our caring truly helpful we must understand the Biblical, theological, ecological, demographic, economic, and scientific principles and theories that provide foundation for environmental views and policies, and we must supply reliable data by which to flesh out the implications of the theories. Whatever one's opinions about environmentalism as a whole— and it is a multifaceted movement, some branches of which disagree strongly with others on a wide variety of issues—no one familiar with a broad range of technical and popular literature about the environment can miss the fact that many common perceptions about our environment are open to considerable debate.

It is with the hope of contributing positively to the evangelical part in environmental debates that I offer this book. I hope it will provide helpful food for thought not only for evangelicals who consider themselves environmentalists but for all evangelicals who care about the human responsibility to steward the earth in Christ's name. If it can be one of many factors helping to bring about an increasingly fruitful discussion by which evangelicals can identify means of enhancing global stewardship, my hopes will be satisfied.

INTRODUCTION

❧　　❧

"Peace! Be still!" (Mk. 4:39)

WITH THAT SIMPLE COMMAND, JESUS CHRIST SHOWS HIMSELF TO BE Lord of nature such that "even wind and sea obey Him." (Mk. 4:41) As Creator, He rightly addresses His creation and demands obedience. Likewise, the Genesis creation account portrays the Almighty as the One who brings order out of chaos.

Of all His good Creation, it is God's creation of mankind that completes the created order in such a way that He pronounces it to be "very good." (Gen. 1:31) Furthermore, the family of man alone is made in God's "image and likeness." (Gen. 1:26) And God's first command to mankind is "Be fruitful and multiply, and fill the earth and subdue it; and have dominion over the fish of the sea and over the birds of the air and over every living thing that moves upon the earth." (Gen. 1:28) Here, in the first chapter of the Bible, is the core text of Judeo-Christian belief: It is God who creates, human life is valued above all other life, and humanity is distinguished from the rest of Creation over which man is to hold dominion.

Jesus Christ, the "Word made flesh" (Jn. 1:14), stood silent before His accusers who ordered His crucifixion, yet He presumes to address the forces of nature and demands their silence: "Peace! Be still!" God creates, brings order, and demands peaceful quiet from His Creation, while it is left to man to "subdue and have dominion over" it. Herein lies the relationship of God and man: the Creator and the one created who cooperates in the divine *opus* of creation by making something of that entrusted to his "dominion."

All Christians who believe the *evangelium*, that is, the "Good News" of Jesus Christ, are rightly called evangelical. Whether by tradition, history, or submission to a particular authority, we may be known as Orthodox, Roman Catholic, Methodist, Anabaptist, Episcopalian, or Presbyterian. Clearly not every Christian subscribes to the beliefs of a Church not his own, but what all of us must share is an evangelical faith, a faith in the person of Jesus Christ, a faith that He is truly the Son of God, that He is truly both fully human and fully divine, and that the Father has raised Him to eternal Life. Furthermore, our evangelical faith makes a difference for us who are privileged to be His brothers and sisters. His shared humanity with us necessarily gives us a new dignity; His Resurrection offers us the hope that eternal life, too, may be our destiny.

It is only right, then, that Calvin Beisner's *Where Garden Meets Wilderness* should appeal to an audience far broader than only those who call themselves Evangelical; his treatment of environmentalism is well-grounded in the Gospels and, so, is truly evangelical. To underscore the truly ecumenical nature of Beisner's work, I should like to develop four topics addressed by him: human life, human culture, the Creator's plan, and the dignity of human work. I should like to relate each of these to Roman Catholic teaching by way of reference to the "Message of His Holiness Pope John Paul II for the Celebration of the World Day of Peace, January 1, 1990, Vatican City," published in *"And God Saw That It Was Good": Catholic Theology and the Environment*, ed. by Drew Christiansen and Walter Grazer (Washington: United States Catholic Conference, 1996). Furthermore, it is my hope that I may provide an overview of environmental concerns that reflects the full Judeo-Christian tradition and is, therefore, truly catholic.

Human Life

Pope John Paul II observes: "The most profound and serious indication of the moral implications underlying the ecological problem is the lack of *respect for life* evident in many of the patterns of environmental pollution." (p. 218) Tragic is the neglect for the value of human life shown by so many environmentalists who seek to advance a concern for nature at the expense of human life.

Nothing could be further removed from the faith of Judaism and of Christianity, that faith of Saint Francis of Assisi, than the New Age worship of the environment which replaces reverence for the Creator with reverence for Creation. Consequently the value placed on human life is secondary to the value placed on animal (and even plant) life. In the Judeo-Christian tradition that spans nearly four millennia, Saint Francis rightly stands above all other religious thinkers for his high regard, his love, for the environment, but he acknowledges that nature is no more than the gift of the Creator, given for human dominion, development, and stewardship, while God the Creator is alone deserving of worship. Like all Christians, Saint Francis knows that only humanity, of all creation, has been ennobled by the Incarnation; it was the Father's will for our salvation that His Son should be one of us, a man.

For a single human being to starve or to lack the means of livelihood because of deference shown to any other created being, animal or plant, is a denial of the dignity that humanity alone enjoys, that dignity which Saint Francis recognizes to be uniquely the highest in all the created order. As advanced by environmentalists, the refusal to develop resources would tragically result in the loss of employment for hundreds of thousands of workers. Lacking this, they in turn would be unable to provide a livelihood for themselves and their families, resulting in a poverty so great that the family itself is threatened as the poor worker is forced to consider contraception or abortion as his only alternative to bringing a child into this life of poverty. Thus, the value put on the environment is made at the expense of human life itself.

The natural replenishment of resources looks for its mandate to a beneficent Creator. The most valuable resource in Creation of course remains the human person, who alone of all Creation has the potential for renewing resources, a fact sadly lost sight of by those who promote the destruction of human life within the womb, thereby diminishing the potential for renewed natural resources rather than merely the depletion of natural resources. By preserving the resource that is the human person, the natural resources can be further sustained. With the loss of human life through abortion, there is in economic terms also the loss of the most valuable natural resource, the one that can alone replenish other resources.

Not only does this extreme sensitivity for environmental matters endanger human life and jeopardize human livelihood, but it denies the human person his dignity as advanced with consistency in the Judeo-Christian ethic. Work of itself seems to be part of the original divine plan; otherwise, God would not have charged man with dominion over Creation; for that requires and presumes work on the part of man. It is only with his fall that man brings upon himself the "sweat of the brow" as a human consequence of the divine gift of work. Work is not a punishment, the sweat is. As a worker, man has an *opus* to perform; as such, he can be said to be a cooperator with God, who, as Creator of the *opus* that is the universe, must be the archetypal Worker.

Human Culture

Like the Old Testament prophets, Pope John Paul II identifies culture with justice tempered by compassion and humility; more precisely: "The ecological crisis reveals the *urgent moral need for a new solidarity*, especially in relations between the developing nations and those that are highly industrialized. States must increasingly share responsibility, in complementary ways, for the promotion of a natural and social environment that is both peaceful and healthy." (p. 219)

Consistent with his teaching elsewhere, the pope relates the environmental question to the involvement of the state and obviously to the form of government and economic system. As Beisner develops his views from a consideration of the etymology of culture, it would be appropriate to consider this as well.

The very notion of culture itself is rooted etymologically in work. "Culture" comes from the Latin verb *colo*, which evolved in meaning from "to till the soil," then "to dwell," and finally "to worship," so we have such different concepts as "agriculture," "cultivation," "culture," and "cult" all derived from the same Latin root. I should like to suggest that this linguistic evolution is in no way a mere coincidence; rather, it reflects the actual historical circumstances: where people planted seeds from which they could derive nourishment and a livelihood, there they would be safe to settle and establish a permanent dwelling; with work and home provided for, then they could allow themselves the "luxury" of religion. Culture, then, embraces where you live, your work ethic, your religion and religious values.

In the area of environmental concerns, the modern state tends also to take an aggressive role in its involvement, often to the extent that it intrudes into the private sector. This frequently entails a diminishing of the value placed on human dignity and individual civil rights to promote the assumed good to be realized for the environment. One need only think of the failure to build dams that would improve (and possibly even save) the lives of people in order to preserve the habitat of snail-darters.

The Creator's Plan

Pope John Paul II observes: "Adam and Eve's call to share in the unfolding of God's plan of Creation brought into play those abilities and gifts which distinguish the human being from all other creatures. At the same time, their call established a fixed relationship between mankind and the rest of Creation. Made in the image and likeness of God, Adam and Eve were to exercise their dominion over the earth (Gen. 1:28) with wisdom and love." (p. 216)

In speaking about man and nature, I like to condense Genesis 1:28–31 into the phrase, *Omnia dabo vobis*, "I shall give you all things, have dominion over them." The phrase *dabo vobis* has a fascinating history in the Latin Vulgate; it occurs almost 200 times, and with the greatest frequency in the prophetic books, where God is usually the speaker and, therefore, the giver; the object given can be a variety of things, literally *omnia*.

The phrase occurs over eighty times in Jeremiah and Ezekiel. They especially see a spiritual renewal as God's gift to His Creation; among the objects of *dabo vobis* are: one heart and one path (Jer. 32:39), one heart and a new spirit (Ezek. 11:19), a new heart and a new spirit (Ezek. 36:26), my holiness (Ezek. 37:26).

Especially intriguing is the phrase in Jeremiah 3:15: *Pastores dabo vobis*. In the context of evangelical environmentalism, I should like to suggest that we see the concept from Genesis of *Omnia dabo vobis* as necessarily joined with *Pastores dabo vobis*, such that the goods of Creation are given over to human dominion but a dominion which is basically "pastoral." In other words, we are called to provide a stewardship of the Creation given to our dominion.

We might, then, see in the Genesis account of the Garden of Eden the divine bestowal of three gifts to man: the human mind, each other, and the gifts of nature. *Omnia dabo vobis. Pastores dabo vobis.*

The Dignity of Human Work

The pope rightly evaluates human dignity in the light of the Incarnation: "Christians believe that the Death and Resurrection of Christ accomplished the work of reconciling humanity to the Father, who 'was pleased... through (Christ) to reconcile to himself all things, whether on earth or in heaven, making peace by the blood of his cross.' (Col. 1:19–20). Creation was thus made new (cf. Rev. 21:5). Once subjected to the bondage of sin and decay (cf. Rom. 8:21), it has now received new life while 'we wait for new heavens and a new earth in which righteousness dwells' (2 Pt. 3:13)." (p. 216)

Beisner correctly observes that much of the environmental movement is decidedly non-theocentric; we must be careful not to lose sight of the value and dignity of the human person in the order of creation. Too often the environmental movement prizes animal and plant life at the expense of human life.

Pope John Paul II develops this in his address to workers on March 19, 1994, the feast of St. Joseph the Worker (*L'Osservatore Romano*, English edition, April 13, 1994, p. 2):

The most important product of work is man himself. Through his own activity, man forms himself as he discovers his own abilities and puts them to the test. At the same time, he gives himself to others and to society as a whole. Thus he established his own humanity through work, and becomes in a certain sense a gift for others, totally fulfilling himself.

As the pope knows too well from his own experience of totalitarian regimes, work can be dehumanizing, so he is concerned to add:

Work should be carried out by man for man. Only then does it correspond to the proper order. Otherwise the Creator's plan is foiled and destroyed.

He concludes:

This is the day of the great prayer with the workers: it is the prayer for work. It started one day in your Italian land. Indeed it was here that St. Benedict taught people to work while praying, and the monks who followed him, faithful to the principle *"Ora et labora!"* brought about a great revolution, which was certainly not inferior to the modern industrial revolution. The result of this revolution was the holiness of man. Work made men, sanctified man, ennobled family life, created social links, shaped the history of nations.

Let us give thanks for the extraordinary fruit of many centuries of human toil in Italy, in Europe and throughout the world. Let us demand at the same time that prayer may have a place within human work, even in our time. The laicization and secularization of work only contribute to making man almost detest his work and treat it exclusively as a source of profit. Working in this way, he can no longer see man in himself and he is unable to see him in others who are striving beside him.

There is then a need for "work upon work". What does this mean? No more than this: "Pray and work!" Work upon work means to work upon the person who is working, so that through work, as the Polish poet Cyprian Norwald said, he may rise again to discover the fullness of his humanity.

Man, rising to the fullness of his humanity, exercises those original gifts in the Garden: the human mind, each other and nature, exercising rightful dominion over these of which the Creator has said: *Omnia dabo vobis.* In his development and responsible stewardship of nature, man enjoys his God-given dignity.

Conclusion

In the first year of his pontificate, Pope John Paul II declared Saint Francis of Assisi as the patron saint of those who seek to promote environmental concerns; in his words: "He offers Christians an example of genuine and deep respect for the integrity of creation." (p. 222)

As I complete this introduction to Beisner's excellent theological study of the environment, the Catholic Church observes the feast of Saint Boniface, who is celebrated for establishing the Christian faith in what is today Germany. He promoted Christianity to the indigenous pagan population by chopping down the tree, revered as sacred, that they had worshipped for generations. In doing so, Boniface, like the prophet Hosea, demonstrated that man is mistaken in worshipping the created order instead of the divine Creator. Not unlike the pagans of a millennium ago, today's New Age adherents in the environmental movement advance a cult that is neither theocentric nor appreciative of the dignity of the human person or the value of human life. Like Boniface, Beisner develops a truly evangelical approach to the environment that is centered on Christ and sees humanity as made in God's image and appointed to steward Creation.

Rev. John Michael Beers
Mount Saint Mary's Seminary
Emmitsburg, Maryland

The Feast of Saint Boniface
June 5, 1997

CHAPTER 1

❧ ❧

The Rise of Evangelical Environmentalism

IF WE RECOGNIZE THE INHERENT BREADTH OF THE WORD *ENVIRONMENT*—which, derived from the French *envirroner*, "to surround," simply denotes one's surroundings, i.e., everything[1]—Jewish and Christian concern for the environment reaches back into the misty past. From the time Noah, at God's instruction, acted to save all the species endangered by the Flood and to begin repopulating the world (Gen. 6–9), to the time Abraham and Lot worried about what many of today's environmentalists would call the "carrying capacity" of the Promised Land (Gen. 13), to the apostle Paul's assurance that although "the creation was subjected to futility" still it "will be delivered from the bondage of corruption into the glorious liberty of the children of God" (Rom. 8:20–21), to the Church Father Tertullian's horror that human beings "weigh upon the world; its *resources hardly suffice to support us*"[2] at the turn of the third century A.D., to the labors of St. Francis of Assisi on behalf of birds and beasts, to our own times, Jews and Christians have thought, spoken, and acted in awareness of the environment. But *environmentalism* as a movement among evangelicals, like its non-evangelical counterparts (secular, New Age, mainline Protestant, and Catholic), is a recent phenomenon.

Broadly speaking, environmentalism grew out of the conservation movement, which was rooted in the ideas of writers like Henry David Thoreau (1817–1862) and in the studies and actions of naturalists like John James Audubon (1785–1851), Sierra Club founder John Muir (1838–1914), and John Burroughs (1827–1921), and outdoorsmen like President Theodore Roosevelt (1858–1919) and United States Forest Service founder Gifford Pinchot (1865–1946). It was, in the words of radical environmentalist and Earth First! founder

David Foreman, "a child . . . of the Establishment. The founders of the Sierra Club, the National Audubon Society, the Wilderness Society, and the wildlife conservation groups were, as a rule, pillars of American society."[3] Conservationists tended to look at nature as a resource on which people could draw to meet their physical, social, aesthetic, and spiritual needs. Thus, they were concerned not so much to *preserve* nature as they found it but to *conserve* it, that is, to ensure that people used it carefully to ensure that it would still be around for coming generations to use. Theirs was, in short, a people-centered approach to the environment.

Conservationism began its transformation into environmentalism in the second quarter of the twentieth century (although the term *environmentalism* would not be coined until much later), particularly under the influence of Aldo Leopold (1887–1948), a forester, wildlife management specialist, and one of the founders of the Wilderness Society. Throughout his career, Leopold held largely to the conservationist perspective: human management of nature for human benefit for the long term. But alongside this perspective and modifying it Leopold developed another: nature for its own sake as a complex web of interdependent biological and physical relationships the result of which is, ipso facto, good.[4] Slowly, almost imperceptibly, conservationism began to give birth to what was first called *preservationism* but from the 1970s on came under the name *environmentalism*. A leader in this transformation was David Brower, executive director of the Sierra Club during the 1950s and 1960s, who was fired by the Club's board of directors in 1969 because of his increasingly radical, anti-establishment sentiments.

From the late 1960s through the 1980s a wide variety of environmental organizations took shape, many expressly repudiating the conservationist perspective as anthropocentric, embracing instead a biocentric or even ecocentric view. This outlook, dominant in such groups as Greenpeace, the Green political parties, Friends of the Earth, and the ecotage-promoting Earth First!, holds the environment itself (by which it means not everything in our surroundings but everything not of human origin), and each thing in it, as having intrinsic value apart from any human use for it. This perspective has been especially strong in what has come to be known as Deep Ecology, a movement and idea rooted in the thought of Norwegian philosopher of ecology ("ecosopher") Arne Naess and with strong influence in much feminist, New Age, and neopagan environmentalism. Deep Ecology, according to Naess, differs from Shallow Ecology in that the former values and protects nature for its own sake, while the latter does so only for nature's usefulness to man. (For a list of some of the more important American environmental organizations and their years of founding, with special attention to those related to evangelical environmentalism, see table 1.1.)

Significant evangelical attention began to turn toward the environment in the 1980s. Especially important was the decision, in 1980, to start the Au Sable Institute for Environmental Studies, in Mancelona, Michigan. Under the direction of University of Wisconsin environmental studies professor Calvin B. DeWitt, Au Sable and its thirty-five faculty and research staff members (listed for 1992–1995), most of whom serve there part-time while holding positions at other institutions, offers a wide variety of college-credit courses, certification programs, and internships in ecological and environmental studies. Through its association with the Christian College Coalition it has unparalleled influence on evangelical higher education about the environment. It has faculty representatives at thirty-nine participating colleges, each of which can send students to Au Sable for credit courses, and forty-eight other Christian College Coalition member schools are also eligible to send students to participate in programs. The Institute also conducts annual forums focusing on various aspects of environmental studies, in which small groups of scholars participate, often generating published anthologies, position papers, or declarations. Among the influential books issuing from Au Sable Forums are *Tending the Garden: Essays on the Gospel and the Earth*, edited by Wesley Granberg-Michaelson (Grand Rapids: Eerdmans, 1987), *The Environment and the Christian: What Can We Learn from the New Testament?*, edited by DeWitt (Grand Rapids: Baker, 1991), and *Missionary Earthkeeping*, edited by DeWitt and Ghillean T. Prance (Macon, GA: Mercer University Press, 1992). By the late 1980s, a survey of 125 church-related colleges revealed that 95 percent offered environmental courses.[5]

Some other milestones in the growth of the evangelical environmental movement have been:

• The selection of "Christian Stewardship and Natural Resources" as the first topic for the newly formed Calvin Center for Christian Scholarship at Calvin College in 1977–1978. Participating scholars were Peter De Vos, then professor of philosophy at Calvin College, later dean of Jordan College; Calvin DeWitt; Eugene Dykema, assistant professor of economics, Calvin College and later (simultaneously) director of the graduate business program, George Fox College; Vernon Ehlers, professor of physics, Calvin College; and Loren Wilkinson, then professor of English, Seattle Pacific College, later professor of philosophy and interdisciplinary studies, Regent Col-

TABLE 1.1
Founding Dates of Selected Environmental Organizations
(Bold face indicates evangelical organizations)

1892	The Sierra Club
1905	National Audubon Society
1919	National Parks and Conservation Association
1922	Izaak Walton League of America
1935	The Wilderness Society
1936	National Wildlife Federation
1947	Defenders of Wildlife
1951	The Nature Conservancy
1954	Humane Society of the United States
1961	World Wildlife Fund (precursor, 1948)
1967	The Fund for Animals
	Environmental Defense Fund
1968	Zero Population Growth
1969	Environmental Law Institute
	Union of Concerned Scientists
	Friends of the Earth
1970	Natural Resources Defense Fund
	Environmental Action Foundation
	League of Conservation Voters
1971	Clean Water Action
	Greenpeace USA
1972	Center for Marine Conservation
1973	The Cousteau Society
1974	Worldwatch Institute
	Inform, Inc.
1975	The Keystone Center
1977	Foundation on Economic Trends
1978	**(Evangelicals for Social Action)**
1980	People for the Ethical Treatment of Animals
	Earth First!
	Au Sable Institute for Environmental Studies
1982	Earth Island Institute
	World Resources Institute
	Rocky Mountain Institute
1984	National Toxins Campaign
1985	North American Conference on Christianity and Ecology
	The Rainforest Action Network
	Global Forum of Spiritual and Parliamentary Leaders
1987	Conservation International
1990	Joint Appeal by Religion and Science for the Environment
1993	National Religious Partnership for the Environment
	Evangelical Environmental Network
1994	**Christian Society of the Green Cross**
	Christian Environmental Association
	Christian Environmental Council

Note that of the forty-five organizations listed, only nine predate 1961, reflecting the fact that environmentalism is a movement of the late-twentieth century. There are literally hundreds of other environmental organizations in the United States and around the world, the vast majority founded since 1960. These are just (a) some of the largest and most influential in the United States or (b) those most important to evangelical environmentalism.

lege. The study generated *Earthkeeping: Christian Stewardship of Natural Resources* (Grand Rapids: Eerdmans, 1980), with Wilkinson as principal writer and Ehlers as editor/manager. The book quickly became influential among evangelicals, as demonstrated by frequent citations from it in other evangelical writings on the environment.

• The regathering of the same group of scholars, again under the auspices of the Calvin Center, to readdress the same themes in 1990, issuing in a thorough revision and augmentation of the book under the new title *Earthkeeping in the Nineties: Stewardship of Creation* (Grand Rapids: Eerdmans, 1991), with Wilkinson as principal editor and rewriter. This revision seems likely to eclipse the first edition in influence among evangelicals studying the environment.

• The holding of a joint forum in 1992 by Au Sable and the Ethics Unit of the Theological Commission of the World Evangelical Fellowship at Au Sable. Papers presented there eventually were published in a special issue, "Evangelicals and the Environment: Theological Foundations for Christian Environmental Stewardship," of the *Evangelical Review of Theology* (vol. 17, no. 2; April 1993), under the guest editorship of Au Sable Senior Research Fellow J. Mark Thomas. The Forum issued a report, "Evangelical Christianity and the Environment," that summarized participants' main concerns and the theological, ethical, political, and scientific perspectives they believed should guide thought and policy regarding them.

• The establishment in 1993 of the Evangelical Environmental Network (EEN), under the auspices of Evangelicals for Social Action, as one branch of the National Religious Partnership for the Environment, which grew out of the Joint Appeal by Religion and Science for the Environment, led by cochairmen Carl Sagan, Cornell University professor of astronomy, and James Parks Morton, Dean of the Episcopal Cathedral of St. John the Divine in New York City. (Other branches are Jewish, Catholic, and mainline Protestant.) On October 4, 1993, a delegation led by Asbury Theological Seminary President David McKenna, ESA President Ronald J. Sider, InterVarsity Christian Fellowship president Steve Hayner, and World Vision Vice President of U.S. Advocacy and Education Paul Thompson met with Vice President Al Gore at the White House to launch the EEN, briefing

Gore on "a comprehensive three year program designed to nurture awareness and action within the evangelical community on environmental issues."[6] Included in the EEN's intentions were:

a.) assistance in convening a Christianity Today Institute on the environment October 28–29, 1993, to help foster an evangelical response to the environment.

b.) completion by October 30, 1993, in coordination with the Christianity Today Institute, of an *Evangelical Declaration on the Care of Creation* as "a definitive document outlining a biblical framework on appropriate evangelical action on the environmental crisis," followed by solicitation of endorsements of the *Declaration* by prominent evangelical pastors, theologians, and activists.

c.) development, under the auspices of World Vision, of "a deeper understanding of sustainable development for evangelistic relief and development agencies."

d.) establishment and support of "'Covenant Congregations' committed to a program of environmental stewardship, study and action."

e.) mailing of twenty thousand copies of *Let the Earth Be Glad: A Starter Kit for Evangelical Churches to Care for God's Creation* to evangelical congregations. (All together, Catholic, mainline Protestant, and Jewish branches of the NRPE mailed resources to approximately 53,000 congregations in 1994.)

f.) establishment of an annual summer institute to train clergy in environmental issues and programmatic responses.

g.) assistance to the Christian College Coalition, in cooperation with Au Sable, on environmental curriculum development.

Members of the EEN's advisory council in addition to McKenna, DeWitt, Sider, and Hayner were Eastern College President Roberta Hestenes, World Vision President Robert Seiple, Christian College Coalition President Myron Augsburger, *Sojourners* magazine editor Jim Wallis, and National Association of Evangelicals Office of Public Affairs Director Robert Dugan (who because of disagreements declined to sign the *Declaration* and later resigned from the EEN).

• Founding of other evangelical environmental organizations in the early 1990s: (1) Christian Society of the Green Cross,[7] a ministry of ESA. The Society publishes *Green Cross*, which calls itself "A Christian Environmental Quarterly" and lists Sider as publisher. (2) Christian Environmental Council, sponsored by the EEN and Au Sable, with DeWitt as president. (3) The Christian Environmental Association, with Gordon Aeschliman, former editor of both *Green Cross* and *Prism*, the latter a new quarterly magazine of ESA, as president.

The remainder of this book will interact with various theological, ethical, political, scientific, economic, and polemical aspects of some of the more important literature emanating from these and other evangelical environmental groups and individuals. While there is much to commend about evangelical environmental activities, our goal will be to identify some of its weaknesses and to suggest ways to correct them.

CHAPTER 2

Evangelical Environmental Worldview and Theology:
Strengths and Weaknesses

EVANGELICAL ENVIRONMENTAL NETWORK LEADER RONALD SIDER AND I were guests on Dick Staub's "Chicago Talks" radio program in January 1994, discussing the *Evangelical Declaration on the Care of Creation*. Like any effective talk show host, Staub hoped for spirited debate. At the outset Sider explained one of the underlying motives of starting the EEN:

> One of the important things is that there are environmentalists out there who are saying some very crazy things, in terms of religion and theology. They're New Age, they worship the earth, mother goddess, and so on. And at the same time it's important to realize that they're groping for spiritual meaning, they're groping for a religious foundation, but they don't think Christianity is the way to get it. And what we're saying is, Biblical truth is exactly the foundation that we need for working seriously at our environmental problems.

Staub then asked for my response, and I said:

> . . . I share Ron Sider's concern for responding to the desire for spiritual meaning and reality in life that we see among a lot of environmentalists. I share also his concern that we not fall into some New Age concepts about the earth—the Gaia mentality, the idea that personalizes and spiritualizes all of nature and essentially brings the rest of nature to the same level as humanity and neglects the fact that God made *man* in His image and not other things. . . .

There was indeed spirited debate, but not much over theological issues. On those, for the most part, Sider and I saw eye to eye.

I relate this story to make it clear that my criticisms of some theological, Biblical, and ethical aspects of evangelical environmentalism are mostly at or near the margin. On the majority of theological issues—especially those at the defining center of the Christian faith—evangelical environmentalists have maintained orthodoxy while addressing environmental concerns that have, for the most part, been brought to public attention from outside the evangelical or even the broadly Christian camp. They are to be commended for this. Later in the same program Sider put the point precisely:

> I think we shouldn't miss a very important evangelistic opportunity here. There is a very important change going on in our society. The intellectual community used to be very secular and naturalistic and didn't believe in anything other than what science could talk about. There's a groping for spiritual meaning and depth going on in our society. But only if Christians get out there with a full Biblical faith and show how it meets the things that they're struggling with can we really respond to that, so there's a crucial evangelistic opportunity.[1]

Sider is right, and he and various other evangelical environmentalists have thoughtfully set forth how Christian faith and ethics offer the best solution to environmental problems. Perhaps the best effort at this is Richard Young's *Healing the Earth*,[2] which deftly and winsomely answers secularist and New Age attacks on Christianity as promoting environmental degradation by teaching man's dominion over nature and explains why in reality Christianity offers the only worldview that simultaneously upholds human dignity and leads to sound environmental policy. Also very helpful in this regard is Loren Wilkinson's "New Age, New Consciousness, and the New Creation," in *Tending the Garden*.[3] Certainly Sider, Young, Wilkinson, and others in the evangelical environmental movement—indeed, many non-Christian environmentalists, including New Agers—are right in insisting that a secularist, technicist worldview cannot provide an adequate foundation for environmental reform.

Nonetheless, there are some significant points at which the application of worldview, theology, ethics, and Scripture to environmental questions among evangelical environmentalists should improve. Recognizing that these categories overlap, nonetheless this chapter focuses on worldview and theology, while the next focuses on ethics, and the fourth on Scripture.

How Should We Perceive Our World?

An important part of debates over environmentalism has to do with just how we should understand our world. Evangelical environmentalists frequently insist at the start that we must not perceive it as "our world," since "The earth is the LORD's, and everything in it" (Ps. 24:1).[4] Of course, this is true, and it provides a critical premise for a Biblically grounded understanding of environmental stewardship. But as in many doctrinal matters emphasizing one truth (Christ is God) to the exclusion of a balancing truth (Christ became Man) can lead to error (Christ's human form was a mere appearance), so here evangelical environmentalists rarely acknowledge an important balancing truth: "The highest heavens belong to the LORD, but the earth he has given to man" (Ps. 115:16).

Human stewardship of the earth takes place in a context of subordinate ownership. All too often, the truth of Psalm 24:1 is brought forward as if it negated any claim of human ownership—and hence of decision-making prerogative—over land. But Psalm 115:16 and the many passages of Scripture (such as the eighth commandment) that assert or imply the reality of human ownership—albeit subordinate—also necessarily imply human freedom and responsibility to make many decisions about what will be done with the earth.

Indeed, that people will make such decisions is inevitable. The great questions are, who will make them, on what grounds, and with what consequences? Will most land-use decisions be made by individuals, private bodies, or civil governments? Will they be made on utilitarian or absolutist ethical grounds, with the benefit of the individual, the human community, or the whole biosphere in mind? To whom are people accountable for the use of creation? How and to what extent can we know and ensure the consequences of our decisions? These questions are where the rubber meets the road in environmental decision making, and mere insistence either that the earth belongs to God or that God has given it to men does not yield clear answers to them.

What is certain, however, is that emphasizing either of the two balancing truths without the other will lead us astray. Emphasizing only that the earth is the Lord's, while neglecting or denying that He has given it to men tends to lead toward making decisions at broad, societal levels, often encroaching on people's legitimate rights to determine the use of their own property. The disastrous record of socialist countries on environmental protection is grim testimony to how poorly such a policy works. But emphasizing only that God has given the earth to men while neglecting or denying that it still ultimately belongs to God tends to lead toward asserting human autonomy in the use of the earth and exalting individual prerogative over the needs of the commu-

nity. The sad environmental record of late-nineteenth-century Social Darwin-
ist capitalism should warn us away from that policy. To respond to this dilemma adequately, the evangelical environmental movement needs to work
out a sound, Biblical political philosophy that properly balances the one and
the many, the community and the individual.[5]

Ownership and decision-making authority over the creation, however, are
not the only questions that need careful consideration. Another is whether the
creation as we find it, before it has been transformed by human action, should
be left as it is. Secular environmentalist Barry Commoner asserts as the third
of his four laws of ecology, "Any major man-made change in a natural system
is likely to be *detrimental* to that system."[6] Unfortunately, some evangelical
environmentalists tend to accept this assumption uncritically. For example,
Vincent Rossi writes (summarizing and explicitly embracing Commoner),
"nature knows best."[7] Similarly, Lionel Basney writes, "left to itself, [nature]
knows what to do" and ". . . it is this 'looking after itself' that is nature's
mark. To be what it is, to be the delight of the One who made it, it does not
need our interventions or (for that matter) us."[8] "What we must insist on is
nature's independence of us—its independent glory as a child of God."[9]

But two Biblical teachings lead to a different understanding of nature[10]
and man's relationship to it. One, that God cursed the earth because of man's
sin, we shall consider more below. For now let it suffice to say that it certainly
implies that much of what we find in nature untouched by human hands is *not*
good and *should* be improved. The other is that even before the Fall and the
Curse, God gave man a stewardly responsibility to subdue and rule the earth
(Gen. 1:26–28), and when He placed man in the Garden of Eden, He instructed
him to cultivate and guard it (Gen. 2:15), implying that it is right and good in
principle for people to interfere with nature. True, because of our sin and
ignorance, sometimes our interference causes more harm than good. But this
only means that we need both to learn how to use creation wisely and to have
our hearts so transformed as to have the will to do so. It does not imply that
we should not interfere.

One reason for confusion over the kind and extent of legitimate human
transformation of the earth seems to me, after reading many evangelical environmental writings, to be a failure to distinguish properly between the earth
as a whole and the Garden of Eden. I have made this mistake myself.[11] For
instance, the authors of *Earthkeeping* (note the second part of the compound
title), in discussing the nature of the subduing and ruling to which Adam was
called in Genesis 1:28, point to Genesis 2:15. After pointing out how "forceful" the words *subdue* and *rule* are in Genesis 1:28, they argue that the two

verbs in Genesis 2:15, *till* and *keep*, are much milder. From this they conclude, "Human ruling, then, should be exercised in such a way as to *serve* and *preserve* the beasts, the trees, and the earth itself—all of which is being ruled.... The original command to subdue and rule is not contradicted, but the *type* of ruling is explicitly directed. There is never any doubt that humans are masters; but the concept of mastery itself here begins to be clarified and reversed in a process which will culminate only in the crucifixion of Christ."[12]

We shall discuss the meaning of man's dominion over the earth more below. Here it is important to note that the Biblical text makes it quite clear that the Garden Adam was told to till and keep was not the same as the earth he was told to subdue and rule. God "planted a garden in the east, in Eden" (Gen. 2:8). A river watering the Garden "separated into four headwaters" (2:10) that flowed *out of the Garden* to water the earth. It was specifically the *Garden* that Adam was to till and keep (2:15). In contrast, it was the *earth* that he was to subdue and rule (1:28). All of the earth was "very good" as God created it (1:31), but Eden was specially good, the Garden within Eden was even more specially good, and the trees of life and of the knowledge of good and evil in the midst of the Garden were still more specially good.[13] Adam's dominion mandate involved his transforming, bit by bit, the rest of the earth from glory to glory. Thus, in keeping with the Biblical teaching that the purpose of all creation is to glorify God (i.e., to display His glory), James Jordan points out that "The task of Adam's descendants would be to . . . [bring] the world from primordial to eschatological glory."[14] The need for transformation by human action does not stand against God's declaration in Genesis 1:31 that all that He had made was very good; it only recognizes that what God made good He intends to make better, and He intends to use people to do it. (For expanded treatment of this theme, see Appendix 1.)

In short, it would have made little sense to tell Adam to subdue and rule the Garden. It was already in perfect order, and succeeding Biblical imagery indicates that it was a type of both the sanctuary and the New Jerusalem—and through them of heaven itself.[15] But the rest of the earth apparently lacked some of the fullness of the perfection of the Garden. It was Adam's task to transform all of the earth (to subdue and rule it) into a Garden while guarding the original Garden lest it lose some of its perfection and become like the unsubdued earth.

Is this a mere technical point of Biblical interpretation? No, it has important implications for our understanding of the environment and our role in it. Among other things, it implies that much that we find in the earth would not, without human transformation, have been as God intends it to be *even had the*

Fall and the Curse never occurred, and therefore that transforming the earth from its natural state is, in principle, good. It also implies that the extension of human dominion over more and more of the earth is to be not lamented but celebrated. And it should remind us that, contrary to romantic notions of the natural abundance of the earth, people really must transform the earth in order to support very many of us. Regardless how simple and attractive it may sound, it is simply befuddled to say, as Basney does, "Neither industry nor the market can, of course, produce a single carrot or a slice of beef. If we want food, we must turn to the natural endowment of fertility and animal growth—what E. F. Schumacher called the 'irreplaceable capital which man has not made, but simply found, and without which he can do nothing.'"[16] Similarly, Calvin DeWitt's picture of the earth's natural bounty is mistaken:

> In creation's garden—so abundantly yielding blessed fruits, sustainably supporting humankind and all life in its God-declared goodness—the social, economic, and political structures we created have themselves been overtaken by the world market and the dynamics of science and technology.[17]

If *industry* and *the market* mean anything, they mean human beings working and trading together in some fashion, and while nature would indeed produce some carrots and slices of beef without human industry and trading, it would not produce nearly enough to meet the needs of today's population. Without science and technology, without industry and trade, "the life of man" is, as Thomas Hobbes put it, "solitary, poore, nasty, brutish, and short."[18] Mere hunting and gathering, after all, can only support one or two people per square mile in the best natural habitats. Were we to restrict ourselves to the food obtainable that way, human population could not rise above, perhaps, 30 million—about 1/166th of our present population.

The Meaning of Dominion

Repeatedly now we have bumped up against the Biblical teaching that God has given man dominion over the earth (Gen. 1:28). It is a commonplace of environmental literature—secular, feminist, deep ecology, New Age—to blame Christianity and the Bible for environmental degradation because of this teaching.[19] Evangelical environmentalists have sought to answer this charge not by repudiating the doctrine of dominion but by developing a more nuanced understanding of it than the common caricature that sees it as justifying wanton destruction of the natural world. Such clarification is an important step in responding to the anti-Christian charges of many environmentalists.

However, some evangelical environmentalists appear to set forth new misunderstandings of dominion in their effort to avoid the caricature. This happens in two ways.

First, some argue, as we have seen, that the meaning of *subdue* and *rule* in Genesis 1:28 is specified by *till* and *keep* in Genesis 2:15.[20] But the distinction seen above between earth and Garden makes this a questionable procedure. Furthermore, the meanings of the words themselves simply are too divergent for the latter to define the former. Subduing and ruling are quite different from tilling and keeping.[21]

Second, on the supposition that the command to till and keep does define the command to subdue and rule, some emphasize that the meaning of *'âbad*, the word translated *till* or *cultivate* in Genesis 2:15, is to serve. Thus Orin Gelderloos writes, "*Abad*, the word used to instruct Adam to 'till' or to cultivate the garden is the root for the words of 'servant' or 'slave'; its literal meaning is 'to serve'."[22] Similarly, the authors of *Earthkeeping in the Nineties* state that *'âbad* "is often translated 'till,' but it is sometimes translated 'work' or 'serve.' And in fact, [it] is the basic Hebrew word for 'serve' or even 'be a slave to.' . . . The kind of tilling which is to be done is a *service* of the earth."[23] From this it is a short step for these authors to turn to Christ's teaching that though He is Lord, He came not to be served but to serve, and to insist that Christ's suffering servanthood is therefore the real model of human dominion over the earth.

Now, we must not reject this insight entirely, for it does rightly remind us that Christ's model of lordship is one of servanthood. Yet it is open to serious objections. First, as we have seen, is the illegitimacy of assuming that Genesis 2:15 defines the dominion mandate in Genesis 1:28, since earth and Garden are not synonyms but are, in fact, contrasted in Genesis geography. Second, although *'âbad* may rightly be translated *to serve* or *work for* another in some contexts, it is properly translated thus only when it is followed by the accusative of a *person* or *persons*. When it is followed by the accusative of *things*, it is properly translated *to labor, work*, or *do work*, e.g., to till the ground, a vineyard, or a garden, or to work in flax.[24] While indeed all of man's tilling of the earth should be service to God, it is inaccurate to say that it is service to the earth itself. Rather, man's cultivating the earth is designed, as Old Testament commentators C. F. Keil and Franz Delitzsch point out, to cause the earth to serve man:

In paradise he was to dress ([Latin] *colere*) the garden; for the earth was meant to be tended and cultivated by man, so that without human culture, plants and even the different varieties of corn degenerate and grow wild. Cultivation therefore preserved . . . the divine plantation, not merely from injury on the part of any evil power, either penetrating into, or already existing in the creation, but also from running wild through natural degeneracy. As nature was created for man, it was his vocation not only to ennoble it by his work, to make it subservient to himself, but also to raise it into the sphere of the spirit and further its glorification. This applied not merely to the soil beyond the limits of paradise, but to the garden itself, which, although the most perfect portion of the terrestrial creation, was nevertheless susceptible of development, and which was allotted to man, in order that by his care and culture he might make it into a transparent mirror of the glory of the Creator.[25]

In this as in various other matters, Richard Young shows greater exegetical care than many other evangelical writers on the environment:

The word translated "work" (NIV) or "till" and "dress" (KJV) in Genesis 2:5 and 15 is *abad*, the common Hebrew verb for *serve*. The most common meanings are (1) to work, used especially when there is no object (Ex. 5:18); (2) to cultivate, when the object is the ground, vineyard, or the like (Gen. 3:23; 4:2; 4:12; Deut. 28:39; Prov. 12:11; 28:19; Ezek. 36:34); (3) to work for someone either as a servant (2 Sam. 16:19) or slave (Ex. 21:2–6); and (4) to serve or worship a deity (Ex. 3:12; Judg. 2:11; Ps. 100:2); or to serve in a place of worship (Num. 4:37, 41).

Normally when *ground* is the object, *abad* means to till or cultivate, implying cultivation for one's own sustenance. The context of Genesis 2:5, however, suggests a different focus. God's concern is not with people managing the garden for their own sustenance, for they had not been created yet, but with the need for a manager to help keep order and harmony in creation. The service is to be rendered to God, not to ourselves.[26]

Third, even Christ's lordship, characterized as it was by self-sacrifice (Phil. 2:5–11), is not always and toward everyone a lordship of service. Toward those He is saving, the Lord is tender and gentle (Isa. 53), but those who rebel against Him He will rule "with an iron scepter" and "dash . . . to pieces like pottery" (Ps. 2:9). As the good Shepherd He keeps His flock (Ps. 23; John 10), but when wild beasts threaten the sheep this entails His subduing or killing the beasts (one of the primary uses, after all, of a shepherd's rod and staff; Ps. 23:4; 1 Sam. 17:34–37). Similarly, while tender cultivation is suited to a garden, forceful subduing is suited to all of the earth that has not yet been transformed into the garden.

In short, subduing and ruling the earth should metamorphose gradually into tilling and keeping the garden as the earth is progressively transformed into the garden. This metamorphosis in treatment is even reflected in the creation accounts in Genesis. It is not difficult to conceive of the forcefulness of God's handling of the newly created heavens and earth when, for instance, He separated light from darkness, made an expanse between the waters, and separated the waters from the dry land. A gentler action seems inherent in His calling forth vegetation from the ground and then commanding the land to produce living creatures. A still more delicate action occurs when He plants a garden in Eden. And the most gentle and intimate action takes place when the Lord God forms man out of the dust of the ground and breathes into his nostrils the breath of life.

The dominion mandate, properly understood, gives man legitimate authority to subdue and rule the earth, progressively conforming it to his needs and the glory of God. That people do and will rule the earth is unavoidable. *How* they rule it is the crucial question. Will they rule it consistently with the commandments of God's law, or with some secular humanist notions of right and wrong, or with the values of Eastern religions? Biblical law does teach significant things about dominion—caring for animals (Ex. 23:5, 12; Num. 22:32–3; Deut. 5:14; 22:1, 3–4; 22:6–7, 10; 25:4), trees (Deut. 20:19–20), and land (Lev. 25:2, 4; 26:34, 43), for instance. Biblical dominion is not autonomous, it is theonomous—restricted by God's law, not man's, and empowered by God's Spirit, not man's.[27]

One problem with the doctrine of dominion, however, is that it simply does not give direct, pat answers to lots of the specific questions that arise in environmental discussions. Should we drill for oil? Here? How? Should we mine coal? There? By boring (which is much more dangerous to the miners), or strip-mining (which can leave ugly scars on the land, although the scars can be restored to beauty)? Should we log old-growth forests? Where? How much, if any, should we preserve? Inferring specific answers to these and many other specific environmental questions from specific passages of Scripture, or even from general principles of Scripture, is not only not easy, it is impossible. The implicit condemnation of certain activities in the following statement carries considerable emotive impact, but it cannot be supported by clear inference from Scripture:

> It is, perhaps, an indication of our fallen condition that we humans have not only seized the Genesis commandment to rule as a permit to use nature only for *human* comfort, but have also interpreted the sacrificial death of Christ as being only for *human* salvation. Thus the most compelling argument in

favor of any degradation of the environment, whether it be strip-mining a hill, clear-cutting a mountain, or butchering a whale, is always the contribution such an action will make to *human* survival—if not the actual survival of individuals, at least the survival of a certain kind of comfort or security. ·

The unique message of the Christian gospel, however, is not only the proclamation of the infinite worth of human life (for God, in Christ, died to redeem it); it is also the importance of being willing to give up that life—or at least to forgo one's comfort and material security—for the sake of another.[28]

There are, in fact, several problems with such reasoning. First, the Bible does put a priority on human survival (e.g., Ex. 21:28), and there is nothing wrong with our doing the same.[29] Second, it is not always clear that strip-mining a given hill, clear-cutting a given mountain, or butchering a given whale is wrong. Anyone who has traveled through the lush, rolling farmland of southern Illinois and observed the thousands of small lakes and ponds that dot the landscape, providing excellent stopovers for migratory birds, not to mention great bass fishing and lovely scenery for people, is observing the long-term impact of strip-mining in that region, for most of the lakes and ponds are played out strip mines.[30] Some species of trees grow back best after logging when there is no canopy, i.e., after clear-cutting; others do better under a canopy, i.e., after selective harvesting. And there is no reason why sensible hunting of whales need threaten their survival as a species. Third, there is a difference between giving up one's life to save another human being and giving it up to save a hill, a forest, or a whale. The one makes sense; the other is, to say the least, questionable. The Bible does, after all, make a clear difference between human and other kinds of life. It forbids taking innocent human life (Ex. 20:13), but under the Mosaic system it required killing some innocent animals as sacrifices (e.g., Ex. 34:20).

That we are, therefore, to think through issues of environmental stewardship with the Biblical doctrine of dominion in mind is certainly true. It should provide some guiding boundaries for our thinking, but it cannot by itself give us all the specifics we need. Generations of thought and experience must teach us how to answer the specific questions.

Can We Ignore the Curse?

"Cursed is the ground because of you," God said. Adam had sinned; "through painful toil you will eat of it all the days of your life. It will produce thorns and thistles for you, and you will eat the plants of the field. By the sweat of your brow you will eat your food until you return to the ground, since from it you were taken; for dust you are and to dust you will return" (Gen. 3:17b–19).

There is a marked tendency among evangelical environmentalists to ignore the Biblical doctrine of the Curse. Repeatedly we encounter references to God's evaluation of creation in Genesis 1:31: "it was very good."[31] But most evangelical books on the environment never mention the Curse. *The Evangelical Declaration on the Care of Creation* never mentions it. When I pointed this out to EEN leader Ronald Sider, he replied, "the *Declaration* does very clearly talk about the Fall, and it clearly talks about the fact that in Jesus Christ all things are going to be restored, and that's not just individuals but it's the groaning creation." I responded:

> But there is a difference between the Fall and the Curse. The fall is man's sin, and the Curse is God's response to man's sin. The Curse is on the earth, and the Curse specifically mentions a degradation of the earth that makes it less fruitful than it initially was. The *Declaration*, for instance, quotes Genesis 1:31 as saying God declares all creation good. The only degradation that the *Declaration* mentions occurring to the earth is all through human action.[32]

What difference does this make? All the difference in the world regarding what we expect to find in nature. We have already seen that God made a difference between the Garden of Eden and the rest of the earth; the former was more glorious than the latter, and Adam was commissioned to transform the earth into the Garden while cultivating and protecting the Garden. These truths implied that not everything Adam found outside the Garden even before the Fall and the Curse would already be as they ought to become. It would need to be subdued and ruled in order to be transformed into greater glory. The Curse intensifies this recognition. The earth outside the Garden, already less glorious than the Garden, was by the Curse made even less glorious than it began. Indeed, it was "subjected to frustration" and the "bondage to decay" (Rom. 8:20–21). Instead of submitting readily to Adam's dominion, it would rebel against him. Instead of producing abundant fruits for Adam's sustenance, it would produce thorns and thistles. In other words, it would behave toward Adam as Adam had behaved toward God—a fitting punishment for Adam's sin.

In this light, romantic longings for some pristine planet beautiful that existed before the twentieth century, or the Industrial Revolution, or European civilization, or Western civilization, or perhaps even before any real civilization, are seen to be empty. From the Fall and the Curse on, there never has been such a place. Thus, when DeWitt laments, "Creation's garden abundantly yields blessed fruits, sustainably supporting us and all life in its God-declared goodness. We 'disciples of the first Adam' have made the choice to extract more and yet more of the fruits of creation—even at the expense of destroying creation's protective provisions and blessed fruitfulness,"[33] we might sympathize, but we must not mistakenly think he describes a historically real option. We cannot choose between "creation's protective provisions and blessed fruitfulness," on the one hand, and civilization's agricultural, industrial, and market activities, on the other. Because of the Curse, creation by itself simply does not abundantly yield blessed fruits. It does yield fruits, some good and some (thorns and thistles) bad, but it becomes abundantly fruitful only under the wise and resolute hand of man.

Since the Curse, earth no longer is "this Eden of a planet."[34] (Indeed, it never was; only a tiny part of it was Eden.) It is legitimate, therefore, for Adam's race, particularly under the redeeming rule of Christ, to seek to transform cursed ground back into blessed ground.[35] It should be no surprise, in light of the Curse, that "even from the time of Adam and Eve, humanity has not been satisfied with the fruitfulness and grace of the Garden—the productive and beautiful creation that God has provided for us."[36] A dissatisfaction (which must not be confused with discontent) that DeWitt understands as sinful is instead a proper response to a cursed ground.

Even when evangelical environmentalists do mention the Curse, they usually cannot invest it with any particular significance. For instance, *Evangelical Christianity and the Environment*, a summarizing committee report of a 1992 forum jointly sponsored by the World Evangelical Fellowship Theological Commission and the Au Sable Institute for Environmental Studies, after boldly confessing, "We wholeheartedly affirm that the universe, as created by God, is good," immediately added, "We experienced some uncertainty and disagreement as to the nature and presence of evil in relation to creation. We did not attain clarity as to whether death as experienced before humankind's fall should be regarded as natural or evil, or as to exactly what the 'curse' brought with this fall, or how it operates."[37] Admirable as the second statement might be for its candor, it highlights precisely what I am getting at here: the failure of evangelical environmentalists to come to grips with the implications of the Curse. Indeed, obscured in the first statement is a hint at the problem. It would have been entirely true to affirm "that the universe, as created by God, *was* good." But the universe *is* not now as it *was* when it was created by God, and man's sin is not the only thing that has changed it; God's Curse has, too, and not for the better. (But we need not despair. Christ's redeeming activity also is transforming it, and not for the worse. More about this later.)

The difficulty in coming to grips with the Curse stems, I think, from a false prior assumption common to evangelical and other environmentalists—one mentioned above. It is, in the words of Vincent Rossi, restating Barry Commoner's third law of ecology, the notion that "nature knows best,"[38] or as Lionel Basney put it, that "left to itself, [nature] knows what to do" and ". . . it is this 'looking after itself' that is nature's mark. To be what it is, to be the delight of the One who made it, it does not need our interventions or (for that matter) us."[39] Environmentalists of every stripe have a tough time admitting that nature can do anything wrong or destructive. Yet as Gregg Easterbrook painstakingly and repeatedly details, nature's destructive powers—demonstrated in ice ages (Ever stopped to think what three-hundred-foot-thick ice sheets did to habitats and species when they covered all of North America, Europe, and Asia down to the 40th parallel—that is, as far south as San Francisco [almost], Salt Lake City, Denver, Chicago, Cleveland, Philadelphia, New York, Madrid, Ankara, Tashkent, and Beijing?), hurricanes, tornados, droughts, floods, volcanoes, earthquakes, tsunamis—far outstrip anything humanity has done or can do.[40]

One evangelical environmental writer has given the Curse much more careful thought than most. In *Healing the Earth*, Richard Young insightfully wrote:

> It is clear from Scripture that nature was affected by the fall and that the curse on the ground marks a relational skewing between humanity and the earth. The problem is to comprehend the precise cause-effect relation. Is the curse on the ground to be understood as a direct pronouncement of God or the natural consequence of humanity's deviant behavior? That is, did God directly cause a change in the ground and vegetation so that they would not yield as before, or did God indirectly allow a change in productivity by letting humanity's chosen path take its natural course?
>
> . . . . The wording [of Genesis 3:17, "Cursed is the ground because of you."] is ambiguous. It could mean that the ground will produce poorly because of divine action or human abuse. In either case the notion of a curse as judgment is upheld, either direct or indirect. Yet one cannot ignore the potency of a divine pronouncement nor the Hebrew notion that a curse carried with it the power to make it happen. Behind the utterance in Genesis 3 stands the omnipotent God, the God who spoke things into existence (Heb. 11:3), who healed with the spoken word (Matt. 8:8), and who pronounced a curse on a barren fig tree and it withered to the ground (Mark 11:14, 20–21). This suggests that the curse is more than merely the natural consequences of human abuse of nature.

Young then considers a common evangelical environmentalist interpretation of the Curse and finds it wanting:

> It is very appealing today with crimes against the environment making headlines to interpret God's curse on the ground as indirectly resulting from human wrongdoing. The authors of *Earthkeeping in the Nineties* contend that "the ground is cursed because we are set against it. . . . In short, the curse describes not a quality in the earth itself, but human misuse of dominion." Granberg-Michaelson agreed, saying, "Adam's disobedience does not intrinsically change the character of God's good creation. Instead, the picture presented is that human rebellion will infect and mar the creation; yet God's grace acts to restore the proper fellowship between God, humanity, and all creation." If the curse represents the natural consequences of our abuse of the environment, then Paul's statement in Romans 8:20, "the one who subjected it," must refer to us (represented by Adam) rather than God. That is, God did not subject the earth to futility, we did. The intrinsic goodness of creation, however, can be maintained without having to dissipate the curse into "human misuse."
>
> Traditionally, the curse on the ground has been understood as a direct action of God in which He holds back the natural productivity of the land. Genesis 5:28–29 reads, "When Lamech had lived 182 years, he had a son. He named him Noah and said, 'He will comfort us in the labor and painful toil of our hands caused by the ground the Lord has cursed.'" The unproductiveness of the ground was not only attributed to God but also characteristic of the antediluvian era. The antediluvian unproductiveness could not be the result of pollution from modern technology or centuries of harmful agricultural practices. . . .
>
> Romans 8:20–21 also tends to support the traditional view: "For the creation was subjected to frustration, not by its own choice, but by the will of the one who subjected it, in hope that the creation itself will be liberated from its bondage to decay and brought into the glorious freedom of the children of God." The agent that caused creation to be subjected is not stated, which leads some to contend that humans, by their irresponsible environmental behavior, have subjected creation to bondage. Against this is the parallelism of the two passive verbs. The same One who subjected creation to bondage will be the One who liberates it from that bondage. Traditional understanding recognizes God alone as the Liberator and Savior of humankind and all creation.
>
> The biblical evidence supports the idea that God directly cursed nonhuman aspects of creation as part of the judgment upon the human race. The curse did not change the inherent quality of nature, only its relational status. With the fractured harmony of the original ecosystem, the death process began for all creation, and the present ecological structure emerged. Be-

cause of the integrity of the created order, God could not have pronounced death upon humans and not include [sic] the rest of creation. Paul says in Romans 8:22 that all creation groans, being under the curse.

. . . . God's curse should be understood as His easing up on His sustaining influence on the natural order so that it begins the process of disease and decay. As such, the curse affects relations within the creation order, not the quality of creation. God's creation remains intrinsically good.

If all creation is suffering under a divine curse, then it might be inferred that nature is also in a fallen state and that there was a cosmic fall; but if so, nature's fall cannot be analogous to the fall of humanity. Nature is not morally responsible and could not fall on account of its own crime. It might be better to say that humanity morally fell, and nature was implicated in that fall, not that nature fell. It is only in this sense that we can speak of a cosmic fall and the need for a cosmic salvation. The solidarity of humanity and the environment necessitates the idea of a cosmic disordering as the result of Adam's sin and a cosmic reordering through the work of Christ (Col. 1:20).

Does this mean that nature is now somehow inherently evil? Does it imply that man can do as he pleases to it? Certainly not:

This perspective retains the inherent value and goodness of nature. There is no evil in nature that precipitated its fall, nor did the curse render the physical realm evil and something to be shunned. . . . Nature lost neither its value nor its inherent goodness; God still values it, and we are still responsible for taking care of it.[41]

Other writers would do well to think seriously about Young's observations. Evangelical environmentalism could not help but be strengthened by incorporating them.

Cosmic Redemption: What Does It Entail?

One theological issue on which evangelical environmentalists have contributed some excellent insights is the scope of redemption. Sometimes drawing on the insights of Greek Patristic thought, sometimes on that of contemporary Eastern Orthodox theologians, they have insisted that both the Old and the New Testaments depict redemption as encompassing not only human souls but the whole created order.[42] In this they undoubtedly are right (Rom. 8:18–25; Col. 1:15–20; Rev. 21; Isa. 65:17–25). It is one of the most important contributions of evangelicals to environmental thought and provides a helpful alternative to New Age thought.

Closely related to the cosmic scope of redemption is man's role in it.

Obviously Christ is Redeemer. But what role, if any, do the redeemed play in the restoration of the earth to glory? Most evangelical environmental writings have not addressed the question, but *Earthkeeping in the Nineties* did so in an insightful way:

> [I]n Christ, both as Creator and as Redeemer, God is immanent in creation. The "equality with God" enables the creating Word to share the flesh of his creation in an immanence which does not grasp at either glory or survival, but which leads ultimately to death. Likewise, though Christians transcend the world, they are also directed to become a redemptive part of what they transcend. Humans are to become saviors of nature, as Christ is the savior of humanity (and hence, through humans, of those parts of creation placed under their care).
>
> This idea of men and women being, along with Christ, the saviors of nature is not simply theological speculation. It is implied in all of those many Scripture passages which speak of redeemed humans as 'fellow heirs' with Christ. As Christ is Ruler, Creator, and Sustainer of the world, so also are we to be. Being heirs with Christ involves (as Paul saw) being crucified with Christ; it also involves sharing in Christ's sustaining, suffering activity in creation.
>
> Most specifically, this startling—but orthodox—idea of humans sharing in the redemption of creation is taught in [Rom. 8:19–22].[43]

Similarly, the *Evangelical Declaration on the Care of Creation* affirms:

> Because in Christ God has healed our alienation from God and extended to us the first fruits of the reconciliation of all things, we commit ourselves to working in the power of the Holy Spirit to share the Good News of Christ in word and deed, to work for the reconciliation of all people in Christ, and to extend Christ's healing to suffering creation.
>
> Because we await the time when even the groaning creation will be restored to wholeness, we commit ourselves to work vigorously to protect and heal that creation for the honor and glory of the Creator—whom we know dimly through creation, but meet fully through Scripture and in Christ.

Every Christian should embrace these insights. What evangelical environmentalists need to do now, however, is to harvest fruits from them, for they are ripe. The effects of the atoning death, victorious resurrection, and triumphant ascension of Christ sweep over all of creation, including man, animals, plants, and even the ground itself. They include the restoration of the image of God in the redeemed and through them—and by common grace even through many who are not redeemed—the restoration of knowledge, holiness, and creativity in working out the cultural mandate, including human multiplication, subduing and ruling the earth, transforming the wilderness by cultivation into a garden, and guarding that garden against harm.

No doubt some evangelical environmentalists will disagree with me sharply here, but the point deserves discussion: In my view, the amazing leaps in economic productivity and human material prosperity stemming from the application of the Christian worldview through the legal, political, economic, scientific, and technological advances propelled by Medieval and Reformation churchmen and scientists are a foretaste of the restoration of the cursed creation foretold by Paul and entailed by the incarnation, death, and resurrection of Christ.[44]

What we ought to expect, if we believe in the transforming power of Christ in the lives of the redeemed and, through them, on the cultures in which they live, is an increasing reversal of the effects of the Curse, a progressive transformation that parallels the growth—both intensive and extensive—of Christianity through the centuries. While Biblically sound social analysis repudiates the secularist ideology of inevitable Progress,[45] nonetheless the Christian doctrines of creation, fall, curse, redemption, and consummation equip us with a linear concept of time and a Biblically grounded faith that God is indeed working in time and space to restore this fallen and cursed world to glory (Matt. 13:24–43), and we ought to see—and can see if we are looking—evidences of this in history.[46]

Indeed, the cosmic implications of Christ's redeeming work, coupled with our understanding of the image of God in man (see chapter 7), suggest a specifically Christian perspective on the troubling question of resource depletion over which so many people wring their hands. For generations people have worried about the world's running out of various resources—especially energy resources. Yet, paradoxically, the long-term price trends of all extractive resources—animal, vegetable, and mineral (including energy resources)—are downward (save one).[47] I say "paradoxically," because falling prices indicate falling scarcity, which is precisely the opposite of what we intuitively expect as people consume finite resources. What explains this paradox? It is a combination of the Curse-reversing effects of redemption and the creative aspect of the image of God in man—the latter enhanced by the former.

Christian economist Gary North has argued that many Christians—especially scientific creationists[48]—have made a great mistake in embracing the secularist understanding of the universe as a closed system and therefore of the Second Law of Thermodynamics—entropy—as applying unvaryingly throughout time and space.[49] The universe is *not* a closed system. Its Creator is distinct from it and—we are not deists, after all—constantly interacting with it. Many of Christ's miracles involved reversals of entropy (turning water into wine, healing diseases and injuries, calming storms, raising the dead). Not only this, but we must keep in mind that entropy applies only to the *physical* world (matter and energy); it does not apply to the spiritual world. And Scripture teaches[50] that there is a domain of spirit—including the human soul, or mind[51]—that interacts constantly with the physical world, causing matter and energy to behave in ways they otherwise would not, that is, in anti-entropic ways.[52] It is precisely for this reason that C. S. Lewis argued that every effect of the mind on the body—and through it on any physical thing outside the body—is, strictly speaking, a miracle, i.e., something that nature, left to herself, could not do (but not something contrary to nature).[53]

In short, Christians have a worldview (Christian theism, metaphysical realism, mind/body dualism) and doctrinal (creation, curse, and redemption) foundation from which to offer a fresh perspective on the effect of human economic activity on the availability of resources. This fresh perspective, which sees resource supplies as increasing rather than decreasing as human civilization becomes increasingly adept at using the God-given powers of the mind to manipulate nature, is more consistent with both Biblical doctrine (e.g., God's abundant provision for His creatures' needs) and historical data (falling resource prices) than the gloomy perspective of those (whose predictions regarding resource supplies have consistently proven not only premature but pointed in the wrong direction) who insist that the world is fast running out of resources.[54]

CHAPTER 3

❧   ❧

The Hazards of Developing an
Ethic of Environmental Stewardship

O NE OF THE CHALLENGES FACING THE EVANGELICAL ENVIRONMEN-
tal movement is developing an ethic of earth stewardship. Both the dominion mandate and the simple fact of human intelligence make human rule
of the earth inescapable. How that rule will be exercised and to what ends is a
matter for careful exploration.

The authors of *Earthkeeping in the Nineties: Stewardship of Creation*—
the most important and substantive evangelical environmentalist book to date—
after discussing a variety of Biblical principles, develop an ethical structure
for earth stewardship, much of which makes good sense. Yet precisely because the book is in many respects so good, and because it has had and will
continue to have great influence on evangelical thinking about the environment, perhaps critical interaction with it will reveal some ways in which its
ethical structure can be improved—or at least in which some weaknesses might
be removed from it.[1]

*"1. The exercise of power inherent in our dominion must be rooted in
wonder—that is, it must be humble. . . ."*[2]

Saint Augustine once wrote, "When a certain rhetorician was asked what
was the chief rule in eloquence, he replied, 'Delivery'; what was the second
rule, 'Delivery'; what was the third rule, 'Delivery'; so if you ask me concerning the precepts of the Christian religion, first, second, third, and always
I would answer, 'Humility.'"[3] This principle is unexceptionable, but its implications, whether for environmental stewardship or for anything else in life,
are not always obvious. On the one hand, one might argue from it that the free
marketeer's insistence on personal freedom in industry, trade, and land use is

prideful and that he ought to submit humbly to economic planning. On the other hand, one might argue—as did Nobel Prize-winning economist Friedrich A. Hayek—that the economic planner's belief that he knows enough about people's needs and wants and capacities, and about the incredibly complex network of relationships that constitute the market to plan the economy is prideful and that he ought humbly to leave people free to choose their own paths within the boundaries of the rule of law.[4] Humility applied to environmental stewardship should lead us, in light of the vast complexity of human society and the earth's ecosystems, to hesitate considerably at the notion that we know enough about them to manage them (as opposed to enforcing the rules of justice)[5]—particularly that we are confident enough of our knowledge to assert our management preferences in place of the free choices of those who disagree with us.

"2. We have the responsibility to work toward a just human sharing of creation. The consumption of 40 percent of the earth's energy and mineral resources by 6 percent of the population is unjust."[6]

That everyone should do justice is undoubtedly true (Micah 6:8). But precisely what this entails is notoriously difficult to agree on. In this instance, these authors have applied an unbiblical, distributivist notion of justice that focuses on the outcome rather than on procedures the fairness of which is determined by their conformity to Biblical law.[7] No distributivist theory of justice will, in a world of dynamic relationships, yield any objective criteria for determining who should enjoy what shares of total wealth at any given time. The focus on distribution rather than on Biblically lawful procedures seems prone to incite discontent, envy, and resentment, not justice or generosity. The claim that "The consumption of 40 percent of the earth's energy and mineral resources by 6 percent of the population is unjust" is open to serious questions: What if those who consume those resources also produce them? What if their consumption does not limit the amount that other people can produce and consume, either now or in the future? Both of these questions can at least arguably be answered in the affirmative. The authors of *Earthkeeping* seem to have felt the discomfort of questions like these, even if they were not able to free themselves from the enticement of the redistributivist notion of justice, since after this assertion they immediately added, "This does not necessarily mean redistribution, for wealth is not simply gathered from the earth; it is created by human action and ingenuity." But if this does not simply vitiate their prior judgment, it is hard to imagine what would.

By all means let us do justice. But let our justice be Biblically defined. As the *Oxford Declaration on Christian Faith and Economics* put it, "Biblical justice means impartially rendering to everyone their [sic] due in conformity with the standards of God's moral law. . . . [T]he civil arrangements in rendering justice are not to go beyond what is due to the poor or to the rich (Deut. 1:17; Lev. 19:15). In this sense justice is ultimately impartial."[8] The point is not to justify the greed and materialism that drives many Americans (Greed and materialism are just as possible for the poor as for the rich, after all.) but to suggest that the justice of a situation is to be judged not by distributive outcomes but by the legitimacy of the procedures that yielded them.

"3. Stewardship implies responsibility for both human and nonhuman creatures. . . ."[9]

Here again, the principle is unassailable, but its practical implications are difficult to specify, to say the least. In a world of finite options, there are bound to be conflicts between (at least apparent) human interests and (at least apparent) interests of other creatures. Resolving those conflicts is only slightly easier when we remember that as God's stewards we should think not only of the human but also of the nonhuman creatures. How many snail darters—in absolute numbers, or as a proportion of the local or total population of the species—must be threatened (and at what probability?) with (a) death, (b) discomfort, or (c) dislocation to justify refraining from building a dam to protect people (and other creatures) against floods and to provide hydroelectric power to help people (and other creatures dependent on them) to live long and healthy at affordable costs? I ask the question not because there is any clear answer to it but precisely because there is not. That is the point. The principle of caring for human and nonhuman creatures by itself contributes little to our ability to make such difficult decisions. When we add to this observation the thoughts about humility, recalling how little we understand about the earth's ecosystems, we find ourselves even more in the dark.

"4. We should use creation in a sustainable way, providing for future generations at least the same opportunities for stewardship of a healthy creation that we have had. . . . An obvious implication of this principle is that we cannot simply use up fossil fuel 'savings' as though there will be no more need for them when they (and we) are gone."[10]

Here what seems at first blush an obviously right principle—Who wouldn't be in favor of sustainability?—and an "obvious implication" of it turns out, on careful examination, to have serious weaknesses. Given the dynamic character of human activity, it is difficult to see just what is meant by sustainability. Presumably—and this notion comes from reading of a wide variety of evangelical and other environmental literature—a procedure is sustainable if it can be continued indefinitely into the future. But exceedingly few human procedures—technologies—continue unchanged even for a few generations, let alone into the indefinite future. At one time most industries burned wood or peat for energy; then they turned to coal; then to mechanical water power; then to hydroelectric power and petroleum; some now use biomass, wind, tides, geothermal, solar, or nuclear fission. Suppose four hundred years ago someone had objected to using so much wood for industrial energy. "We should use creation in a sustainable way," he says, "providing for future generations at least the same opportunities for stewardship of a healthy creation that we have had. An obvious implication of this principle is that we cannot simply use up wood as though there will be no more need for it when it (and we) are gone. Just think how fast we'll run out of wood as our population and industries grow! Regrowth of forests won't be fast enough to keep up." Suppose he'd managed to persuade everyone to abandon or sharply curtail the use of wood for industrial fuel. That would have virtually halted industrial progress, leaving the whole human race at the subsistence level, condemning everyone to a brief and disease-ridden life. But as it turns out, it doesn't much matter whether burning wood for industrial fuel was using creation "in a sustainable way." The technical achievements made possible by the industrial activity once fueled by wood soon freed most industry from dependence on wood.

There is ample room for argument about judgments of sustainability. Consider another energy source—coal—as an example. "In 1865," writes Julian Simon,

> W. Stanley Jevons, one of the last century's truly great social scientists, wrote a careful, comprehensive book predicting that England's industry would soon grind to a halt due to exhaustion of England's coal. . . . And Jevons's investigation proved to him that there was no chance that oil would eventually solve England's problem.
>
> What happened? Because of the perceived future need for coal and because of the potential profit in meeting that need, prospectors searched out new deposits of coal, inventors discovered better ways to get coal out of the earth, and transportation men developed cheaper ways to move the coal. Other countries did the same. At present, the proven U.S. reserves of coal are enough to supply a level of use far higher than the present level for many hundreds or thousands of years. Though the labor cost per unit of coal output has been falling, the cost of other fuels has dropped even more. This suggests that *not enough* coal was mined in the past, rather than that the future was unfairly exploited in earlier years. As to Jevons's poor old England, this is its present energy situation: "Though Britain may reach energy self-sufficiency late this year or early next, with its huge reserves of North Sea oil and gas lasting well into the next century, the country is moving

ahead with an ambitious program to develop its even more plentiful coal reserves."[11]

Why would Simon have proposed that *not enough* coal had been mined in the past? Because energy consumption is, in the short run, a crucial constraint on economic development. Economic development fueled the technical advances that now enable us to use every energy source much more efficiently than we did in the past (and will enable us to use them all still more efficiently in the future). Had England and other industrialized countries clamped fierce restrictions on energy consumption in response to Jevons's fears, we might still be using energy at the efficiency levels of the late nineteenth or early twentieth century—i.e., consuming far more energy for every unit of economic output. Then either our total economic output (and consequently the availability of food, clothing, shelter, health care, education, transportation, communication, and all the other things we consume—some important and some frivolous) would be much less than it is now, or our total energy consumption would be much greater, or we would have some combination of lower output and higher energy consumption. The flip side of this coin is that if *more* coal had been consumed in the late nineteenth and early twentieth centuries, economic development probably would have been faster, and consequently technical advances would have occurred earlier, bringing greater energy efficiency earlier, leaving us with more remaining reserves of energy sources now rather than less. We cannot know precisely what would have resulted from more coal consumption, since unrealized contingencies are not susceptible to human knowledge, but theoretical understanding can point strongly toward a general conclusion.

"Another implication of this responsibility to future generations," the authors of *Earthkeeping* add, "is that we should not use creation today so as to leave hazards for the future. Thus we need to exercise great care in our disposal or storage of toxic and radioactive wastes. Such an obligation does not necessarily mean that we should never create such wastes, but it does imply that we should do so only if we are sure of a safe method of very long-term storage."[12] There is good common sense to this extrapolation, but there is still great difficulty in applying it to specific decisions.

First, at least subsequent to the Fall, safety is not an absolute but a relative term. There is no risk-free environment. This means that rather than insist on absolute safety as the proper standard for any given technology, we must compare risks and benefits from various achievable options. Thus we may choose to use some technologies despite their present or future risks because we believe their probable benefits outweigh their probable costs. Such judgments will rarely be noncontroversial, and sometimes we're bound to make what will in hindsight turn out to have been wrong choices, but choosing is inevitable.

There is no *absolutely safe* method of very long-term storage of toxic or radioactive wastes, for instance. There are more and less safe methods, the costs of which vary. There are also risks associated with refraining from the activities that generate the wastes. (Refraining from building more nuclear power plants out of fear of the risks associated with nuclear waste, for instance, involves accepting the risks and costs of alternative electricity generating technologies: more sulfur and CO_2 emissions from coal and petroleum plants, more loss of wild river habitat because of added hydroelectric dams, and so forth. Or it may involve accepting the risks and costs associated with producing less electricity: higher electricity prices leading to less urban street lighting and more urban crime, or less affordable food refrigeration leading to more food spoilage and consequently to more malnutrition and disease, and so forth.) The point is simply that some risk taking is inevitable.

Second, it is at least worth asking whether we can reasonably expect future technological developments to make future generations better able to deal with toxic and radioactive wastes than we are—perhaps even to turn them into valuable resources. Two hundred years ago, petroleum was not a resource, it was a sticky, smelly nuisance wherever it bubbled up out of the ground. Today, of course, it is a valuable resource. Why? Because people have developed ways to use petroleum for energy, lubrication, synthetic fibers, plastics, fertilizers, medicines, and a wide variety of other purposes. Similarly, some places now have affordable technologies to turn large amounts of raw sewage into valuable fertilizer; in others these technologies are not yet affordable. Thus, in some places raw sewage is a smelly and disease-bearing nuisance, while in others it is a valuable resource. Gregg Easterbrook tells just how valuable sewage sludge can be:

> In the 1980s cities making fertilizer from sludge had trouble finding buyers. Product quality, if that's the right term, was uneven, if that's the right adjective. Except for the brand-named Metrogro marketed by Madison, Wisconsin, sludge fertilizer often contained excess levels of cadmium. Farmers feared consumers would boycott foods grown with sludge fertilizer. Beginning in the late 1980s, knowledge-based improvements in the processing of sludge to fertilizer transformed the market. Corn grown in fertilizer made from Milwaukee sewage now contains less than on part per million of heavy metals, a safe level.

Once quality improved farmers began to demand sludge-based fertilizer, which sells for less than petrochemical fertilizers. By 1992 the percentage of U.S. sludge recycled to fertilizer had risen from about 20 percent to 48 percent and was still headed up. Today New York City ships sludge fertilizer to Arizona, Colorado, and Texas, where soils are often deficient in the very copper, nitrogen, phosphorous, and zinc that urban sludge contains. In 1993 farmers in Lamar, Colorado, wrote to New York City officials complaining about missed sludge shipments and asking when more would arrive. That's right: Lamar was experiencing a SLUDGE SHORTAGE.[13]

Is it crazy to imagine that a generation or two from now, after someone has devised a wonderful use for radioactive waste, people might be wondering, "Now why did those folks back in the 1990s have to go and bury that stuff so deep in that granite? They made it awfully expensive to retrieve, and we could use a lot more of it than our present nuclear plants are putting out!"? (Already, by the way, there are some uses for certain types of radioactive waste. One is as the active agent in smoke detectors. Another is in radiation therapy for cancer.)

"5. Our planning horizon must be unlimited. As Christians, we believe that there will be an end to this world as we know it, but we 'know not the day nor the hour' of that end. And since we have no way of knowing when it will be, we must proceed as though there will be no end to our need to exercise stewardly care."[14]

While we must think of future generations in our earth stewardship and not excuse profligate waste and wanton destruction on the grounds that the rapture's right around the corner, nonetheless, to think in terms of an *unlimited* planning horizon for economic and ecological activities is of limited usefulness. To put it simply, the technological circumstances of the world a century—let alone a millennium—from now are far beyond our ken. Even science fiction writers of the late nineteenth century could not have predicted much of what today we take for granted. Thousands of *types* of technologies—each with dozens or scores of name brands or models—exist today that no one had dreamed of a century ago. And the rate of technological development is increasing, which means that if we could travel through time we would probably feel more at home in the world of the late nineteenth century—or perhaps even the late seventeenth—than in that of the late twenty-first. If we would think our great-grandparents' plans for our world were a bit quaint, how might our great-grandchildren think of our plans for their world? Certainly we want to leave the world a better place for posterity. But we're jesting if we consider ourselves capable of planning in light of their hypothetical future circumstances.[15]

     6. We need to know as fully as possible where the things which sustain us come from and how they are produced. What is the source of the food we eat, the fuel we burn, the materials we use for shelter, clothing, and transportation? . . . To know the forest that grew the beams in our house, the soil that grew the vegetables in our salad, the ore which was the origin of our automobile—all of these increase our knowledge of and participation in the production of what we use, as does growing or picking our own food, for example. Even a little of such an activity is a valuable reminder that we are participants in a wide community of life."[16]

     Are there good reasons for us to learn where what we buy comes from and how it is made? Yes. The development of our imagination is one good reason. Awareness of options is another. Environmental stewardship is yet a third. But we would be naive to think we could know very much at all about where all but a few of the things we use each day come from and how they are made and brought to us.

     One of the classic essays in economics is Leonard Read's brief and simple "I, Pencil,"[17] a genealogy of a lead pencil written in the first person. Its lesson is *"not a single person on the face of this earth knows how to make me."* Read demonstrates this by describing the sources of the wood, minerals, and chemicals that make up a lead pencil, the processes by which those materials are extracted from the earth, transported, refined, and combined, and the vast web of enterprises involved in all the various steps, combining the work of millions of people from many countries in hundreds of industries, almost none of whom intends to make a pencil.

     I, Pencil, am a complex combination of miracles: a tree, zinc, copper, graphite, and so on. But to these miracles which manifest themselves in Nature an even more extraordinary miracle has been added: the configuration of creative human energies—millions of tiny know-hows configurating naturally and spontaneously in response to human necessity and desire and *in the absence of any human master-minding!* Since only God can make a tree, I insist that only God can make me. Man can no more direct these millions of know-hows to bring me into being than he can put molecules together to create a tree. [Emphasis original.]

     This principle inherently contradicts the first one the authors of *Earthkeeping* proposed: humility. As Hayek put it, "in the study of such 'essentially complex' phenomena as the market, which depend on the actions of many individuals, all the circumstances that will determine the outcome of a process . . . *will hardly ever be fully known or measurable.*"[18] What frees us to specialize in doing what we can do well is the confidence that, entirely apart from our knowing or directing what they do, others will do what they can do well, we can trade our surplus with them for theirs, and all will enjoy more with less effort than if we tried to make everything for ourselves. In short, putting this principle into rigorous practice would mean transporting ourselves back to the time (which probably never occurred) when no one traded with anyone but everyone made everything he himself consumed. It would also mean forgetting that the different gifts God has given to different people enable them to play different roles in the Body of Christ (Rom. 12; 1 Cor. 12). Remember Christ's reply when Peter asked him what was in store for John: ". . . what is that to you? You must follow me" (John 21:22).

"7. We should not undertake a process of agriculture, mining, transportation, energy generation, waste disposal, recreation, and so forth until we have evaluated its consequences for the household of life. This does not mean that ecosystem-disturbing activities should be abandoned, but that they should continually be redesigned toward the ideal of an earthly creation which can meet human needs without being diminished in intricacy, vigor, and diversity. . . ."[19]

As stated, this principle is unobjectionable. The authors exercise admirable restraint by insisting only that consequences be *evaluated* and that the principle does not require that particular activities be abandoned but only that they be redesigned toward an ideal. Still, we must be careful not to slide from this realistic principle to the unrealistic goal of knowing *every* consequence for *every* part of the household of life and postponing the use of any process until we have such knowledge, or even until we have so refined the process as to be certain it will have only such consequences as we are prepared to accept. For the consequences will be affected by such complex interrelationships that they will be literally unpredictable for finite minds. Each new process will spur changes in other processes, which in turn will spur changes in still other processes, *ad infinitum*. It is simply impossible to know all such consequences and to balance their costs and benefits. Further, while the general principle of cost/benefit analysis is legitimate, it is not always easy to apply, as we saw above, particularly when either benefit is clearly visible while cost is not, or vice versa. Fallible judgment calls are inevitable. It behooves us to remember not to import the certainty of moral absolutes to disagreements over such matters.

"8. We should show particular concern for the animals we have brought into the human world through domestication and use. . . . [W]hen we make

use of them we should do so with as little pain as possible. . . ."[20] Bravo.

"9. The lands which produce our food and provide important ecosystem functions must be protected from destruction. We should develop policies which prevent the urbanization of the very lands upon which we ultimately depend for our well-being. . . . Above all, we should establish and support policies which encourage the preservation of the soil. . . ."[21]

With the general concern to ensure adequate agricultural land to provide plenty of food for everyone there should be no quarrel. Neither should we reject the importance of land that performs "important ecosystem functions," although well-meaning people will disagree over just how important various functions are in relation to alternative functions, and we must be humble in our evaluations of their preferences.

There is some risk, however, of adopting a static perspective toward land use that is historically unrealistic and economically and ecologically unwise in its inflexibility. If the development of new farmland in Brazil, or the improvement of yields in India, relieves market demand for agricultural products from Canada, there is no reason why all the farmland previously under cultivation in Canada should remain so indefinitely. Farmland is not natural; it is the fruit of cultivation that might require nothing more than plowing under wild grasses and planting seed that will grow adequately with water supplied by rain, or removing trees and rocks, leveling hills, draining swamps, irrigating arid soils, and adding fertilizers. This means that it is possible, ordinarily, to replace farmland lost in one locale with new farmland developed elsewhere. If a thousand acres of farmland will bring a higher price when converted to residential or industrial use than when retained as farmland, it may well make sense to convert them and use the profits to meet the cost of developing new farmland elsewhere.

As for soil conservation practices, these already are in effect in the United States and most other developed nations. Certainly they should be adopted increasingly in other countries as well, but patience is in order as we await the growth of understanding on the part of many farmers in less-developed countries—and of their ability to pay for erosion control measures. At any rate, worldwide upward trends in crop yields spanning centuries and with no end in sight seem to indicate that on the whole topsoil loss to erosion does not seriously threaten the adequacy of the world's food supply.[22]

"10. We must limit human population to a level which can be sustained within a healthy and diverse creation. . . . [E]very environment has a carrying capacity. For some time now we have been increasing the earth's capacity to sustain humans by diminishing its capacity to sustain other creatures. . . ."[23]

"We must limit" is an innocuous-sounding phrase that has frightening implications for political and social relationships. It is far preferable for husbands and wives to make their own choices about reproduction than to be coerced or even subject to governmental pressure (through tax policies favoring small families, for instance) to limit the number of children they have. What is to be done to those who decline to embrace the small-family policies promoted to slow or stop population growth? Certainly in something so sacred and intimate as procreation, choices are best left in private.[24] (Chapter 7 argues that population growth does not threaten the earth's carrying capacity, so we shall leave that issue until then.)

"11. In planning for future energy needs, it is essential to consider the end use of energy and to determine an appropriate source for it. . . . In a house, for example, it is desirable to have an air temperature near 70 degrees Fahrenheit. To produce that temperature, it may be necessary to have a medium somewhat warmer—perhaps a 120-degree radiator. Yet to produce that low temperature heat . . . we must burn coal, oil, or gas in a furnace at temperatures up to 2,500 degrees. Solar energy, on the other hand, delivers low temperature heat—somewhat below the boiling point of water—and thus is ideally suited for one of the main needs of such heat: space and water heating in homes. Such matching of end-use needs to appropriate energy sources requires some flexibility in the design of both homes and utilities, but the potential for saving, both economically and ecologically, is very great."[25]

This principle is reasonable, and economic factors will ordinarily prompt people to adopt the most cost-effective matches of energy source to energy use available to them.[26]

"12. We need to choose carefully those sources of energy which do the least damage to creation. . . . Many good reasons have been advanced for opposing nuclear power, but such opposition is misguided if it assumes that any alternative—especially coal-fired power plants—is superior. The risks of increased coal burning (such as more acid rain and more carbon dioxide in the atmosphere) might be greater than the risks of nuclear power. But other alternatives—such as more conservation and various uses of solar energy— would be better than either. We also need to remember the net energy cost. The amount of energy that goes into building, maintaining, and dismantling any energy system—from nuclear to solar—may in the long run be so high as to render it environmentally unacceptable."[27] And,

"13. Energy conservation is the single most important part of any energy program. . . ."[28]

The first of these eminently sensible principles could go far toward alleviating popular antipathy toward nuclear power among environmentalists. The relative risks of nuclear power generation versus other large-scale power generation technologies are minuscule, even in estimates of such antinuclear lobbying groups as the Union of Concerned Scientists.[29] Certainly, too, the development of increasingly efficient technologies so as to reduce energy input per unit of output is a sensible goal—one that private persons and businesses, seeking to minimize costs and maximize gains, are pursuing around the world. (That they are pursuing other goals, too, means they won't always put the same priority on this one that we might wish, but humility should make us shrink from imposing our priorities—as distinct from moral absolutes—on them.)

"14. The fossil 'fuels'—coal, oil, and natural gas—are a unique chemical treasure and, as much as possible, should not be burned as fuels but rather should be used as sources of synthetic material. Oil, coal, and natural gas are our primary source of plastics. Yet currently we burn 95 percent of these hydrocarbons for fuel and use only 5 percent for synthetic materials, including medicines. Since there are many other potential sources for heat, but no comparable source for the chemical properties of these fossil materials, a stewardly use of these resources would be to stop using them for fuel and save them for these higher uses."[30]

In general, this principle makes sense. However, if the demand for coal, oil, and natural gas as sources of synthetic material were greater, their prices would rise, depressing their consumption as fuels and thus freeing more of them for use as synthetics. It probably is not necessary to adopt any government policy to do what the market is already capable of doing very well.

"15. Since it is clear that we must rapidly shift from use of 'savings' resources (fossil fuels) to use of 'income' resources [solar], we should give our greatest attention to the development and widespread use of solar energy conversion devices. . . . [T]he order for our research and development priorities, should be something like this:

I.   Income (and Short-Term Savings) Resources
   A.   Solar-passive
   B.   Solar-active
      1.   Hydroelectric
      2.   Solar thermal
      3.   Biomass—e.g., wood, methane from wastes, alcohol or petroleum from plants or plant products
      4.   Wind
      5.   Solar electric

> 6. *Ocean temperature differential*
> C. *Tidal*
> II. *Inheritance Resources*
>   A. *Geothermal*
>   B. *Nuclear fusion*
>   C. *Nuclear fission*
> III. *Savings Resources (Long-Term)*
>   *Fossil fuels"*[31]

The rapidity with which the shift from fossil fuels to other energy resources must be made will become evident only with time, and technical developments will determine what, at any given time, seems the best order of priorities for research and development. (Unforeseen developments—a new form of internal combustion engine, for instance, that triples or quadruples vehicle mileage, or an affordable and low-risk method of using hydrogen as a vehicle fuel, or a breakthrough in battery technology that makes electric cars cheaper and more convenient to operate—could justify major changes in priorities at any given time.) But in general this principle seems reasonable. However, this guideline is prudential/pragmatic, not principial/ethical. That someone might prefer a different order of priorities is not cause for moral judgment, as happens all too often in debate over environmental issues.

"16. Christians should seek to reform those societal structures which damage the ecosphere and produce injustice among humans. . . ."[32]

This is eminently reasonable. It should go without saying also, however, that honest Christians will disagree on both the moral question of what constitutes injustice and the practical questions of which societal structures damage the ecosphere and why, and of how best to go about reforming those that do.

"17. We must maintain a clear distinction between price and value. Price is set by the market system and is a result of the available supply and of demands made on the basis of wants. Value, on the other hand, depends not on someone's cash-backed yearnings but on a quality intrinsic to the thing or to its function. To dispose of an object on the basis of price alone is to continue in that misunderstanding of dominion which says that humans are the only source of value and meaning on earth. . . ."[33]

This principle raises the very difficult issue of how best to ascribe value to objects or functions. The hesitation to let market price be the primary measure of value is understandable. However, at least in the understanding of some economists, market price—in a free market—reflects not simply "economic" considerations but all the various ideals, needs, wants, preferences, objectives, and even moral commitments people bring to the valuing process.

This does not mean, of course, that every individual would attach the same market price to something; it only means that the market clearing price(s) will reflect the concerns of the wide variety of people who constitute the market. Economists think of economic value as *subjective*, even though they (most of them, anyway) affirm the reality of *objective* moral value. (An economist who believed pornography was morally wrong would refuse to buy or sell it no matter how low or high the price. And even if he believed it ought to be outlawed, he would still recognize that its market price reflected the subjective economic value ascribed to it by those who *were* willing to buy and sell it.) Thus, economists tend to resist ascribing *intrinsic* value to anything but moral principles and human lives.[34]

Certainly, however, if what is intended by this principle is to remind people that concerns other than the "bottom line"—money profits and losses—ought to guide our choices, then no one should object to it.[35]

"18. All people should be free to exercise stewardship over a fair share of creation. The commandment to exercise dominion was given to 'the Adam': all humankind. Yet, because of the present inequities of the distribution of power over the earth's resources, vast numbers of people lack not only the basic means for sustenance, but also the very privilege to exercise stewardship."[36]

Here the question of what constitutes justice arises again (see point 2). There is no need to repeat the discussion here. However, lack of ownership of land or movable property does not deprive anyone of the "privilege to exercise stewardship." Everyone can and must be a steward of himself: his soul and body, energy and time, abilities and relationships—all of these things far more important than material possessions. Indeed, good stewardship of oneself can lead to acquiring property in (stewardship over) land and other objects—a lesson illustrated in the life of Joseph, who, though sold into slavery in Egypt, quickly became steward of an officer's house, and though wrongly imprisoned, soon became steward of the whole kingdom. It is significant that in the parable of the talents, the master (who represents God) distributes money to his stewards according to their abilities (Matt. 25:15), rewards them according to their performance (vv. 21, 23, and 25–28), and upon taking from the unprofitable servant the one talent he had and giving it to the most profitable servant explains, "For everyone who has will be given more, and he will have an abundance. Whoever does not have, even what he has will be taken from him" (v. 29). Differences of wealth and income are neither inherently unjust (Matt. 20:1–15) nor insuperable obstacles to faithful stewardship.

"19. Our aid to developing nations should not impose Western ideas of

development, but should encourage and enhance both the cultural unique-
ness of the peoples of those nations and the diversity of creatures within them."[37]

Depending on what is included in the category of "Western ideas of de-velopment," this guideline might be sound or silly. If attitudes about such things as personal hygiene, pollution of rivers and streams with human and animal waste, treatment of women and children with dignity, or diligence ver-sus sloth are included, then it is silly. And yet attitudes about such things differ greatly from culture to culture, and they have enormous effects on eco-nomic development. On each of them, *Christian* ethics has important things to say. And it is an unavoidable fact of history that Christianity has deeply influenced Western culture. There are, of course, aspects of Western culture toward which Christian ethics may be largely neutral (type of dress, for in-stance—except when it transgresses the bounds of modesty), and some as-pects of it that Christian ethics must condemn (materialism, nihilism, ethical relativism, and so forth). But there are other aspects of Western culture that Christian ethics must affirm and the denial of which it must condemn.

Culture, after all, is rooted in the cult. As T. S. Eliot pointed out in 1946 in *Notes Towards the Definition of Culture*,[38] the words *culture* and *cultivate* share the same root, *cultus*, a Latin word derived from the verb *colere*, which means both to worship and to till the soil. At the very core of culture is reli-gion, with its concepts of God and of transcendent morals, concepts so pow-erful that they shape every other element of culture, for good or ill. It is mistaken, therefore, simply to condemn all export of Western culture, shaped as it has been by Christianity, to other lands. By all means let us separate what is truly Christian from what is not in Western culture, and export the one and not the other. But let us not rush into the one extreme of cultural relativism in our effort to avoid the other extreme of cultural chauvinism.[39]

"20. Our lives as stewards should make clear that the achievement of the central purposes of life is not directly proportional to our level of consump-tion. . . . [Q]uality of life does not necessarily improve with increased con-sumption. Western statistics on divorce, suicide, and drug and alcohol abuse make it plan that trying to 'have it all' leads to misery."[40]

Amen to that.

What can we say in summary about these guidelines for creation steward-ship? While many make good sense, all require careful, nuanced application, and some are questionable on Biblical grounds. One interesting observation is the extent to which these guidelines for "stewardship over creation" spread to cover a great deal of ground that we might not normally think of under the heading *environment*. We have visited humility and justice; human and non-human life; present and future generations, indeed an unlimited planning horizon; the need to know whence things come to us and how our economic processes affect the whole "household of life"; domestic animals; land, population, and energy resources; societal structures; value and price; foreign aid and its effect on varied cultures; "the central purposes of life"; even "divorce, suicide, and drug and alcohol abuse." On the one hand, this aptly illustrates the interrelatedness of all of life. It reminds us, as we so badly need to be reminded, that we cannot isolate one aspect of life from all the others and pretend it neither affects them nor is affected by them. On the other hand, it also illustrates the tendency of environmentalism to becoming "everythingism"—i.e., to lead to totalitarian visions of social reform.[41]

Two final comments: First, many of the very specific suggestions (e.g., reducing energy use through efficiency, recycling, minimizing unneeded packaging, car pooling, buying long-lasting products rather than disposables) given by the authors of *Earthkeeping* in their appendix "What You Can Do"—particularly in the section "Individuals and Families"—are clear and sensible, and the criticisms of the principal guidelines above do not imply rejection of those suggestions.[42] Their implementation by anyone would almost certainly help to improve the state of our environment.[43]

Second, time and again these guidelines have been found open to serious debate either as to principles or as to application. This should make all of us cautious about blanket moral judgments when others disagree about how best to exercise creation stewardship. A marked tendency, particularly in popular publications, toward moralizing about environmental issues may express the fervency of personal commitment that some people feel, but it is rarely justified by careful ethical or empirical consideration. Indeed, what we call good stewardship may change over time as technologies change, a point demonstrated in appendix C of *Earthkeeping in the Nineties*, "A Case Study—Recycled Paper," in which the authors conclude, after discussing the costs and benefits of paper recycling, both financial and environmental, that while in the past, "because recycled paper requires de-inking and bleaching, the pollution generated in the recycling process was often greater than that for virgin paper," present recycling processes are significantly cleaner. Nonetheless, even now "the use of recycled paper appears to be only slightly more stewardly than the use of virgin materials."[44] If so tentative a conclusion is warranted in regard to paper recycling, it is surely much more so in regard to many other environmental issues about which we know even less. Patience, charity, and open minds are definitely in order.

CHAPTER 4

🐌   🐌

The Use of Scripture
by Evangelical Environmentalists

THE MOST IMPORTANT SOURCE OF UNDERSTANDING EVANGELICALS CAN bring to environmental issues is the Bible. From it, above all other sources, we learn about Creator and creation, about ourselves and our relationship with the rest of creation, about righteousness and sin and judgment and redemption, about the beginning and the end and the purpose of it all.

Evangelical environmentalists make much use of Scripture, often in insightful ways. As we saw in chapter 2, they have written extensively about such major Biblical issues as the dominion mandate (Gen. 1:26–28), Adam's role as cultivator and keeper of the Garden of Eden (Gen. 2:15), the effect of sin on the earth and man's relationship with other creatures and the ground itself (Gen. 3), God's ultimate ownership of the earth (Ps. 24:1) over which He has given man stewardship (Ps. 115:16), the wonder we should feel toward creation (Job 38–41; Ps. 104), and the inclusion of creation in Christ's redemption (Rom. 8:19–23; Col. 1:15–18). No doubt there is room for added insights and for some adjustments in the understanding of these and other major issues, but by and large the Bible plays a strong and positive role in shaping the thought of evangelical environmentalism.

Evangelical environmentalists are to be commended particularly for their effective refutation, by use of Scripture, of various charges by non-Christian environmentalists that Christianity is to blame for environmental degradation. Some secular and New Age environmentalists, for instance, charge that Christianity's anthropocentrism leads to neglect of other forms of life. Evangelicals rightly respond (a) that Christianity is not anthropocentric but theocentric, (b) that God holds man accountable for his stewardship of cre-

43

ation, (c) that the Bible teaches us to appreciate creation and praise God for it, and (d) that the earth was not made just for man but for the pleasure and glory of God.

Other non-Christian environmentalists charge that Christianity's affirmation of human dominion over the earth justifies misuse of ecosystems. Evangelicals reply (a) that a proper understanding of dominion involves careful stewardship of the earth, not its degradation, and (b) that cultures shaped largely by other religions have done at least as much damage to the environment as has Western culture. Several evangelical environmental publications, including *Earthkeeping in the Nineties*, from the Calvin Center for Christian Scholarship; *The Environment and the Christian: What Can We Learn from the New Testament?*, edited by Calvin DeWitt of the Au Sable Institute; and perhaps best of all *Healing the Earth: A Theocentric Perspective on Environmental Problems and Their Solutions*, by Richard A. Young—who set out with this specific purpose in mind—do an excellent job of answering such charges.

As good as much of the use of Scripture is in evangelical environmental writings, however, it can be improved. This chapter, therefore, will look critically first at how some evangelical environmentalists use particular passages of Scripture to bolster some of their ideas but misunderstand or misapply the passages, and second, at some relevant passages that seem to be overlooked in the writings of evangelical environmentalists. The aim is not to quibble over small matters of interpretation with only narrow implications but to discuss how our handling, mishandling, or neglect of a few specific passages of Scripture can affect our understanding of certain broad principles related to environmental stewardship and ethics.

Does the Bible Really Mean That?

1. ISAIAH 5:8. Aside from the texts mentioned above, one that comes up very frequently in evangelical writings on the environment is Isaiah 5:8: "Woe to you who add house to house and join field to field till no space is left and you live alone in the land." After citing it, Orin Gelderloos writes, "Placing house next to house reduces biodiversity and leaves humankind disconnected from the created world and without the companionship of the other species of creation."[1] *Earthkeeping* uses it as an epigram to a chapter titled "The Human Deluge," which argues that human population growth threatens to crowd the planet, deplete resources, and drive many species extinct.[2] Calvin DeWitt uses it to condemn "deforestation and habitat destruction" and the conversion of agricultural land to residential and other uses:

By clearing tropical forests we are able to enjoy inexpensive items like ply-wood, bathroom tissue, hamburger meat, and orange juice, among other things. All this comes at the cost of destroying the long-term sustainability of soils, forest creatures, and resident people. . . . In the United States, about 3 million of the 400 million acres of cropland that is used for agriculture is converted to urban uses every year. . . . And houses are replacing some of the best cropland.

The Bible has a verse that speaks to this particular abuse of creation: "Woe to you who add house to house and join field to field till no space is left and you live alone in the land" (Isa. 5:8).[3]

Before discussing whether the verse properly applies to such questions, two other things deserve note. First, it is unlikely that, as Gelderloos put it, "placing house next to house reduces biodiversity." On the contrary, by living close together, people reduce their overall intrusion on natural habitats, thus minimizing whatever negative effect they might have on biodiversity.[4] Second, whether these writers have accurately described the empirical situation (e.g., DeWitt's claim of the rate of farmland conversion to urban uses is highly debatable) and whether the empirical situation even as described is actually a problem are distinct questions from whether they have rightly used this verse. Even if they have used the verse properly, it might not lend added (Biblical) authority to their empirical claims.

But does the verse itself even properly apply to such concerns? Certainly not directly. Gelderloos, for instance, thinks it condemns building many houses close together, but the verse says the result of joining "house to house and field to field" is that "no space is left and *you live alone in the land.*" What does this mean? That people—lots of them—live densely packed together without other species? That does not seem to have been the concern God intended to express through Isaiah. (Certainly nothing in the context hints of a concern for other species. Israelites are the focus.)

The judgment pronounced in this verse is rooted in the Jubilee land tenure law (Lev. 25),[5] which forbade the permanent sale of agricultural land outside a family line, requiring instead that it be sold only for as many years as remained until the Jubilee (every fiftieth year) and for a price equal to the combined value of the intervening annual crops, after which it must be returned (its sale price having been repaid by the crops) to the original family of ownership. If obeyed, this law would have ensured that every family retained over long periods of time, albeit perhaps with temporary interruptions, possession of productive land. It also would have prevented the amassing of large agricultural landholdings in a few hands while many Israelites were left without land on which to earn a living.

Here Isaiah writes of Israel's disobedience to this law and of its conse-quences. (Micah, a contemporary of Isaiah, mentions—with more obvious reliance on the Jubilee law—the same oppression by some rich Israelites: "They covet fields and seize them, and houses, and take them. They defraud a man of his home, a fellowman of his inheritance" [Mic. 2:2]). By "till no space is left," then, Isaiah means "no space [for brother Israelites, particularly the poor who have been dispossessed of their landed inheritance,] is left,"[6] because the oppressors have taken all their lands from them, contrary to the Jubilee law. As commentator John Oswalt put it, "those who possessed the means were dispossessing the poor and reducing them to servitude on their own land."[7] Hence the oppressors "live alone in the land," not densely but sparsely populating it because they have driven the poor from their lands.

The difficulty is harmonizing "join house to house," which Gelderloos and some other environmentalist authors take to imply lots of dwellings close together, with "you live alone in the land." The solution seems to be that the highly elastic word *bayith*, translated *house*, in this instance probably denotes not a physical dwelling but a *place* or *property* associated with a family.[8] Perhaps the best translation would be "join estate to estate" or—as suggested by a comment by George Buchanan Gray—"homestead to homestead."[9]

Nothing in this passage condemns building dwellings on agricultural land. The prophetic concern is not about deforestation or conversion of farmland to residential land or having lots of houses close together but about some people unlawfully defrauding others of their property—whether dwelling or field, whether urban or rural. To apply it to questions of land conversion is to import Biblical moral authority illegitimately.

2. JEREMIAH 2:7–8. Wesley Granberg-Michaelson describes a conversation with a geography teacher during an airline flight. Looking down at the scars of clear-cut areas, the teacher said, "The Scripture verse I'm reminded of is from Jeremiah. . . . It says, 'I brought you into a plentiful land to enjoy its fruits and its good things. But when you came in you defiled my land. . . .' That's exactly what we've done."

"Later I looked up the reference," Granberg-Michaelson continues, "and found it in Jeremiah 2:7–8. This is one of numerous biblical references por-traying the unfaithfulness and sins of humanity *expressed in the destruction of the environment*."[10]

Now, wanton destruction of the environment is undoubtedly a form of unfaithfulness to the stewardship God has given to man and thus is sin. And

Jeremiah 2:7–8 does indeed attribute environmental destruction to the sins of Israel. But there is an important difference between what Jeremiah says and what Granberg-Michaelson says. Granberg-Michaelson says that this and other Biblical passages portray human unfaithfulness and sin as "expressed in the destruction of the environment." If this were so, what sorts of acts might we expect Jeremiah to list as sins that "defiled [God's] land"? Wasteful killing of forests and animals, careless farming that caused rapid soil erosion, failure to give the land its sabbaths by leaving it fallow every sabbath year, and so on. But what sorts of acts does Jeremiah actually name? "They followed worthless idols and became worthless themselves. They did not ask, 'Where is the LORD, who brought us up out of Egypt and led us through the barren wilderness, through a land of deserts and rifts, a land of drought and darkness, a land where no one travels and no one lives?' I brought you into a fertile land to eat its fruit and rich produce. But you came and defiled my land and made my inheritance detestable. The priests did not ask, 'Where is the LORD?' Those who deal with the law did not know me; the leaders rebelled against me. The prophets prophesied by Baal, following worthless idols. . . . My people have committed two sins: They have forsaken me, the spring of living water, and have dug their own cisterns, broken cisterns that cannot hold water"[11] (Jer. 2:5b–8, 13). What sins "defiled the land"? Not poor environmental practices, but idolatry and infidelity to the covenant.

Jeremiah explains that Israel's theological infidelity has brought God's judgment: foreign invasion (2:15; compare 4:6–7) and drought (3:3), leading ultimately to the once fruitful land's becoming "formless and empty" with "no people" or even birds, "a desert" with "all its towns . . . in ruins" (4:23, 25–26).[12] This leads to an important observation about the interrelationship of God, man, and the environment: God is personally involved, acting in covenantal judgment on the environment in response to man's covenantal loyalty or treason (just as He cursed the earth in response to Adam's sin in the Garden). Notice that when Israel had been faithful, God had blessed it by bringing it out of foreign oppression in Egypt, leading it safely through a barren wilderness, and settling it in "a fertile land to eat its fruit and rich produce" (2:6–7). But now that Israel has turned in betrayal from the covenant, God is judging it by putting it under foreign oppression again and making its land infertile. Certainly sound agricultural practices are important to the land's fertility, but they will be of no avail when a nation, by turning from God to idols and spurning His law, brings God's judgment on itself.

If we are to preserve or restore the earth from environmental degradation, then, the most important message evangelicals can communicate will focus not on carbon dioxide or chloro-fluorocarbon emissions, not on soil erosion or deforestation, not on species extinction or toxic wastes, but on fidelity to God and His law. Our most significant message is not pragmatic (use contour ploughing, reduce carbon dioxide emissions, reduce dependence on fossil fuels) but ethical: Worship and obey the God of Abraham, Isaac, and Jacob. Pragmatic instructions are useful, but they are secondary. Ethics is primary— ethics defined by the revealed law of God in Scripture, not by current "best wisdom" about pollution control and ecology. Those who live in faithful obedience to the God of the covenant will experience His blessing even on the environment:

> If you pay attention to these laws and are careful to follow them, then the LORD your God will keep his covenant of love with you, as he swore to your forefathers. He will love you and bless you and increase your numbers. He will bless the fruit of your womb, the crops of your land—your grain, new wine and oil—the calves of your herds and the lambs of your flocks in the land that he swore to your forefathers to give you. You will be blessed more than any other people; none of your men or women will be childless, nor any of your livestock without young. The LORD will keep you free from every disease. [Deut. 7:12–15a]

But those who live in unbelieving sin will experience God's curse even on the environment:

> However, if you do not obey the LORD your God and do not carefully follow all his commands and decrees I am giving you today, all these curses will come upon you and overtake you: You will be cursed in the city and in the country. Your basket and your kneading trough will be cursed. The fruit of your womb will be cursed, and the crops of your land, and the calves of your herds and the lambs of your flocks. . . . The LORD will send on you curses, confusion and rebuke in everything you put your hand to, until you are destroyed and come to sudden ruin because of the evil you have done in forsaking him. The LORD will plague you with diseases until he has destroyed you from the land you are entering to possess. The LORD will strike you with wasting disease, with fever and inflammation, with scorching heat and drought, with blight and mildew, which will plague you until you perish. The sky over your head will be bronze, the ground beneath you iron. The LORD will turn the rain of your country into dust and powder; it will come down from the skies until you are destroyed. [Deut. 28:15–24]

God Himself blesses or curses the environment in response to man's faithful obedience or faithless rebellion (Lev. 26:1–14; Deut. 8). This, too, is a pregnant observation for environmentalism: Since God willingly causes devastation to the natural environment in response to man's sin (e.g., in the worldwide flood of Noah's day), (a) God's highest priority must not be environmental preservation but the restoration and maintenance of His covenantal relationship with wayward sinners, (b) in God's grand purposes, human beings take precedence over the natural world, and (c) environmental degradation must sometimes be attributed to God's direct judgment—in response, indeed, to human sin, but with God, not man, as the efficient cause.

By all means let us teach man's accountability to God for his dominion over the earth. Let us develop and teach sound principles of resource use and conservation, of pollution abatement, of recycling. Let us recognize that Scripture reveals environmental consequences of sin. But first and foremost, let us call mankind to repentance for sin and faithful obedience to God according to His laws, and let us be careful not to read environmental degradation into passages of Scripture that talk instead of idolatry, spiritual adultery, and other such sins that may be committed just as much by someone who uses best available practices in soil conservation or waste disposal and recycling as by someone who ignores or flouts such wise methods.

Another implication of this principle is that where we see great and ongoing environmental devastation, we should at least ask, "Can this devastation be God's response to unfaithfulness and sin in this society? In what ways are these manifested?" And where we see great and ongoing environmental improvement, we should at least ask, "Can this improvement be God's response to faithfulness and obedience in this society? In what ways are these manifested?" It will be difficult—sometimes impossible—to pinpoint the connections between disobedience and devastation or between obedience and improvement, but our faith in Scripture requires us to try. And our own faithful application of this principle requires us to stand against the political correctness of our times in two ways. First, we will reject the cultural relativism that refuses to make moral distinctions between cultures. Second, we will reject the automatic preference for non-Western (especially non-American) cultures that dominates much of the secular and New Age streams of environmentalism. Instead, we will judge cultures impartially by the standards of God's law, and we will recognize that despite its weaknesses, despite the fact that it has a long, long way to go before it can be called truly Christian, Western culture has been more thoroughly influenced by Biblical worldview, theology, and ethics than any other culture, and that the consequent progress it has made in guaranteeing basic human rights, enhancing liberty and the rule of law,[13] improving human health and longevity, reducing hunger and disease, and increasing material wealth while diminishing pollution[14] bears testimony to that influence.[15]

Calvin DeWitt cites Jeremiah 2:7 as applying to "global toxification" by the discharge of chemicals into air, water, and soil. Like Granberg-Michaelson, he misidentifies the human action and overlooks the divine judgment as efficient cause of the environmental damage described in Jeremiah's prophecy.[16] Similarly, after discussing global warming caused by the release of carbon dioxide and other greenhouse gases, and ozone depletion caused by CFC emissions—processes he says are causing "alteration of planetary energy exchange"—DeWitt cites Deuteronomy 32:6: "Is this the way you repay the LORD, O foolish and unwise people? Is he not your Father, your Creator, who made you and formed you?"[17] But the sin Moses had in mind was not chemical air pollution or any other action evangelical and other environmentalists name as threatening the environment but—just as we saw in Jeremiah—idolatry, spiritual infidelity (Deut. 32:15-18, 21), and here again God's judgment is expressed in His bringing devastation on the environment (Deut. 32:22-24).

The point is not to excuse clear-cutting or greenhouse gas and CFC emissions (the wisdom or folly and the safe levels of which are to be determined by scientific investigation, not by appeal to Scripture, and will vary from place to place and in relation to other changing conditions) but to point out that these verses do not properly apply to the empirical issues Granberg-Michaelson and DeWitt have in mind. Citing them as if they did both obscures the important moral and theological truths they properly convey and illegitimately imports their moral authority to what are debatable scientific questions.

3. ISAIAH 24:4. In *The Environment and the Christian*, DeWitt writes, "In the midst of creation's garden—so abundantly yielding blessed fruits and supporting life in its God-declared goodness—we have made the choice to extract more and more, even at the expense of destroying creation's protective provisions and blessed fruitfulness.... Under this arrogant assault on the fabric of the biosphere, to use the words of the Old Testament [Isa. 24:4], 'the earth dries up and withers.... The earth is defiled by its people.'"[18] The implication is that poor ecological practices defiled the earth. But the context of Isaiah 24:4 indicates otherwise and contains what must be, from the perspective of environmentalism, a surprising note:

> See, the LORD is going to lay waste the earth and devastate it; he will ruin its face and scatter its inhabitants—it will be the same for priest as for people,

for master as for servant, for mistress as for maid, for seller as for buyer, for borrower as for lender, for debtor as for creditor. The earth will be completely laid waste and totally plundered. The LORD has spoken this word.

The earth dries up and withers, the world languishes and withers, the exalted of the earth languish. The earth is defiled by its people; they have disobeyed the laws, violated the statutes and broken the everlasting covenant. Therefore a curse consumes the earth; its people must bear their guilt. [Isa. 24:1–6a]

The surprising note from the perspective of environmentalism—even, unfortunately, most evangelical writings on the environment, which rarely mention it and never give it prominence—is that *God*, not man, devastates the earth. The important lesson behind this is one we saw in dealing with Jeremiah 2:7–8: Divine judgment is expressed on the natural world in response to human sin. In Biblical terms, *defilement* and *devastation* of the earth are different things. Human sin *defiles* the earth—makes it morally polluted and impure—regardless whether it takes place in the midst of sound or unsound environmental policy. Divine judgment *devastates* the earth—makes it infertile and inhospitable—in response to human sin regardless of man's environmental practices.[19] In addition, here, as with the verses discussed in the previous section, these writers illegitimately import Biblical moral authority to their position in the environmental debate by misusing Scripture.

4. THE LAW OF JUBILEE. Some evangelical environmentalists appeal to the Old Testament Jubilee law (Lev. 25) to support the belief that wealth should be more evenly divided among people than it is, and that somehow greater equality of wealth would reduce environmental harm.[20] Gelderloos, for instance, writes, "The Year of Jubilee . . . [included] a redistribution of wealth...." and "The concept of the Sabbath, particularly the year of Jubilee, leads to sustainability as it deals with inequality.[21] The year of Jubilee is based on an initial equitable distribution, fair dealings, zero interest rate, sabbatical fallow, minimal rights of the poor, tithes, and so forth."[22]

This reading and application of the Jubilee law, however, is mistaken in at least three ways: (1) The law was not based on an initial equal distribution of land in Israel;[23] (2) it did not deal with inequality and did not redistribute wealth; (3) there does not appear to be any correlation between inequality of wealth distribution and degrees of environmental degradation or economic sustainability.

First, the initial distribution of land to the tribes of Israel (described in Joshua 13–21) was by no means equal. Simeon, the smallest tribe (22,200 males aged 20 or over), received about five times as much land as Benjamin (45,400), about four times as much as Zebulun (60,500) or Issachar (64,300), and about three times as much as Dan, the second largest tribe (64,400). Manasseh (52,700) received about six times as much land as the slightly larger tribe of Asher (53,400) and about sixteen times as much as Zebulun, which had about 15 percent more people.[24] Even if land were equally divided within tribes, then, there would have been gross inequality between families of different tribes (A family of Simeon, for instance, would have received a piece of land more than eleven times the size of one received by a family of Issachar, while a family of Manasseh would have received a piece of land more than eighteen times the size of one received by a family of Zebulun.), and nothing in Scripture indicates that it was evenly divided within tribes. Furthermore, the land must have varied greatly in fertility and other important determinants of value (e.g., weather, security from enemies, proximity to trade routes and cities), from the arid desert of southern Judah to the rugged mountains of Benjamin to the fertile Jordan valley shared by Manasseh, Issachar, and Gad. Yet this distribution was by divine order, so it cannot have been unjust. Justice, therefore, by no means requires an equal, or even an approximately equal, distribution of property.[25]

Second, the Jubilee law, if obeyed, would not have reduced inequalities of wealth in Israel. Certainly it could not have resulted in a more equal distribution of land than the highly unequal original distribution. Neither would it have had an impact on wealth distribution other than land (money, livestock, buildings, ships) or on the value of land as worked by its owners (land carefully farmed versus land left wild). Even the return to its original owner of land once "sold" did not redistribute wealth, since the price of the land at the sale (the combined annual value of the prospective harvests) would have been repaid to the buyer by the value of its harvests, meaning there was no net gain or loss from the transaction to either buyer or seller simply in the exchange of land and money.[26] (Either, however, might gain from the use to which he put the land or the money, and that gain would not be equalized between them by the application of the Jubilee law.)

Third, the degree of inequality of the distribution of wealth does not seem to be related to environmental quality in a society. There is, however, a strong relationship between economic development and environmental quality.[27] As a country's economy makes the transition from subsistence agriculture to industry, pollution emissions tend to rise, although improving health and longevity indicate that the benefits of the polluting activities to health and longevity outweigh the costs. As it makes the transition from industry to service and technology, pollution emissions tend to fall, while health and longevity continue to improve. One economic study indicates that pollution emissions increase until an economy tops $5,000 per person, after which pollution begins to decline.[28]

Does the Bible Really Say This?

1. NATURE IN THE WORDS AND ACTS OF JESUS. Vernon Visick, in his essay "Creation's Care and Keeping in the Life of Jesus," writes, "Jesus mentions nature in only a few places: (1) in a contrast between the beauty of flowers and Solomon in all of his grandeur, concluding that flowers are more beautiful [Matthew 6:29]; and (2) in a comparison between the respective value of sparrows and human beings, asserting that in God's mind human beings are more important than sparrows [Matthew 10:29–31]."[29] (No doubt Visick would agree that people are more important than flowers [Matt. 6:30], too—this prioritization of people over plants and animals being an important point evangelicals should make in the face of the biological egalitarianism that has come to dominate Deep Ecology and other parts of the environmental movement.) Perhaps Visick did not intend for this to be taken as an exhaustive list, although it appears that he did ("only a few places:"). Whichever is so, it certainly neglects some words and acts of Jesus that have interesting implications for environmental thought. Consider several examples.

Might we infer from the parable of the sower (Matt. 13:3–23; Mark 4:3–25; Luke 8:5–18) that the earth requires careful cultivation that transforms it significantly from the natural state (rocky, thorny, or packed) into a useful state ("good soil") in which it bears much fruit for man's benefit and God's glory, and might this imply that we should be careful not to overstress the abundance of the earth's natural fruitfulness under the Curse? Might we infer from the parable of the wheat and tares (Matt. 13:24–30, 36–43) that man is justified in considering some plants a nuisance rather than a blessing, and working to minimize their presence?

Might we infer from His cursing the barren fig tree (Matt. 21:18–22; Mark 11:12–14) that nature really should be expected to meet man's needs, or that destroying a natural object may be justified even if only to illustrate a lesson? Or from His stilling the storm (Matt. 8:23–27; Mark 4:37–41; Luke 8:22–25) that nature should submit to man's authority, even though because of the Fall and the Curse it does not, and that man's increasing subjugation of nature (Gen. 1:28) is a good thing? Granted that Christ is the last Adam, the new paradigm Man whose dominion over creation demonstrates what redeemed and glorified mankind will enjoy, what might His turning water into wine

(John 2:1–11), producing the great catches of fish (Luke 5:1–11; John 21:1–14), walking on water (Matt. 14:25–33; Mark 6:48–52; John 6:15–21), or multiplying food for thousands (Matt. 14:15–21; 15:25–33; Mark 6:35–44; 8:1–9; Luke 9:10–17; John 6:1–14) teach us about our relationship to the environment?

One other point bears making about Jesus' ministry and its relevance to man and the environment. Sometimes silence and inaction speak as loudly as words and deeds. In setting priorities between human needs and those of animals, plants, or the earth itself, we do well to remember that Jesus healed multitudes of people and taught much about how we should treat them, while we have no record of His healing animals or plants or restoring devastated ecosystems (like the Valley of Hinnom, the great waste dump of Jerusalem, or the salinized lands surrounding the Dead Sea, or the plain of Sodom and Gomorrah) or directly teaching how we should treat other creatures.[30] Scripture does indeed declare the cosmic effects of Christ's redeeming death and resurrection, but it places a clear priority on human redemption and transformation, teaching even that full cosmic redemption awaits the consummation of human redemption (Rom. 8:18–23). From this perspective, as well as in light of the principle discussed above of God's devastating the earth for man's unbelief, idolatry, and other sins, the greatest service we can do for the environment is to "go and make disciples of all nations, baptizing them in the name of the Father and of the Son and of the Holy Spirit, and teaching them to obey everything [Christ] has commanded" us (Matt. 28:19–20). In short, the missionary mandate is rooted in and restores man's ability to perform the cultural mandate.[31]

2. NATURE UNDER THE WRATH OF GOD. A particularly discomfiting class of Scriptures for environmentalists who mourn the desacralization of nature comprises those that tell of God's pouring out on nature His wrath for human sin. The two most obvious cases are the Curse on the earth following man's Fall (Gen. 3:17–19) and the Flood by which He destroyed nearly all life on earth, and greatly changed its topography, in response to the pervasive decadence of humanity (Gen. 6–8). Some others are:
  • the destruction by fire and brimstone from heaven of the cities of Sodom and Gomorrah and the surrounding plain (Gen. 19);
  • the plagues on Egypt (Ex. 7–12), including turning surface waters to blood, sending great infestations of frogs, lice, flies, boils, hail, and locusts (some of which hurt men, animals, and even plants alike), darkness, and finally the death of the firstborn (not only of men but

also of animals);

• the dividing and rejoining of the Red Sea (Ex. 14), the violent aqueous actions of which would have harmed many sea and shore creatures and plants;

• the disruption of ecosystems involved in turning rivers into deserts and vice versa (Ps. 107:33–34; compare Isa. 35:6–7; 41:17–19);

• the destruction of forests and fields in God's judgment on Assyria (Isa. 10:18–19);

• the ecological devastation of Babylon (Isa. 13:13, 20–22);

• the destruction of the harvests of Cush (Isa. 18:4–6);

• the devastation of harvests and the Nile in Egypt (Isa. 19:5–10);

• wild animals destroyed in God's judgment on Edom (Isa. 34:6–11);

• sending drought in judgment on Judah (Jer. 14), Babylon (50:38–40), and Israel (Hosea 13:15–16);

• sending locusts and drought on Judah and Jerusalem (Joel 1:4, 6–12);

• sending earthquakes, storms, floods, droughts, and plagues on various places in judgment (Amos 9:5–6; Mic. 1:3–4; Nah. 1:3–5; Hab. 3:1–12);

• causing crop failure by drought because of neglect of God's house and worship (Hag. 1:5–11).

In short, ecological as well as cultural devastation is a common part of God's judgment on sinful peoples. Consider this warning through Zephaniah: "'I will sweep away everything from the face of the earth,' declares the LORD. 'I will sweep away both men and animals; I will sweep away the birds of the air and the fish of the sea. The wicked will have only heaps of rubble when I cut off man from the face of the earth,' declares the LORD" (Zep. 1:2–3). Here God's words clearly reflect those spoken at creation: "Let us make man in our image, in our likeness, and let them rule over the fish of the sea and the birds of the air, over the livestock, over all the earth, and over all the creatures that move along the ground" (Gen. 1:26). Man's rebellion against God has judicial consequences not only for man but also for the earth of which he is the covenant head; therefore God's judgment on human sin has ecological consequences. This principle is illustrated in the mixing of human and environmental devastation in the pouring out of the seven bowls of God's wrath in Revelation 16:

• sores on people;

• sea turned to blood and everything in it dying;

• rivers and springs turned to blood and everything in them dying;

• intense heat from the sun causing burns on people;
• the throne of the Beast plunged into darkness;
• the Euphrates dried up;
• a tremendous earthquake and storm destroying Babylon the Great, followed by plagues and famine (Rev. 18:8).

Unlike secular and New Age environmentalists, who have no allegiance to Scripture, evangelical environmentalists must think through how God's repeated devastation of the earth in judgment on human sin fits into a Biblical view of environmental ethics. However, in my reading of evangelical environmentalists, I have thus far found no discussion of this issue. I do not know myself just how to answer this challenge. Certainly it has implications for our causal analysis of ecological troubles (e.g., that not every ecological problem can be traced directly to human polluting or depleting activities) and for our evaluation of the desirability of maintaining present ecological conditions. (Should deserts be irrigated, swamps drained, wildlands explored and made accessible by road building? The considerations above indicate that we cannot simply give instant, principled answers that apply across the board. Prudential judgments based on empirical studies and balancing a variety of preferences and values must be made instead.)

3. OTHER CURIOUS PASSAGES. Certain other Biblical passages pose uncomfortable questions to environmentalists—sometimes including evangelicals—for a variety of reasons.

Some environmentalists protest the killing of animals for their skins to make clothing; what are we to make, then, of the fact that God was the first to do this (Gen. 3:21)? Certainly we are to care for and generally show compassion to animals, yet Old Testament law required Israelites to break the neck of firstborn donkeys in connection with the Passover (Ex. 13:13) and to kill thousands of animals as sacrifices; how do we reconcile these two Biblical teachings? Many environmentalists—including some evangelicals—decry monocultural agriculture[32] (planting large areas with single crops) because it fails to take advantage of the natural pest control inherent in polyculture, yet God's law forbade the Israelites to plant more than one type of seed in a single field (Lev. 19:19; Deut. 22:9–10); even assuming that God gave this law for ceremonial reasons (as a sign of Israel's distinction from the Gentiles), it is difficult to think that God would have advised Israel to use a farming method that was inherently inferior—certainly not one that was morally condemnable.

In Exodus 23:20–30 God explains that He will not drive the wicked

Canaanites out of the Promised Land all at once lest wild beasts take over again, making its occupation by Israel more difficult; does this imply that the earth is better off under the dominion even of horribly degenerate peoples like the Canaanites than under that of wild animals? In Exodus 34:13 (cf. Deut. 7:5; 12:3) God commands the Israelites to cut down the sacred groves[33] of the pagan peoples of the Promised Land as part of their work of extirpating spiritual wickedness from the Land, and at various times Jewish rulers did just this and were commended for it (Judg. 6:25; 2 Kings 18:4 [cf. 2 Chron. 31:1]; 23:14–15 [cf. 2 Chron. 34:3–7]; 2 Chron. 14:3; 17:6 [cf. 19:3]), yet some evangelical authors criticize the same practice by Christian missionaries of the Middle Ages;[34] what is the right way to relate care for forest ecosystems and spiritual warfare in Christian missions and earthkeeping?

The issues considered in this chapter indicate that evangelical environmentalists, although in many instances they make good and fruitful use of Scripture in developing an ethic of earth stewardship, still need to improve their use of Scripture in significant ways. In particular, they need to be careful (a) not to misuse some passages by interpreting them improperly or applying them in inappropriate ways, and (b) not to overlook passages that suggest important—or sometimes even small—considerations that would help to distinguish the worldview, theology, and ethics of evangelical environmentalism from those of secular and New Age environmentalism.

CHAPTER 5

❧　　❧

The Problem of Environmental Misinformation

An important weakness of much environmentalism is its tendency to present false or highly debatable claims of environmental problems and their significance as if they were unquestionably true.[1] Usually, environmentalists use such claims to frighten people into accepting a message of environmental crisis, after which they will be more likely to embrace policy recommendations environmentalists make. Unfortunately, evangelical environmentalists frequently accept such claims uncritically and often—as we saw in the previous chapter—pass them along to their fellow believers with the added moral authority of Scripture. And they, too, tend to use such claims to promote the crisis mentality.

This chapter will examine some examples of empirical errors and scare tactics both to offer readers another view of the alleged problems and to suggest points at which evangelical environmentalists need to be more careful about empirical claims.

A convenient starting point for discussion is a membership recruitment letter issued in April 1995 by the Christian Society of the Green Cross. We focus on it first because (a) it is a type of environmentalist literature that more evangelicals are likely to see than the more academic literature we shall discuss later, and (b) it brings together, in brief compass, a number of examples of mistaken or debatable environmental claims:

> Increasingly, both church leaders and leading scientists see issues of
> the environment as the most serious which our society faces. Some of the
> facts which depict this predicament follow: Here are a few examples: [sic]

59

*   Since 1945, Americans have consumed more of the world's resources than have all previous generations who have ever lived on the planet put together[.] <u>We have used more than our fair share</u>.

*   Every day Americans turn 9 square miles of rural land over to development. Every year, our agricultural practices waste over 1,000,000 acres of topsoil through erosion. As there are more people, there is less farmland on which to grow food. <u>We are using up our resources in a way that cannot continue</u>.

*   Within the lifetime of a child born in this decade, virtually all of the world's petroleum will be burned. Still common minerals will be exhausted, such as copper, tin, zinc, lead and nickel. Water is increasingly tainted with chemicals. Over 60% of the world's great forests have been cut. Half of this has occurred in the past thirty years. <u>We are leaving a legacy of degradation and depletion</u>.

*   Atmospheric levels of heat-trapping carbon dioxide are 26% higher than pre-industrial concentrations and continue to climb; the results will be higher temperatures. The ozone shield in the upper atmosphere is thinning; the result is increases in skin cancers. Entire species of plants and animals are vanishing. <u>We are creating trends which will change the world as we have known it</u>.

The letter's litany could have continued through a long panoply of complaints: acid rain killing forests and fish; pesticide residues on foods giving us cancer; species going extinct at the rate of three a day, or a thousand a day, or eight thousand a year, or 35,000 a year, or 75,000 a year (pick any number; you can find it in the literature); asbestos in schools causing cancer; radon in basements causing cancer; toxic wastes causing cancer; dioxin causing cancer; smog causing cancer or heart disease or respiratory ailments; nuclear power causing cancer; electromagnetic fields causing cancer; oil spills causing "irreversible" damage to ecosystems; human population busting at the seams, exceeding the earth's carrying capacity.

But the letter didn't have to list all these things. It had listed enough to do its job: scare the unsuspecting (as if they needed any more scaring after the last twenty years of media hype) into joining the Society. Why say "scare the unsuspecting"? Because anyone who reads regularly about the environment from a variety of perspectives—from the more numerous doomsayers to the so-called "cornucopians"—would recognize that the letter's claims are all highly debatable as to either fact or significance:

• Americans do consume more of some resources per capita than most people (but typically not the rich) in most other countries, and we do consume more per capita than people of the past (although it is difficult to imagine just how one might accurately compare total American consumption since 1945 with total human consumption from Adam and Eve until 1945). But we also *produce* more resources per capita than most people in most other countries and than people of the past; we consume no more than we produce; and our consumption doesn't reduce the ability of others to consume. The long-term downward real price trends of extractive raw materials (mineral, plant, and animal) show that our consumption of resources neither exceeds our production of them nor interferes with the ability of others to consume or produce them. (For a truly representative example, inflation-adjusted copper prices fell by about 70 percent, and its price divided by wages by about 99 percent [meaning its affordability rose by 99 percent], from 1801 to 1990.) In this case, the empirical claim (misleading at that) is logically irrelevant to the moral charge based on it.

• Precisely what it means to say that every day we "turn 9 square miles of rural land over to development" is difficult to guess, since—depending on who uses the term—"development" might mean anything from a skyscraper to a housing tract to a park. Furthermore, such raw numbers, though they may sound scary in isolation, become meaningful only when set in a larger context.

The United States comprise 3,536,338 square miles of land, of which about 97 percent is undeveloped. (The U.S. Bureau of the Census defines "developed" land as including urban and built-up areas in units of ten acres [a square 660 feet wide] or greater, plus rural transportation.) The conversion of 9 square miles of rural land each day therefore translates into 3,285 square miles (a square 57 miles wide) per year. (That is 9/100ths of 1 percent of total U.S. land.) At that rate, total undeveloped land would be reduced by only about another 9 percent—to about 88 percent of total land—in a hundred years. (In case you're interested, it would take 1,076 years to develop all U.S. land at that rate.)

Actually, although it is meant to be scary, the Green Cross's land conversion figure is probably low. From 1960 to 1990 the conversion rate was about double what the Green Cross claims as the present trend, although it was faster earlier and slower more recently. But there is good reason to expect that as U.S. population stabilizes and continues to become more concentrated in cities and suburbs rather than rural areas the conversion rate will fall yet more. Also, from 1960 to 1990, during the same years when we were developing land at about 6,500 square miles per year, the National Wildlife Refuge system grew from about 15 million to about 95 million acres; the National Parks system from about 20 million to about 70 million acres; and total public recreation lands from about 225 million to about 375 million acres. In other words, we protected an additional 437,500 square miles of refuges, parks, and public recreation lands (not including similar state, local, and private lands) from development in thirty years, or 40 square miles per day—more than four times the rate of land development the Society bemoans. The data, then, support no crisis of land conversion.[2]

• What the Society means by "wasting over 1,000,000 acres of topsoil" through erosion every year is unclear. Taken literally, it would seem to mean that every year erosion completely eliminates about a million acres of usable agricultural land. But that is certainly not true. America's farmers harvested 309 million acres of crops in 1993 compared with 324 million in 1960—a decline of 15 million acres (less than half a million per year). But in the interim, harvested acres rose and fell, with jumps in both directions of as much as 20 million acres from year to year. Farmers respond to market prices and government policies. When crop prices rise, they harvest more acres; when crop prices fall, they harvest fewer.

Probably this claim is meant to convey something about an amount of topsoil lost per year through erosion from all acres under cultivation. But it fails to communicate because topsoil is not measured in acres but in tons or cubic feet. (An *acre* of topsoil 5 inches thick, after all, is eighty times heavier than an *acre* of topsoil 1/16 inch thick.) Furthermore, the Society does not tell us whether this is *gross* or *net* loss. The distinction is crucial. Because of routine erosion control measures, according to University of Maryland agricultural resource economist Bruce Gardner, on almost all cropland in the United States new topsoil formation (from the combination of plant fiber decay and the breakdown of deeper, denser soil and rocks) roughly matches loss from erosion, yielding almost no annual net change in topsoil (up slightly in some cases, down slightly in others; on average, practically no change). Additionally, most eroded topsoil is not lost; it moves from one piece of farmland to another. All of this is consistent with the fact that over the last fifty years higher and higher percentages of

U.S. cropland have met the "prime" grade according to the U.S. Soil Conservation Service, and with rising yields per acre.

• The letter implies that growing population causes diminishing farmland in America. But American farmers are planting fewer acres not because fewer acres are available to plant but because agricultural production here and worldwide is so high that prices won't support cultivating more acres. While harvested U.S. cropland declined 11 percent from 1978 through 1987, total crop production rose 25 percent, meaning that yield per acre rose 40 percent. With yield rising almost four-and-a-half times more than population and crop prices falling, taking some land out of production makes perfect sense.

• Predictions have been made about running out of oil for nearly a century, and always they have proved false. (See table 1.) They are contradicted by (a) falling long-term real prices of petroleum (down about 70 percent from 1870 to 1990) and (b) rising world oil reserves (up from about 100 billion barrels in 1943 to about 10 trillion barrels in 1989). Yes, there is a finite amount of oil in the earth. No, we don't know when cost-effective sources will be used up. But past experience with other resources indicates that when supplies begin to dwindle significantly relative to demand, rising prices will prompt discovery of additional sources, increasing efficiency, and invention of new natural and artificial substitutes—which, if they follow the pattern of substitutes for other dwindling resources in the past, will be much more abundant, much less expensive, and much more effective.

Perhaps the claim that "virtually all of the world's petroleum will be burned" in a lifetime—say, by the year 2060—rests on dividing present known reserves by annual consumption, allowing for projected increase in consumption. (At 1990 consumption—22 billion barrels—the 10 trillion barrels of known reserves would last about 450 years.) But while this formula allows for expanding demand, it forgets about expanding supply. Continued exploration and discovery—not to mention substitution of other substances for the same purposes, increasing efficiency, and changed processes—counterbalances extraction from known reserves. So far, discovery and innovation have outpaced consumption, and it appears that oil companies find it economically rewarding to keep discovery about fifty to sixty years ahead of consumption. Thus the expectation that *presently* known reserves will be exhausted in fifty to sixty years (let alone a lifetime, or even 450 years) is true by definition but meaningless in

TABLE 1.1
Past petroleum prophecies and realities

Date	U.S. prod. (bil. bbl/yr)	Prophecy	Reality
1866	.05	Synthetics available if oil production ends (U.S. Revenue Commission)	In next 82 years U.S. produced 37 billion bbl. with no need for synthetics
1885	.2	Little or no chance for oil in California (U.S. Geological Survey)	8 billion bbl. produced in California by 1975
1891	.5	Little or no chance for oil in Kansas or Texas (U.S.G.S.)	14 billion bbl. produced in Kansas and Texas by 1975
1908	1.8	Maximum future U.S. supply 22.5 billion bbl. (officials of U.S.G.S.)	35 billion bbl. produced with 26.8 billion bbl. proven reserve by January 1, 1949
1914	2.7	Total future production only 5.7 billion bbl. (official of U.S. Bureau of Mines)	34 billion bbl. produced from 1914 to 1975
1920	4.5	U.S. needs foreign oil and synthetics; peak domestic production almost reached (U.S.G.S.)	1948 U.S. production in excess of U.S. consumption and more than four times 1920 output
1931	8.5	Must import as much as possible to save domestic supply (Secretary of Interior)	During next 8 years imports were discouraged and 14 billion bbl. were discovered in U.S.
1939	13	U.S. oil supplies will last only 13 years (Interior Department)	New oil found since 1939 exceeds the 13 years' supply known at that time
1947	19	Sufficient oil cannot be found in U.S. (State Department)	4.3 billion bbl. found in 1948, largest volume in history and twice our consumption
1949	2.0	End of U.S. oil supply in sight (Secretary of Interior)	Recent industry shows ability to increase U.S. production by more that a million bbl. daily in next 5 years

Source: U.S. House of Representatives, Subcommittee on Energy and Power, Committee on Interstate and Foreign Commerce, February 17-21, 1975. Adapted from William M. Brown, "The Outlook for Future Petroleum Supplies," in the Ultimate Resource, ed. Simon and Kahn (New York: Basil Blackwell, 1984), 362.

Table 1. The dismal track record of past predictions of petroleum exhaustion.

relation to when we might expect exhaustion of total recoverable reserves.

Similar considerations weigh in against the fear of running out of the other minerals mentioned. Their prices, like oil's, are in long-term decline, indicating diminishing scarcity. And despite intervening consumption, known reserves of copper rose by 179 percent from 1950 to 1970; of tin by 10 percent; and of lead by 115 percent, for reasons like those for oil. Figures for nickel, and more recent figures for the other minerals named, are not readily available, but historical and theoretical considerations indicate that there is no good reason to think that we face any reasonable prospect of exhausting any of these minerals without our first finding substitutes that serve our purposes better.

• The vast majority of chemicals that taint our water are harmless in the doses found in drinking-water supplies, making risks from drinking-water in developed nations minuscule. And access to safe water worldwide has risen dramatically in the last century (up from 40 percent to 65 percent just from 1970 to 1990 in low- and middle-income countries, according to the World Bank), and it continues to rise with increasing speed. (The real danger in drinking-water is contamination by bacteria and untreated sewage, a problem found mostly in less-developed countries, where it causes hundreds of thousands of early deaths.)

• Have over 60 percent of the world's forests been cut? Perhaps, although for any time before about 1980 there are no reliable world-wide statistics. But it hardly matters. After all, 100 percent of last year's wheat crop was cut in a single year! Yet next year there will be a whole new crop. Forests and wheat are analogous; the principal differences are that trees grow larger and more slowly, while far more acres of wheat are harvested each year than of trees. What the alarmists at the Christian Society of the Green Cross don't mention is that total world forested area and total growing board feet of wood both appear to be greater now than they were fifty years ago—and on the increase—and that the annual rate of deforestation has been falling worldwide due to public pressure for conservation and to increased plantation forestry.

• What about rising CO_2 and global temperatures? Probably CO_2 is rising (data for the past are debatable); perhaps global average temperatures have risen slightly in the last century (data for the past are highly uncertain); and perhaps temperatures will rise in the future in response to rising CO_2 (but climatologists differ in their estimates of how much *and whether* global average temperatures will rise based on various assumptions of carbon dioxide increase and its effects on climate through positive and negative feedback mechanisms).

But the letter does not mention (a) that roughly two-thirds of the *apparent* .45 degree C. increase in global average temperatures between 1880 and 1990 was attributable to natural causes, (b) that almost all of that increase occurred before 1940, i.e., before the sharpest increases in carbon dioxide, indicating that there is no direct correlation between carbon dioxide and temperature (i.e., putting the effect before the alleged cause), (c) that the most recent and refined computer climate models predict much lower overall increases than models that produced the frightening scenarios of the 1980s, and (d) that most of any increase will occur in the winter and at night, yielding little or no shrinkage of ice caps (which, contrary to doomsayers' predictions, have been expanding of late, not shrinking), little or no rise in sea levels, some benefit to agriculture because of longer growing seasons and increased water use efficiency (caused by higher carbon dioxide concentrations, which improve photosynthesis and water retention), and less need for heating in winter (thus reducing energy consumption).

• Is ozone becoming abnormally thin? There *seems* to be a slight downward trend in stratospheric ozone concentrations for 1957–1992, but it is not known whether that trend—if real[3]—is down from historically *normal* levels or from historically *high* levels. (Our data go back only to the 1950s, and forty years is statistically insignificant as a sample of a dynamic system thousands or tens of thousands—let alone millions or billions—of years old.) We simply *don't know*, and not knowing is not grounds for taking any particular action. Is skin cancer on the rise as a result of thinning ozone? No reliable data back this claim. Furthermore, the skin cancer associated with increased ultraviolet B exposure (hypothetically resulting from ozone depletion) is mostly non-malignant, and the increased risk associated with the worst-case ozone depletion scenarios is about equivalent with the increased risk involved in moving sixty miles closer to the equator or a thousand feet higher in elevation—a risk so small as not to figure in the vast majority of decisions about where to live. And—oh, yes—ground-level UV-B concentrations seem to be falling, not rising, contrary to doomsayers' predictions.[4]

• Species extinction? The letter does not say how fast it is occurring. But presumably its authors think it is occurring significantly faster than in the past. But the most thorough attempt at a worldwide study of field data on extinction rates—commissioned by the International Union for the Conservation of Nature and by no means skewed by an anti-environmentalist bias—generated this general reckoning (in the foreword) by IUCN Director-General Martin Holdgate: "The coastal forests of Brazil have been reduced in area as severely as any tropical forest type in the world. According to calculation, this should have led to considerable species loss. Yet no known species of its old, largely endemic, fauna can be regarded as extinct. Genetic erosion has undoubtedly taken place, and the reduced, remnant populations may be much more vulnerable to future change, but the study illustrates the need for very careful field documentation to compare with calculation in this and other situations." According to two others of the book's authors, "IUCN, together with the World Conservation Monitoring Centre, has amassed large volumes of data from specialists around the world relating to species decline [worldwide], and it would seem sensible to compare these more empirical data with the global extinction estimates. In fact, these and other data indicate that the number of recorded extinctions for both plants and animals is very small. . . ." and "Despite extensive enquiries we have been unable to obtain conclusive evidence to support the suggestion that massive extinctions have taken place in recent times, as Myers and others have suggested. On the contrary, work on projects such as Flora Meso-Americana has, at least in some cases, revealed an increase in abundance in many species. . . ."[5] Over and over the book's many authors state that, expectations to the contrary, field evidence for extinctions in recent decades is slight to non-existent.

Why be so picky? After all, this is a public relations piece. And everybody knows that PR's standards of truth are—well, not too high. (But what about *Christian* PR?) Does this kind of confusion and misinformation about empirical affairs characterize other evangelical writing on the environment? Sad to say, yes.

Consider the first issue of *Green Cross*, the magazine of the Christian Society of the Green Cross. (The Society, by the way, is a ministry of Evangelicals for Social Action, headed by Ronald J. Sider, who is listed as

Green Cross's publisher.) In a major article, Susan Drake, an environmental policy advisor with the U.S. State Department and a member of *Green Cross*'s editorial board, writes, "In Africa alone, a tropical forest area the size of Ohio is destroyed each year. In Latin America twice as much, in proportion to the total area, is destroyed."

These two sentences convey an ominous feeling. But what do we now know about tropical deforestation in Africa and Latin America that we did not know (or think we knew) before? If we are like most people, we read "the size of Ohio" and thought, *That's big!* But how big is Ohio? How big is it compared with Africa, or with Africa's tropical rainforests? Do we know? Unless we specialize in geography, not likely. What about Latin America? What does Drake mean by "twice as much, in *proportion to the total area*"? Can most of her readers quickly calculate, from what they do not know about the size of Ohio relative to what they do not know about the size of Africa, how much tropical rainforest is being destroyed each year in Latin America—the size of which they also probably do not know? Of course not. But the sentences scare.

Let us examine them. Ohio is about 116,105 square kilometers (44,828 square miles; a square 212 miles on each side). That is about .388 percent of Africa's 29,901,620 square kilometers (a square 3,397 miles on each side). (In other words, it would take 257.5 Ohios to equal one Africa.) Now, if the deforestation rate is twice as high, in proportion to total area, in Latin America, then tropical deforestation there should be about .776 percent of total land, or 159,127 square kilometers (a 248-mile-wide square). Add these two figures together and you get annual tropical deforestation in Africa and Latin America combined of 275,232 square kilometers (a 524-mile-wide square). That is a lot of forest—although most people probably would not guess, if they heard the number in isolation, that it amounts to slightly over half of one percent of the two continents' combined land. If they knew that, they might be concerned, but probably not scared.

But there is more. We are assuming here that Drake's figures are right. Are they? Not if a sidebar to her article, by R. S. Whaley, president of the State University of New York's College of Environmental Science and Forestry, Syracuse, is right. Whaley writes, just two pages after Drake's claim, "During the past decade, about 15.4 million hectares [154,000 square kilometers] of tropical forest have been lost every year." But Whaley is writing about the whole world, not just about Africa or Latin America. In other words, Drake's implied figure for Africa and Latin America alone is 78 percent higher than Whaley's figure for the whole world!

Whaley's figures for the world are very close to those given by the World

Bank in *Social Indicators of Development on Diskette, 1995*, a standard statistical data source, which showed a simple average annual tropical forest loss for 1980 through 1990 for Latin America of 74,781 square kilometers, for Africa of 39,654, and for Asia of 49,126, for a world total of 163,561 square kilometers (a square 404 miles wide)—about 60 percent of Drake's total for Latin America and Africa alone, and about .75 percent of tropical forest area and .225 percent of total land area for the three continents. (This does not make Whaley's figures certain, by the way. There are reasons to think the World Bank's figures are significantly overstated.) If this annual rate continued for a hundred years (and the reforestation records of developed countries indicate that it will instead probably slow, stop, and reverse), it would reduce the world's tropical forests by about 53 percent. (See figure 1.) (By the way, it appears that deforestation has slowed significantly since 1989 in Brazil's Amazon basin.[6])

Who is right? Drake, or Whaley, or the World Bank? Drake appears to be way off. Whaley and the World Bank seem to be closer to right, but still, in

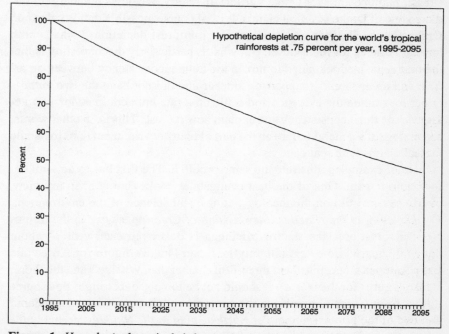

Figure 1. *Hypothetical* tropical deforestation at .75 percent per year, 1995–2095. Developed country patters predict instead that deforestation will slow, stop, and reverse with economic growth.

my judgment, high. But field data simply are not adequate for us to be sure. So why make such a big point about this?

Partly because it illustrates a common problem with facts (or alleged facts) about environmental degradation: a propensity for doomsayers to pick numbers at the scary end of the spectrum while paying little attention to evidence that those numbers may be vastly exaggerated. (At the same time there is a tendency for the doomsayers' critics—often called cornucopians—to pick numbers at the benign end of the spectrum while paying little attention to evidence that those numbers may be vastly minimized. The proper aim for both parties should be truth.) But partly, too, because it illustrates particularly well another common problem about environmentalists' reporting: their propensity to ignore factual inconsistencies that might otherwise alert them to the need for more careful investigation.

This is particularly relevant to this case because Drake's and Whaley's drastically inconsistent numbers were both presented as fact in the same magazine—not as counterbalancing viewpoints but as if Whaley's sidebar provided substantiating details for Drake's article. In reality, Whaley's numbers contradicted one of Drake's central claims. It is, of course, possible that Whaley and Drake simply disagree about the rate of rainforest depletion. Perhaps both have arguments for their views. But what is particularly disconcerting is that the magazine's editor failed to notice the huge inconsistency between an article and an apparently supporting sidebar and did not have the two authors either reexamine the evidence and settle on a rate both could endorse or acknowledge the inconsistency and explain how it arose. This is, in other words, a symptom of a general failure on the part of many environmentalists to handle factual claims with real care.

Other examples illustrate the same problem. The first has to do with deforestation again. One of the best evangelical books (but still, in my view, overly pessimistic) on the theology, ethics, and science of the environment, *Earthkeeping in the Nineties: Stewardship of Creation*, says, "In the tropics alone a forest area the size of Michigan is destroyed each year"[7]—about 250,000 square kilometers (slightly less than Drake's figure for Africa and Latin America alone, but about three-fifths higher than Whaley's and the World Bank's figures for the world). It should not be too disconcerting if this source differs from *Green Cross*, since the two probably were not interdependent.[8] But one of the primary authors of *Earthkeeping in the Nineties*, probably the best-known evangelical environmentalist, Calvin B. DeWitt, wrote in his book *Earth-Wise*, "today . . . tropical deforestation . . . removes about 25 million acres of primary forest each year—an area the size of the state of Indiana."[9]

Now, Michigan is two-and-two-thirds times the size of Indiana. (And Indiana, by the way, is only three-fifths the size of the area Whaley and the World Bank claim is depleted annually.)

This is no small margin of error. It is not the sort of thing that, in scientific work, understandably arises from slight variations in method or measurement. Huge variations like this more often stem from lack of reliable empirical study as the basis for any numbers at all. These discrepancies, in other words, are not just insignificant oddities. They are symptomatic of a larger problem that afflicts a great deal of environmental science and propaganda: a scarcity of long-term, observational field data. All too often the missing field data are replaced by simple guesses that later get repeated as estimates, only to be repeated ever after as proven facts. (For a well-told story of just such a phenomenon, see the sidebar on the origin of specious species extinction figures.)

This tendency might explain the amazing fact that then-Senator Al Gore, in *Earth in the Balance: Ecology and the Human Spirit*, could tell us in the text on page 24 that "species . . . are now vanishing around the world *one thousand times faster* than at any time in the past 65 million years (see illustration)," while the illustration on the same page depicts a pre-Industrial Age extinction rate of around one per century but a present extinction rate of around 8,000 per year (which is not 1,000 but 80,000 times one per century) that is expected to rise to around 70,000 per year (which is 7 million times one per century) by the year 2000, while on p. 28 he claims a present extinction rate of one hundred per day (3.65 million times one per century), and on p. 120 he claims simply "thousands" per year. It is difficult to explain how the same author can make such grossly inconsistent claims in the same book. It might have something to do with pulling numbers out of a hat. Whatever is the case, it is not encouraging to see the extent to which the Evangelical Environmental Network has looked to Gore for encouragement.[10]

A second example brings us back to topsoil. *Earthkeeping in the Nineties* tells us, "The United States . . . still loses an average of twelve tons of topsoil per acre each year, while the annual rate of soil formation, under normal conditions, is only one and a half tons per acre."[11] But DeWitt, one of the book's authors, has written in several places that in "much of this [U.S.] prairie, two bushels of topsoil are lost for every bushel of corn produced,"[12] and in *Earth-Wise* he wrote, "It takes about one hundred years to produce one half-inch of topsoil. And that's the highest rate—sometimes only one-eighth of an inch of soil is produced in a century!"[13] DeWitt's claim about erosion implies the loss of about 9.5 tons of topsoil per acre—21 percent less than *Earthkeeping* claims—while his claim about formation implies a maximum of 1.2 tons per

In 1994, the World Wildlife Fund, in a fund-raising letter and newspaper interviews, repeated what was then and remains today a common claim about species extinctions: that a million species might go extinct in the last two decades of this century. Julian Simon comments:

> WWF backs the million-species claim only with the statement "some scientists believe." This is no scientific evidence at all. You can find "some scientists" who will say they believe almost any proposition you like, even if the established scientific facts are quite the opposite. In the advertising trade... such a statement is known as weasel-wording....
>
> The available evidence on species suggests an astonishingly different picture, however.
>
> The proximate source for WWF's forecast is the 1979 book, The Sinking Ark, by Norman Myers. Mr. Myers gives these two statistics: the estimated extinction rate for known species between the years 1600 and 1900 was about one every four years. And the estimated extinction rate from 1900 to the present was about one a year. Mr. Myers gives no sources for these two estimates, but let us assume they are valid....
>
> Mr. Myers then departs spectacularly from that modest evidence. He goes on to say that some scientists have "hazarded a guess" that the extinction rate "could now have reached" 100 species per year.
>
> Next, this pure conjecture about upper limit of present species extinction is increased and used by Mr. Myers and WWF scientist Thomas Lovejoy as the basis for the "projections" quoted in the fund-raising letter and elsewhere. Mr. Lovejoy—by converting what was an estimated upper limit into a present best-estimate—says that government inaction is "likely to lead" to the extinction of between 14 and 20 percent of all species before the year 2000....
>
> In brief, this extinction rate is nothing but pure guesswork. The forecast is a thousand time greater than the present—yet it has been published in newspapers and understood as a scientific statement.

Simon then explains that at the time there simply were no long-term field studies to support any estimate of extinction rates. As we saw in discussing the Green Cross's fund-raising letter, once such studies were done, under the auspices of the International Union for the Conservation of Nature—in response to Simon's and others' criticisms—the field data supported only a very low extinction rate. But the Myers/Lovejoy/WWF claim continues to be repeated in environmental literature as gospel.

[Excerpted from Julian L. Simon, "Truth Almost Extinct in Tales of Imperiled Species," The Washington Times, September 19, 1984, reprinted in Julian L. Simon, Population Matters: People, Resources, Environment, and Immigration (New Brunswick, NJ: Transaction, 1990). See also Julian L. Simon and Aaron Wildavsky, "On Species Loss, the Absence of Data, and Risks to Humanity," in The Resourceful Earth: A Response to 'Global 2000', edited by Julian L. Simon and Herman Kahn (New York: Basil Blackwell, 1984), 171–83; and Julian L. Simon, "Disappearing Species, Deforestation, and Data," New Scientist, May 15, 1986, reprinted in Rational Readings on Environmental Concerns, edited by Jay H. Lehr (New York: Van Nostrand Reinhold, 1992), 741–49.]

year—20 percent less than *Earthkeeping* claims. Yet DeWitt was one of *Earthkeeping*'s authors. Why the discrepancies? Why are they so large? And do such large discrepancies among cooperating writers foster much confidence in their accuracy?

Actually, despite their disagreements with each other, both *Earthkeeping* and DeWitt probably have greatly exaggerated the rate of erosion and greatly understated the rate of formation of topsoil on U.S. cropland. University of Maryland agricultural resource economist Bruce Gardner commented on DeWitt's statement on erosion losses on corn cropland:

> The latest national survey of cropland erodibilities was in 1987, and it did not address the "two bushels per bushel" calculation, so I don't know where your author got his estimate. Topsoil isn't usually measured in bushels, but with a bushel of topsoil weighing 80 pounds and corn yield of 120 bushels per acre, the statement says about 19,000 lbs. or 9½ tons of topsoil is lost per acre of corn, or about 1/16 of an inch. The Corn Belt has land that <u>could</u> erode (in the absence of erosion control measures) at this rate, but not much—maybe 5 percent. Moreover, all such land is now (since 1990) under "conservation compliance" provisions that require farmers who participate in the corn program (85% do) to undertake erosion control measures, even if the farmers would not have taken these measures on their own accord, which they typically would have. Therefore, I would be very surprised if there is an appreciable acreage of corn land eroding at the 9½ ton rate.
>
> It should be noted also that cropland, by making residual dry organic matter out of air, water, and sunlight, creates roughly 5 tons of soil per acre each year (about 1/32 of an inch).[14]

After mulling his letter over for a while, I called Gardner to ask if I were right in inferring from it that on most U.S. cropland, topsoil formation roughly balances topsoil erosion, resulting in little or no net loss of topsoil. He agreed. This is consistent with other research, which indicates that "average soil loss tolerance [the loss rate at which new soil formation balances loss from erosion] for cropland, pasture, and forestland in the United States is about 5 tons per acre per year."[15] It appears, then, that soil erosion rates on U.S. corn (and other) cropland are significantly lower, while soil formation rates are about three to six times higher than DeWitt and the authors of *Earthkeeping* maintain. There are, of course, variations from the average in both erosion and formation, but the average represents much more cropland than extremes in either direction. (Incidentally, what is most important about farmland is not just the depth of its topsoil but its productivity determined by dividing its total output by total inputs. By this index, the productivity of American farmland has more than tripled since 1910, as shown in figure 2.)

We could go on picking apart the numbers in various environmentalist writings on a wide range of subjects like global warming, ozone depletion, acid rain, and toxic hazards, but I have already done that in two books,[16] and various other people have done it, too. But doing that is not the point of this book. It is not even the point of this chapter.

The point of this chapter has been simply to encourage readers to think critically about environmentalists' claims, to illustrate some of the ways in which factual claims can be tested, and to urge evangelical environmentalists to be more careful about the empirical claims they promote. Not all environmental problems are bogus. The most acclaimed problems, particularly those that are on a global scale (global warming, ozone depletion, species extinction) or a regional scale (acid rain, deforestation, desertification, resource depletion), are vastly exaggerated, and in some cases (like acid rain) almost entirely false. In all of these cases, the actual risk to human beings is very small to vanishing. But there are other problems, mostly on a local scale (air and water pollution, toxic waste disposal, food distribution, local deforestation and desertification), that are very serious in some places (especially low- and middle-

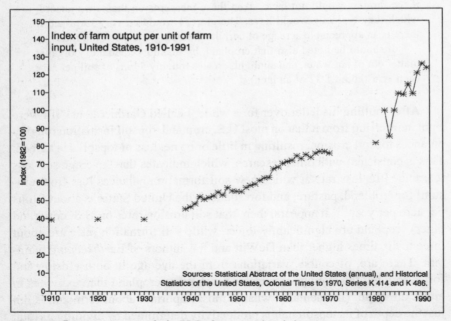

Figure 2. Long-term trends in U.S. farm productivity.

income nations) even though they may be diminishing or nearly ended in others (high-income nations).

For example, despite the gains mentioned above in access to safe drinking water in developing nations, hundreds of millions of people in poor countries continue to drink polluted water, and the diseases they contract from it cause millions of early deaths each year. Even this trend is toward improvement, but it could be hurried along if some funds were diverted from the low-risk and hypothetical global and regional problems to these high-risk and undeniable local problems. A billion dollars invested in waste water treatment plants and municipal and rural water systems would improve the health and life expectancy of many times more people than an equal amount invested in any of those other problems.[17]

Some steps prescribed for fighting some of the global and regional problems seem likely to do more harm than good to the world's poor. Consider just two examples. First, eliminating chloro-fluorocarbon use to protect stratospheric ozone will, perhaps for several decades in developing countries, greatly increase the cost of refrigeration. As a result, low-income people will have to wait longer before they can afford to protect their food from spoilage, which now causes widespread hunger, disease, and death. Second, reducing energy consumption to slow or stop CO_2 buildup in an effort to prevent global warming will slow economic growth in developing countries, since production is heavily dependent on energy use. But there is a strong correlation between economic development and pollution abatement. (Roughly speaking, when a nation's gross national product per capita exceeds $5,000, it begins to reduce pollution because its people can now afford to spend the money to do so.)[18] Slowing economic growth, therefore, will not only slow improvements in human health and longevity in developing countries but also delay pollution reduction.

The failure of many environmentalists, including evangelicals, to prioritize sensibly in terms of actual threats to human health and life is among the most scandalous aspects of today's environmental movement.

In March 1995, several Western economists attending the Oxford Conference on Christian Faith and Economics in Agra, India, were struck by the prevalence of dung. The air in every city and town was thick with it. Disturbing as it was, some tried to joke about it. The biggest laugh came at the end of the week, awaiting takeoff in Delhi, when one of the party said, "Boy, do I ever look forward to getting up to 35,000 feet again so I won't have to breathe dung anymore!"

But the vast majority of India's people have no hopes of getting to fresh, pure air at 35,000 feet on an airliner. They live with the filth, perpetuated by their poverty, all day, every day—until they die with it. Unfortunately, many environmental policies, like those regarding CFCs and the reduction of energy consumption, sentence these poor people to more years in such conditions. This is not to say that developing more energy-efficient means of production, transportation, and so on is a bad idea. It is a great idea. But until those technologies become available at a price poor people can afford, their health and lives will be better served by the economic growth fueled even by inefficient energy use than by the economic stagnation that could be brought on by forced reductions in energy consumption.

Consider these comments by Gregg Easterbrook—a self-professed liberal Democrat environmentalist—in his brilliant new book *A Moment On the Earth: The Coming Age of Environmental Optimism*:

> As anyone who travels the developing world rapidly discovers, the view that Western industrial countries are the polluted ones is a fantasy. Studies show that 1.3 billion people in the developing world live in zones of "dangerously unsafe" air—air alerts at the "dangerous" level having become almost unknown in the Western world. And one billion people in developing countries lack access to drinking water meeting the crudest safety standards.
>
> These figures are not just abstractions. What environmental problems kill human beings in numbers today? Not Alar or ozone depletion. What kills them is dung smoke[19] and diarrhea.
>
> According to the World Health Organization, in 1993 four million Third World children under the age of five died preventable deaths from respiratory diseases brought on in most cases by air pollution. This is about as many people of all ages who died of all causes that year in the United States and European Union combined.
>
> In places such as Bangkok, Calcutta, Karachi, Lagos, Mexico City, and almost any metropolis in China, factories operate without so much as mesh screens on smokestacks, to say nothing of the cost-no-object scrubber assemblies that now adorn the stacks of Western industrial facilities. Third World buses, cars, and trucks run without any emission controls, burning low-quality leaded gasoline made from the sulfurous petroleum unused in the West. Brown coal, shunned for decades in the West, is burned for industrial and electric power. . . .
>
> The developing world also has a pervasive form of air pollution unknown in the West, rural smog. "Most of the child deaths from respiratory distress stem from living in poorly ventilated huts where fuelwood, cow dung, or agricultural wastes are used for heating and cooking. Smoke inside a hut like this can be unbelievable," says Gurinder Shahi, an official of the United Nations Development Programme. "Women and children, who spend

most of their time in the home, are most harmed. Today 40 percent of the global population heats and cooks with biomass in raw form."

Next, according to UNICEF, 3.8 million developing-world children under age five died in 1993 from diarrheal diseases caused by impure drinking water. In the First World, death from diarrhea is about as common as comet strikes; in the developing world diarrhea kills far more people than cancer. This happens because a billion impoverished human beings drink unfiltered water taken from rivers or lakes into which human and animal feces loaded with parasites has been discharged. Most of Africa, the Indian subcontinent, and Latin America have no wastewater treatment facilities....

An estimated 25 billion tons of unfiltered industrial pollutants were emitted directly to Chinese waterways in 1991, meaning more water pollution in that one country alone than in the whole of Western society. Major Chinese rivers such as the Taizai cannot now support fish; they have become biologically dead in the way that was repeatedly predicted for First World water bodies but never actually realized except at the infamous Cuyahoga River near Cleveland [which is now mostly cleaned up]. . . .

Three-point-eight million deaths from dirty water in a single year is substantially more than the combined worst-case mortality estimates for asbestos, dioxin, electromagnetic radiation, nuclear wastes, PCBs, pesticide residues, and ultraviolet rays—the sorts of ecological issues that obsess the First World. . . . Yet Western public consciousness continues to focus on exotic ecological threats while ignoring millions of annual deaths from basic environmental problems of water and air. "Issues like African sewage are not sexy, so they always fall to the bottom of the agenda," says Deborah Moore, a scientist at the Environmental Defense Fund and one of the few Western environmentalists advocating a focus on basic Third World reform.

Western environmental thinking has considerable difficulty coming to terms with such realities. The mere facts that Third World economists call propane and kerosene "clean fuels," and speak longingly of the day when their countries will be wholly electrified, repels ecological orthodoxy, which depicts fossil fuels as hideous and central electric generation as part of a vast plot to engender an artificial greenhouse effect. One reason air pollution is so bad in Mexico, Nigeria, and other nations is that most driving is done on dirt roads. Trucks and buses leave clouds of dust behind them; dust is a pollutant, having the same effect as particulates on the lungs of people and animals and damaging the respiratory stoma of plants. Enviros are dismayed at the thought of paving the developing world, but nature might not be, because the first impact of a paving campaign would be a reduction in dust kicked into the air. What developing-world nations need to free their populations from extreme air pollution is paved roads, catalytic converters, hydroelectric dams, modern petroleum refining, advanced high-efficiency power plants—the sorts of technology green doctrine considers outrageous.

There is a famous statistic that says that the United States has four percent of the world's population and consumes 40 percent of current resources. Environmental orthodoxy says this proves U.S. resource use must go way down. What the statistic really tells you is that Third World resource consumption must go way up. . . . [I]t will be impossible to raise the standard of living of the world's impoverished to anything like a morally equitable level without a significant rise in net global consumption of resources.[20]

The desire of institutional environmentalism to avoid dealing with such issues was manifested in the preliminary negotiations for the Earth Summit. In the years prior to the summit the Group of 77—the bloc of impoverished nations whose name is a play on the wealthy Group of 7—said what it wanted from Rio was for Western countries to commit to investing 0.7 percent of GDP in development aid. [Because of the profligate wastefulness of government foreign aid, I think this would be a largely futile policy. Developing countries would be helped far more by the elimination of trade barriers and by their welcoming multinational corporations to develop factories within their borders. But that is another issue.—E.C.B.] . . .

. . . but . . . environmental lobbyists . . . pounded on the theme that the greenhouse effect was the preeminent issue of Rio. The tactic got out of hand, working so well that greens actually managed to convince the Western heads of state that global warming was more important than drinking-water purity. Some delegates of poor nations left Rio embittered not so much at Western governments but at Western enviros, who not only managed to place the speculative concern of greenhouse warming above the confirmed horror of Third World poverty but who seemed actively pleased to have pulled this coup, allowing as it did the theme music of the summit to suit the institutional purposes of Western environmentalism.

As the Clinton Administration took office, one candidate for a top economic post was Lawrence Summers, chief economist for the World Bank. Summers was furiously opposed by environmental lobbies because he favors Third World industrial development and has said such things as, "Nobody should kid themselves that they are doing Bangladesh a favor when they worry about global warming. Poverty is already a worse killer than any foreseeable environmental distress." Clinton decided not to nominate Summers because green opposition was so strong. Clinton did, however, ask the United Nations to pick as the new head of the U.N. Development Programme James Speth, former head of the World Resources Institute. The Group of 77 nations was dismayed because Speth has a reputation as a doomsayer: For instance, he has called tropical forest loss "an unparalleled tragedy." If the loss of renewable trees is an unparalleled tragedy, what words are left to describe millions of children dead from waterborne disease?[21]

It is tempting to go on quoting Easterbrook. I've seen no one else make the points so poignantly that economic development is what the Third World needs most and that this development will also bear the fruit—in time—of environmental improvement.

What is the bottom line? Responsible environmentalism will (a) be careful to ensure that it has sound empirical and theoretical grounds for its claims, and (b) prioritize in terms of greater and lesser risks first to human beings and then to the rest of creation. It will put the needs of poor human beings first. But too much contemporary environmentalism, even among evangelicals who in the past have made the poor a priority, now (a) promotes scary notions without adequate evidence and (b) focuses on low-risk problems, often on problems not so much for people as for other species, at the expense of addressing the high-risk problems from which poor *people* really suffer.[22] Instead of calling people to the urgent and winnable battle of reducing basic air and water pollution and building drinking water treatment and distribution facilities and improving food production, preservation, and distribution in the developing world, they are raising unwarranted fears about hypothetical problems, the dangers from which are minute by comparison. To put it bluntly:

- No one ever died—no one ever even got sick—from reduced stratospheric ozone.
- No one ever died—no one ever even got sick—from acid rain falling on forests, lakes, and streams.
- No one ever died—no one ever even got sick—from increased carbon dioxide in the atmosphere; from global warming, real or imagined; from the environmental effects of logging old-growth forests in the Pacific northwest; from pesticide residues in American-grown fruits and vegetables; from the toxic waste leaks at Love Canal or any other toxic waste site in the United States; from the dioxin spread on the dusty roads of Times Beach, Missouri; from the accident at the Three Mile Island nuclear power station;[23] from all the years of all the operation of all the civilian nuclear power plants in the Western world; or from the Exxon Valdez oil spill in Prince William Sound.

No one ever died—no one ever even got sick—from most of the biggest, most exotic environmental problems today's Western environmentalists, including evangelicals, hammer on day in and day out. But every year *millions* of poor people all over the developing world die for lack of such simple things as waste treatment plants and water purification and distribution systems and paved roads and refrigerators.

It is time for environmentalism to put its focus in the right place. Evangelicals, with their admirable and effective worldwide missions to the poor, should take the lead in adopting that new environmental focus.

CHAPTER 6

❧   ❧

Observations on the Mind of the
Evangelical Environmental Movement

IN *50 WAYS YOU CAN HELP SAVE THE PLANET*, TONY CAMPOLO AND GORdon Aeschliman wrote, "Confusion, fuzzy thinking and unfriendly name calling surround the Christian community's debate on our responsibility to the environment."[1] Unfortunately, they are right. Earlier chapters documented some of the confusion among evangelical environmentalists about world view, theology, ethics, Scripture, and scientific issues. In order to call participants to a higher level of discussion, this chapter will discuss some of the confusions—including name-calling—that have marred evangelical debate about the environment.

Debate Over the *Evangelical Declaration on the Care of Creation*
On October 30, 1993, the Evangelical Environmental Network (EEN) adopted its *Evangelical Declaration on the Care of Creation*, intending to circulate it to obtain endorsements from well-known Christian leaders (which it later did). In an article published in *World* November 27, 1993 (see appendix 4), I criticized the *Declaration*'s vagueness, pointed out various empirical errors embodied or (with reference to an earlier draft) implied in it, recognized several good points, and took issue with several of its theological perspectives. I concluded that while the *Declaration* rightly reminded Christians of our responsibility for the environment, it fell seriously short on some Biblical principles and empirical accuracy. One of my greatest concerns was that most of the Christian leaders who would be asked to endorse it—pastors, seminary professors, parachurch ministry leaders—would lack the necessary

expertise in the pros and cons of environmental debates to assess the *Declaration*'s view of the current state of the environment adequately before deciding whether to lend to it their prestige and, in many cases, the prestige of the large organizations they led.

Reaction was furious. Aeschliman, a member of the EEN, awarded *World* and me the Toxic Turkey Award of the Christian Environmental Association, of which he was a leader. At the time he was also editor of *Prism*, the new flagship magazine of Evangelicals for Social Action, a parent group of the EEN. In the editorial "Somebody got shot in the head: *Creation after the fall*," he insisted that my critique had concluded that the *Declaration* was "false and misleading because—here is the pillar of [the critique's] argument—there is no substantial environmental problem in the world today."

"Do we just neglect that billions of people live outside the reach of Christ's love because their creativity will eventually lead them to a church door?" he asked incredulously. "Do we ignore the impact of the Fall on marriages and families because people's creativity will eventually lead to fidelity, honesty, gentleness and the keeping of covenants? Do we ignore the stress of drugs and violence upon urban youth because in their creativity they will eventually walk away from those destructive forces? Do we ignore the brutal practices of oppressive governments because in time their creativity will lead them away from their sinful practices?"[2] Precisely how these problems related to the environment, to the *Declaration*, or to my critique was not clear. No such ideas could be found in the article, and I embrace none of them.

It is difficult to imagine how *Prism* could have misrepresented my article more thoroughly. I replied in a letter to the editor:

> Your editorial . . . combines *argumentum ad hominem* abusive [attacking the person] with straw man and outright falsification. How anyone could read my statement that the "*fall has had serious consequences*, physical and spiritual, causal and judgmental, for the whole human race. It plunged us and our world into decay and death" (emphasis added), and then write, ". . . the consequences of the Fall are not so serious, says Beisner," is a mystery. (Decay and death are *examples* of the serious consequences, not the whole show. Explicit mention of them does not equate with denying other effects of the fall, including original sin, total depravity, the corruption of rationality, and so on—all of which I affirm.)
>
> You allege that I said that:
> ". . . there is no substantial environmental problem in the world today." I didn't say that, and it's not true.
> ". . . there is no current problem in the world with land degradation." I

didn't say that, and it's not true.

". . . there is no reason to be concerned about deforestation." I didn't say that, and it's not true.

". . . there is no cause for alarm regarding the impact of global slashing and burning." I didn't say that, and it's not true—except insofar as slash-and-burn agriculture is not global and will dwindle away where it's happening in developing countries, just as (only probably faster than)[3] it did in presently advanced countries, when it becomes economically inefficient for farmers.

". . . there is [no] problem of species extinction." I didn't say that, and (as I did say) the hard field data aren't sufficient yet to say whether it's true.

". . . neither water nor the air is becoming more polluted and hence dangerous to human and animal well being." I didn't say that. What I said was, "Local water pollution is a genuine problem, sometimes severe; but on a global scale, water pollution is insignificant and, in advanced economies, declining, as it will do as other economies grow to afford cleaner technologies."

". . . there is no need to worry about the world's resources—because God created them we will never run out." I didn't say that, and it's not true. What I said was that we won't run out not because God created resources but because God gave mankind the ability to refine, transform, and substitute raw materials and processes by the application of growing knowledge so that resources become more abundant, not more scarce, through time.

". . . we have no reason to believe that environmental problems are causing pain and hardship to human beings and their cultures." I didn't say that, and it's not true.

". . . people who claim there is an increasingly critical environmental problem have been duped by pseudo scientists, and just plain don't want to know the facts." I didn't say that, and it's true only of some people some of the time about some issues, but not of all people all of the time about all issues. I do not assume that it is true of the authors of the *Declaration*.

In addition to its misrepresentations and irrelevancies, the editorial was filled with sarcasm, ridicule, and personal attack. Ironically enough, the same issue of *Prism* included a copy of the *Chicago Declaration II: A Call for Evangelical Renewal*, adopted by Evangelicals for Social Action, *Prism*'s (and the EEN's) parent organization. *Declaration II* included the following: "Too often, recent evangelical political engagement has been uncivil and polarizing, has demonized opponents and lacked careful analysis and biblical integrity." In a letter to Aeschliman, I cited that statement. One of *Prism*'s editorial advisory board members also wrote in protest. Aeschliman responded in a letter addressed to both of us that his "editorial was rather restrained" and charging me, because of my disagreement with the EEN's environmental views, with "racism, sexism and cold heartedness" and with advancing "discrimination against the poor."

Why tell this story? To illustrate how easily emotions can rage and attention can be diverted to side issues in the environmental debate. My critique of the *Evangelical Declaration on the Care of Creation* said nothing racist or sexist, nothing cold hearted toward the poor. Right or wrong, it questioned the accuracy of certain assertions the *Declaration* had made about the physical world and about theology. Sadly, a key spokesman of the EEN cheapened the debate by demonizing his opponents and misrepresenting their views.

The Moral Side of Disagreements

It is tempting to ask, "Why can't we just keep emotions and moral accusations out of this debate and focus on the facts?" But that question ignores the important truth that in God's universe, fact and value are always interrelated. This is no less true in the environmental debate than in any other. British evangelical pastor John Stott wrote, "Despoiling the earth is blasphemy, and not just an error of judgement, a mistake; it's sin against God as well as man."[4] Yet while we may agree with Stott in principle, we must still make some careful distinctions.

First, not everyone agrees about what constitutes "despoiling the earth." Some people believe that irrigating the desert to make it bloom is despoiling the earth; others believe it is a wonderful improvement on a world in which not everything is best untouched by human hands. Some believe building flood-control dams on rivers is despoiling the earth; others think it is good to protect farmland, residential areas, and forests from flooding this way. Some people believe raising crop yields through genetically engineered high-yield seeds and application of artificial fertilizers is despoiling the earth; others believe it not only helps people by making food more abundant and affordable but also protects the earth by reducing the number of acres required to grow enough food for everyone.[5] Difficult and serious factual and ethical questions intertwine with these and scores of other points of the environmental debate. To adopt one perspective and condemn as a blasphemer whoever disagrees not only is arrogant and unhelpful to a debate that might otherwise improve mutual understanding but also might reveal considerable ignorance of just how complex and unclear many of the issues are.

Second, the Bible distinguishes among types of sin. Some sins are "presumptuous" (Ps. 19:13). We know that we are doing wrong, and we stubbornly and arrogantly proceed, presuming on God's grace, just as if we had never been united with Christ and liberated from sin (Rom. 6:1–2). Such sins deserve stern rebuke and, if unrepented, excommunication (Matt. 18:15–21). Some sins we struggle against, sometimes triumphing and sometimes succumbing, always longing for complete deliverance (Rom. 7:13–25). Such sins "overtake" us, and they call for loving and humble correction by our partners in faith, who must humbly consider themselves lest they, too, be tempted (Gal. 6:1–4). Some sins we commit unintentionally, without realizing that we are doing wrong (Lev. 4:2; 5:15–18). Such sins, while we are truly guilty for them (Lev. 5:17), require correction and restitution, but the sacrifices assigned to them under the Old Testament law—much lighter than for intentional sins—indicate that there is a real moral difference between them and either presumptuous or habitual sins.

Third, the Bible's list of sins is not infinite. Sin is lawlessness—violation of God's law (1 John 3:4; Rom. 6:19; 2 Cor. 6:14). It is legalism to call sin what is not contrary to Biblical law. Some primitive forms of agriculture do serious harm to ecosystems, but they are the best agricultural methods some people know. Is it sin for them to use them? There is legitimate debate over the wisdom of pesticide use to improve crop yields. Is it sin to hold any of the many possible views in that debate? What of a disagreement between agricultural scientists over whether the safe level of fertilizer use in a given locale is .5 or .6 ton per acre—is one scientist sinning because he advises .6 ton, while the other is not because he advises .5? It would be difficult indeed to argue that Biblical law unequivocally requires one view or practice over another in such matters.

So it is dangerous to say simply, as Stott does, "Despoiling the earth is blasphemy. . . ." Doing so—and applying it to specific debatable actions—assumes that our understanding of complex empirical problems is right and another is wrong; it fails to distinguish presumptuous from habitual and unintentional sins; and it may well call sin what Scripture does not call sin. Whichever is the case, it encourages us to respond to everyone who—in our judgment—"despoils the earth" as we would to a flagrant and stubborn blasphemer, while many such people might simply need gentle correction—or we might even be mistaken about some, thinking they have done wrong when they have done right.

Five More Fallacious Types of Argument

Thus far this chapter—as to some extent chapter 4—has suggested several faulty ways in which some evangelical environmentalists carry on the debate over environmentalism: personal attack through ridicule, sarcasm, or

questioning of motives; misrepresentation of critics' views; moral condemnation over matters of theoretical or empirical disagreement. The remainder of
this chapter will point out a few other faulty debate tactics used by some
evangelical environmentalists. No one should infer from this that all, or even
most, of the arguments in evangelical environmentalists' writings share these
faults. On the contrary, most avoid these faults. Neither should anyone assume that those who commit these mistakes do so wittingly. This critique
must not be taken as an attack on anyone's honesty. But the following five
categories of defects in argumentation arise often enough that perhaps pointing them out will help to elevate the quality and fruitfulness of the debate.

1. TAKING RATIONAL CRITICISM PERSONALLY. In this book and in several
published articles I have evaluated various aspects of the evangelical environmental movement. Often I have been critical of the movement's theology,
ethics, use of Scripture, and views on theoretical and empirical questions related to population, resources, pollution, and other matters. I have tried to be
a friendly critic.

Sometimes, however, questions about the accuracy of someone's claims
are taken as personal attacks. One prominent evangelical environmentalist,
evidence for one of whose empirical claims I requested repeatedly in letters
spanning more than a year, wrote to me, "In the midst of the battle I am not
used to getting shot at by a fellow soldier in the trench beside me." In his
view, he was fighting the battle between Biblical Christianity and a hostile
secular world, and by questioning his empirical claim about a particular environmental problem and asking for his evidence I was fighting against him in
that battle.

His response, however, confuses a debate about empirical states of affairs
with the battle between Biblical Christianity and its foes (secularism, pagan-
ism, competing religions, and so forth). This scholar does stand firmly for
Christianity in a hostile academic world. He rejects the anti-Christian world
views and ethics promoted by the secular, New Age, and Deep Ecology
branches of environmentalism and offers a genuinely Christian alternative. I
have observed firsthand, and been humbled by, his sincere piety and love for
the Lord.

But none of these was the point at issue. The point at issue was a specific
empirical claim. Fellow believers ought to be able to debate empirical problems—even with a certain passion—without fear of offending each other or
being accused of treason in the battle for the kingdom of God simply because
we ask for evidence to back up a claim with which we disagree. (For that

matter, within the boundaries of historic, orthodox Christianity defined by the early ecumenical creeds, we ought to be able to debate theological and ethical matters as well without fear of being called traitors to King and kingdom.)

2. ATTACKING CREDENTIALS. As liberal Democrat environmentalist Gregg Easterbrook wrote, "A rule of argument is that when opponents attack someone's qualifications or motives rather than rebutting the substance of arguments, this happens because they do not know how to rebut the substance. Increasingly in the 1990s, doctrinaire environmentalists have been impugning the qualifications or integrity of those who disagree with them."[6] Unfortunately, evangelical environmentalists sometimes adopt this tactic.

In an article critical of evangelical environmentalism's critics, Gordon College professor Richard Wright responded in part by pejoratively referring to some of them—Julian L. Simon, Herman Kahn, S. Fred Singer, and Dixy Lee Ray—as "scientific" sources—with the quotation marks.[7] Wright's placing quotation marks around *scientific* is just such a case of *argumentum ad hominem* abusive. As it is, all of those are bona fide scientists—properly credentialed and professionally accomplished—in the fields in which they have written as authorities in the environmental debate.[8]

An ironic twist on the credentials argument is to pronounce one's debate opponent unqualified to discuss a subject because he is not a scientist specializing in a topic, while one lacks those qualifications himself. During a radio talk show, EEN leader Ronald Sider cited Ghillian Prance, director of the Royal Botanical Gardens at Kew in London, in support of his belief in rapid species extinction.[9] When another guest countered that a major worldwide study by the International Union for the Conservation of Nature concluded that there was no solid evidence for rapid species extinction,[10] Sider responded, "Well, I sure would prefer that scientists tell me about biological questions rather than economists or theologians or psychologists."[11] But if Sider's response counted against his opponent's citing scientific authorities on species extinction, it counted just as much against his doing the same. In reality, it counted against neither. It is legitimate for laymen to read, report, and evaluate the work of specialists.

Arguments should address logic and evidence principally, credentials only secondarily. When someone's logic and evidence are credible (even if not finally persuasive), his credentials are largely irrelevant. Credentials (testimonials of presumptive authority) are most relevant when people make mere pronouncements; they are least relevant when people muster arguments; and good arguments should always trump credentialed pronouncements.

3. APPEALS TO MAJORITIES. Determining truth by popular vote has never found much respect among logicians, but it crops up from time to time among evangelical environmentalists. For example, in reply to a critique of the *Evangelical Declaration on the Care of Creation*, Sider wrote, ". . . the vast majority of responsible scientists disagree with Beisner's scientific claims."[12]

First, however, as Edwin Olson, professor emeritus of geology at Whitworth College, puts it, "that is a debatable conclusion. . . ."[13] While the popular notion is that a majority of climatologists, for instance, believes that global warming caused by human activity is a significant threat to the planet, a 1991 Gallup poll of professional climatologists showed the reverse.[14]

Second, even among scientists majority votes are no guarantee of truth. In the 1970s, it appeared that a majority of scientists investigating the matter believed that global cooling was underway and presented a serious threat of an impending ice age. Had everyone succumbed to the "truth by majority vote" argument, no one would have done the research that later led to some scientists' believing now that global warming is an impending threat. And while a majority of scientists once thought acid rain was causing serious damage to forests and lakes in the Adirondack Mountains and New England states, once the ten-year research program of the National Acid Precipitation Assessment Program (NAPAP) was complete and its results became known, the majority reversed.

Third, while appeals to majorities are always fallacious as determinants of truth, they are most fallacious (to relativize an absolute term) when applied to debates in which one side admits from the start that it is a minority—often styled "contrarian"—view. Critics of conventional thinking on environmentalism are by definition a minority—otherwise they would not be criticizing "conventional thinking." But it is precisely the courage of contrarians to buck the trend that, time after time in the history of science, has led to corrections of past mistaken thought. Were it not so, we would all still believe in a flat earth, a geocentric universe, and the reality of ether (a substance regarded by ancient philosophers as filling all space beyond the sphere of the moon), no one would be flying, and the Reformation would never have taken place.

Proponents of conventional views must respond to contrarians not by pointing out that they are contrarians (No one ever doubted that!) but by answering the evidence and logic of their arguments.

4. INTIMIDATION. One way to head off questions is to awe observers by reference to the immensity or sophistication of one's research. For example, in *Earth-Wise* DeWitt writes, "To the best of my ability I have done a computer

search of 700,000 titles of articles on the environment. I have pruned this collection down to those written in the professional, refereed literature, and have organized these into major topics that I call 'Seven Degradations of Creation.'"[15] Many lay readers, on encountering such a statement, would shrink from the prospect of challenging what DeWitt then says about the environment. They need not.

First, it is exceedingly unlikely that DeWitt has given all 700,000 of these titles careful consideration. Suppose one could carefully read, evaluate, and consider how to integrate an article into his thinking about the environment in an average of just ten minutes per article, and that one committed ten hours per day, six days per week exclusively to doing so. At that rate, it would take one person over thirty-seven years of exclusive work to consider all 700,000 articles. No doubt DeWitt has read a great deal about the environment—far more in his long career, I expect, than I have—but the argumentative significance of the number 700,000 is practically nil, except for its intimidating effect.

Second, consider how DeWitt's goal—to find articles that can be organized into major topics called "Seven Degradations of Creation"—provided an automatic filter that might have prevented his seeing contrary evidence. Does an article, even in a refereed journal, purporting to give evidence *against*, say, the CFC/ozone depletion hypothesis, or the enhanced greenhouse effect hypothesis, or the critical soil erosion on U.S. cropland hypothesis, or the rapid species extinction hypothesis, etc., count as an article on one of the "Seven Degradations of Creation"? The temptation simply to overlook such articles must be intense.

Adding to the intimidating effect of DeWitt's claim is his statement that he has "pruned this collection down to those written in the professional, refereed literature." Particularly to people who haven't observed the degree of debate and disagreement in scientific and other professional journals, this can create the impression of nearly monolithic agreement among specialists on such subjects. But nothing could be farther from the truth. The "professional, refereed literature" is filled with conflicting articles on practically every aspect of the debate over the environment—except that articles questioning the basic premise that we face great environmental crisis rarely see the light of day. Furthermore, although many laymen assume that scientists practice scrupulous objectivity and openness to contrary ideas, strong biases often affect what gets admitted for publication even in refereed journals. One of the clearest subjects in which this occurs is the evolution/creation controversy. Bona fide scientists who believe the evidence points toward creation (whether young-earth or old-earth) have a notoriously difficult time getting articles arguing for their views—and sometimes any articles at all, no matter the subject—accepted for publication in professional journals. Indeed, some who have had stellar publishing records before they became known as creationists have found the doors slammed shut afterward.[16] Similar obstacles exist in relation to other scientific controversies.[17] Indeed, it is surprising that DeWitt, a Christian scientist struggling to uphold the cause of Christ in the often hostile atmosphere of a secular university, should place such trust in professional, refereed literature dominated by anti-Christian thinkers.

Environmental orthodoxy is one area in which such publishing bias occurs. The story of how Philip Abelson, then editor of *Science*, rigged the system to keep contrarian Julian Simon's article "Resources, Population, Environment: An Oversupply of False Bad News" from publication for three years despite excellent referees' reports should be enough to persuade anyone that such decisions can be far from objective. The article did finally get published,[18] but only after a hair-raising fight. And as Simon points out, "for each such case such [sic] as mine that by a miracle gets past the gate, there must be many unconventional but worthy writings still outside the fence literally crying to be printed and read. . . ." Worse, however, is the story of how Daniel Koshland, a later editor of *Science*, succeeded in ensuring that an article he initially solicited from Simon not only never got published but never even got submitted to referees—an event followed by Simon's discovering that Koshland had himself published an article arguing for "effective population control" because population growth is "dooming our ecosystem"—i.e., for positions directly contrary to Simon's.[19]

Sometimes the environmental bias affects people's employability. When soil and water chemist Edward Krug, a Ph.D.'d field researcher working with the NAPAP, found to his surprise that most lakes and streams of Connecticut were *not* seriously acidified, that there was *not* a significant correlation between acid rain and soil and surface water acidity, that sediment core samples indicated that surface water acidity in the suspect lakes and streams had been roughly as high in pre-industrial times as it is now, and that there were natural rather than human explanations for the phenomenon, and when he then made those results public, public attacks on him by officials of the Environmental Protection Agency led to his inability later to find employment in any government-funded research programs—although the EPA later was forced to apologize for its unfounded attacks.[20] (Krug, shocked by the furor with which his environmentalist former friends greeted what he thought they would welcome as good news, began wondering, "Why do these people hate truth so much?"

His quest for an answer led to his reading Francis Schaeffer and C. S. Lewis and becoming a Christian.)

Neither the cycle of scientific minorities' becoming majorities and being replaced by later minorities nor majorities' suppressing the work of minorities should surprise people familiar with the history of science. As Thomas Kuhn argued in *The Structure of Scientific Revolutions*, a reigning scientific paradigm tends to dominate academia and publishing for decades while a small number of scientists nibble away, often unaware of each other, at bits and pieces of it. At some point, usually not gradually and piecemeal but suddenly and wholesale, the reigning paradigm collapses and is replaced by a new orthodoxy, and the process repeats itself. (Such a transition seems imminent in the environmental debate as evidence mounts against the conventional doom-and-gloom view. Easterbrook's *A Moment on the Earth* is in many ways a sustained argument for that.) In Kuhn's view, shared by various other historians and philosophers of science, such paradigm shifts are one of the great engines of theoretical progress in science.[21] What is surprising, however, is that Christian scientists—who are used to being minorities and confronting the bias of secular scientists—should put much trust in the objectivity of the scientific academic and publishing communities.

Two other factors also contribute to the dominance of crisis perspectives in scientific literature on the environment. First, in addition to a plethora of national and international agencies all over the world, over 450 private nationwide organizations in the United States alone, plus thousands of local organizations, have been established to promote environmentalism, and for many their *raison d'etre* is to alert people to crises and propose solutions to them; without news of crises, fund raising (leading environmental organizations raised over $400 million in 1991) plummets. They have a vested interest, therefore, in supporting scholars whose work generates the "right" results. Second, this phenomenon exists in a positive feedback loop with the desperate need many scientists feel for research funding. Few donors—private or public—are willing to fund research on non-problems; they want to fund research on crises, the bigger the better. This creates a strong natural incentive for researchers to look for evidence of problems and ignore contrary evidence.[22] Of particular importance is the fact that the federal government has become by far the largest source of funding for environmental research, whether directly (in the environmental activities of its own departments and agencies) or indirectly (in its support of public, private, and mixed universities and research institutions). Climatologist Patrick Michaels points out,

Virtually every active academic researcher in the environmental sciences is supported by the federal government. As large amounts of research support were directed towards the issue of global climate change, it is logical that the research community would not refuse such support. However, this support would stop if that community repeatedly stated that the data indicated that much of the concern about the issue was misplaced. The policy community therefore received little if any signal indicating that the [global climate change computer] models [that predicted large and dangerous global warming] were not being verified by observed data.

Without a healthy mix of public and private funding, political bias and self-preservation are bound to show up in research proposals and findings.

That mix, or dynamic equilibrium, does not exist today in the environmental sciences, particularly with respect to climate change. There is virtually no private funding, and the Federal biases are obvious. As Senator from Tennessee, for example, Albert Gore assumed chairmanship of the Subcommittee on Science, Space and Technology, which oversees the budgets of both the National Science Foundation and NASA. It is difficult to envision these Agency heads testifying at budget hearings in front of the Senator that global climate change is not so important an issue that it merits a substantial increase in their budgets.[23]

In short, what is important is not how many sources one can cite favoring his views, or even that the sources are from refereed scientific journals, but the strength of the evidence and logic constituting the arguments. And nonscientists should never feel intimidated by scientists in evaluating such arguments. As Ben Bolch and Harold Lyons (both Ph.D.'d professors, of economics and chemistry, respectively) put it in *Apocalypse Not: Science, Economics, and Environmentalism*,

The intelligent layperson's responsibility is to evaluate scientific stories, and, as we have tried to point out in this book, people should never be afraid of applying common sense to that enterprise. Nor should anyone be surprised when scientists themselves are the last to see the common sense of an argument opposing their latest story, since they are as apt as anyone to be blinded by love of their own creation.[24]

5. LOOKING ON THE DARK SIDE. (OR: THE GLASS IS ALWAYS HALF EMPTY.) Another common mental habit of environmentalists, including some evangelicals, is viewing things negatively that could as easily be viewed positively. One example, noted above (see note 5), is the complaint many environ-

mentalists have against high-yield farming. While they decry its use of chemical fertilizers and pesticides as threatening some wildlife, they forget that by doubling or tripling yields per acre it reduces by half or two-thirds the number of acres that must be farmed—thus protecting far more wildlife than it threatens. Another example is the lament in *Earthkeeping in the Nineties* that "the same civilization which has brought us knowledge of the earth also seems to threaten it."[25] It would be just as sensible to point out that the same civilization that has threatened the earth has also brought us the knowledge necessary to reduce the threat. Indeed, the authors do essentially that later in the book: "The same gifts of wisdom and power—our science and technology—which have created many of the problems have also opened our eyes to the accompanying degradation."[26] While some writers have pointed out that CFCs function as a greenhouse gas, they rarely point out that their theoretical reduction of stratospheric ozone, another greenhouse gas, offsets their greenhouse effect at least to some degree. While they point out the risks of global warming from increased atmospheric CO_2, they do not discuss the beneficial effects of increased CO_2 on plant growth. While they bemoan population growth, they forget that it is a symptom of falling death rates—i.e., a sign that people are living longer and healthier, which ought to be cause for celebration. A more judicious approach will not neglect the positive side of some (really or apparently) negative phenomena.

Conclusion

The quality of the environmental debate among evangelicals can improve if all sides will commit to logic and evidence rather than misrepresentations, moral condemnations, *ad hominem* arguments, intimidation, appeals to majorities, and unbalanced emphasis of either the negative or the positive aspects of phenomena. It is my hope that this book—regardless whether it persuades any of my brothers and sisters in the evangelical environmental movement of any of the positions I take on the theological, ethical, Biblical, and empirical issues discussed—will help at least to elevate the debate.

CHAPTER 7

🐝　🐝

Imago Dei and the Population Debate[1]

SOMETIME EARLY IN THE NINETEENTH CENTURY B.C.,[2] THE HEBREW patriarch Abram and his nephew Lot dwelt as semi-nomadic shepherds in the region of Bethel and Ai in Palestine. "Abram had become very wealthy in livestock and in silver and gold" (Gen. 13:2), and Lot

> ... also had flocks and herds and tents. But the land could not support them while they stayed together, for their possessions were so great that they were not able to stay together. And quarreling arose between Abram's herdsmen and the herdsmen of Lot. . . .
>
> So Abram said to Lot, "Let's not have any quarreling between you and me, or between your herdsmen and mine, for we are brothers. Is not the whole land before you? Let's part company. If you go to the left, I'll go to the right; if you go to the right, I'll go to the left."
>
> Lot looked up and saw that the whole plain of the Jordan was well watered, like the garden of the LORD, like the land of Egypt, toward Zoar. . . . So Lot chose for himself the whole plain of the Jordan and set out toward the east. The two men parted company: Abram lived in the land of Canaan, while Lot lived among the cities of the plain and pitched his tents near Sodom. [Gen. 13:5–12]

This is the earliest instance recorded in the Bible[3] of the impression that a local human population had outstripped the ability of the land to support it.

Tucked away in this passage is a fascinating lesson for those who will see it: Lot chose for himself what appeared to be the most fertile land. In contrast, Abram, father of the faithful and of many nations (Rom. 4:11, 16–17), ac-

95

cepted whatever land God, in His providence, gave him through Lot's choice. Lot's eyes focused on material circumstances, Abram's on the ability of God to bless His servant regardless of circumstances. Lot's decision was driven by his thoughts about the capacity of the land; Abram's by his faith in God.

After Lot had chosen the richer, more fertile land, Yahweh said to Abram, "Lift up your eyes from where you are and look north and south, east and west. All the land that you see I will give to you and your offspring forever. I will make your offspring like the dust of the earth, so that if anyone could count the dust, then your offspring could be counted. Go, walk through the length and breadth of the land, for I am giving it to you." (Gen. 13:14–17).

Now, there is something ironic in this promise. Abram and Lot had separated precisely because they thought the land could not support their households and livestock. From their perspective, the last thing either would consider a blessing would be a new expansion of population. But that is precisely what God promised Abram: "I will make your offspring like the dust of the earth. . . ." Would not the fulfillment of that promise mean repeating the very dilemma that had caused strife between Abram and his nephew in the first place? Yet before long God repeated the promise as a blessing of the covenant, and "Abram believed the Lord, and he credited it to him as righteousness" (Gen. 15:4–6). And then God did indeed multiply Abram's offspring, so much that by the time of the exodus some 400 years later they numbered some 600,000 adult males, plus women and children, i.e., probably between 2 and 5 million.[4]

If I were to point to one thing that most saddens me about the propensity among many today—including many devout and honest Christians—to fear population growth and its impact on resources and the environment, it would be that in this fear they think more like Lot than like Abram. They focus on the material world rather than on the infinite faithfulness and goodness of God, and their choices—like Lot's—reflect their belief that the present state of the world sets the boundaries of human expectations. In this fear they do not, like Abram, focus on the promises of God and His perfect faithfulness and power to fulfill them. To them I would say with Paul—recognizing that he used the language in a different context—"Set your minds on things above, not on earthly things" (Col. 3:2).

This fear, as we have just seen, has ancient roots, and it has persisted through the millennia. Some 2,100 years after Abram and Lot separated lest they overburden the land of Palestine, the Church Father Tertullian wrote with alarm:

Everything has been visited, everything known, everything exploited. Now pleasant estates obliterate the famous wilderness areas of the past. Plowed fields have replaced forests, domesticated animals have dispersed wild life. Beaches are plowed, mountains smoothed and swamps drained. There are as many cities as, in former years, there were dwellings. Islands do not frighten, nor cliffs deter. Everywhere there are buildings, everywhere people, everywhere communities, everywhere life. . . . Proof [of this crowding] is the density of human beings. We weigh upon the world; its *resources hardly suffice to support us*. As our needs grow larger, so do our protests, that already *nature does not sustain us*. In truth, plague, famine, wars and earthquakes must be regarded as a blessing to civilization, since they prune away the luxuriant growth of the human race.[5]

From our vantage point in history, it seems ludicrous that Tertullian, writing in Carthage around A.D. 200, could have thought his world overpopulated when the whole world's population probably fell short of 500 million—about a tenth of what it is today. But people do say ludicrous things sometimes—like the couple who, unwittingly reflecting Tertullian's complaint that we "weigh upon the world," wrote a letter to the editor of a northwest Arkansas newspaper claiming that human beings are "crushing our planet under the weight of our own population."[6] Consider this for a moment. The roughly 5 billion people in the world have a combined weight of about 375,000,000 tons, or about 1/67 billionth the weight of the earth's crust alone, which weighs about 25 quintillion tons and constitutes only a fraction of the whole earth. To put this into perspective, it's about like saying that something weighing 1/82 billionth of an ounce would crush an adult human being.

Such irrational fears, however, usually arise from more understandable concerns. Tertullian's alarm arose from his conviction that the world's "resources hardly suffice to support us," that "nature does not sustain us." It was not that he looked around him and saw people crammed together like sardines in a can, but that he thought there were insufficient resources in the world to support the people in it—whatever their mathematical/geographical density.

That concern and another closely related to it appear to lie at the root of today's fears about population growth. As Susan Power Bratton points out in *Six Billion & More: Human Population Regulation and Christian Ethics*, environmentalists ". . . agree that if a human population gets too large, it will exceed its environmental carrying capacity."[7] (See appendix 4 for a thorough review of Bratton's important book.) In the words of Laurie Ann Mazur, "At the heart of the environmentalists' perspective on population growth is the concept of 'carrying capacity.' The planet's carrying capacity is, in essence, its ability to sustain life."[8] And the "ability to sustain life," in turn, consists of two components: the ability to provide the resources man needs to consume in order to live, and the ability to absorb the pollution man generates in his productive activities without the earth's biological systems' being overwhelmed. This dual concern is aptly expressed in the subtitle of the book Mazur edited: *Beyond the Numbers: A Reader on Population, Consumption, and the Environment*. It also finds expression in the words of Riane Eisler, a feminist environmentalist:

> The population crisis . . . lies at the heart of the seemingly insoluble complex of problems futurists call the *world problematique*. For behind soil erosion, desertification, air and water pollution, and all the other ecological, social, and political stresses of our time lies the pressure of more and more people on finite land and other resources, of increasing numbers of factories, cars, trucks, and other sources of pollution required to provide all these people with goods, and the worsening tensions that their needs and aspirations fuel.[9]

In short, the two principal concerns of those who fear continued population growth are (1) that in their effort to meet their needs and wants people are using up the earth's resources, and (2) that in the process they are polluting the earth to such an extent that its ability to continue to sustain life, or at least the abundant variety of life that it presently sustains, is catastrophically, perhaps irreversibly, threatened.[10] The vision of mankind that underlies these two concerns is of two parts also: Mankind is principally a consumer and a polluter. And these two traits can be summed up in a single trait: Mankind is fundamentally destructive.

I believe the Bible gives us a very different vision of mankind, that on the grounds of that Biblical vision we ought to take a very different attitude toward population growth from that common among environmentalists, and that sound science and economics—both theoretical and empirical—confirm the Biblical vision and the attitude suggested by it.

A Biblical Vision of Man

A decidedly low view of man dominates the environmentalist and population control movements. They call people the population bomb, the population explosion, the population boom, the population plague, a cancer, or people pollution.[11] But what does the Bible say about mankind?

Look first at Psalm 8:3–8, one of the definitive scriptures on the doctrine of man. Overwhelmed at contemplating God's greatness and the greatness of creation, David writes, "When I consider Your heavens, the work of Your fingers, the moon and the stars, which You have ordained, what is man that You are mindful of him, and the son of man that You visit him?"

Here David commits a logical fallacy, and he is honest enough, under the influence of the Holy Spirit, to record it. He confuses quantity with quality. He wrongly thinks, "God is so great that He made the heavens and everything in them with His fingers, and next to them, what is man? He is so tiny! How can he be important to God? Why should God even think of him, let alone visit him?"

David's fallacy is the same one abortion proponents commit when they argue against the humanity of the unborn from its being so tiny as to be unrecognizable. Far from it! Quantity has nothing to do with it; quality, everything. Indeed, as the celebrated French geneticist Jerome Lejeune has pointed out, the very first cell after fertilization—before any cell division—although tinier than any ensuing stage of the human embryo, "knows more and is more specialized . . . than any cell which is later in our organism." It contains more information, in better order, than any other cell or group of cells at any later stage of development—and that information determines everything about the future physical makeup of that human being.[12] And is it unrecognizable? Any genetics student of Dr. Lejeune who could not tell the difference between a single *cell* of a human embryo and a cell of a chimpanzee or gorilla embryo "would fail his exam."[13]

Quality and quantity must not be confused. Yet David, for a moment anyway, confuses them. But he is not held captive by the fallacy. No, a revelation comes upon him, and instantly he is liberated. "For You made him a little lower than"—

Than what? Many translations read, "You have made him a little lower than the *angels*." But that is not what the Hebrew reads, and John Calvin rightly preferred the Hebrew to the Septuagint here.[14] What the Hebrew says is, "For You have made him a little lower than *God*," harking back to Genesis 1:26, which tells us that God made man in His own image and after His likeness. After all, according to Hebrews 1:14, angels were made to serve men, not men to serve angels, and according to 1 Corinthians 6:3, men will judge angels. So David writes,

> For You have made him a little lower than God,
> And You have crowned him with glory and honor.
> You have made him to have dominion over the works of Your hands;
> You have put all things under his feet,

All sheep and oxen—
Even the beasts of the field,
The birds of the air,
And the fish of the sea
That pass through the paths of the seas.

The Bible, right alongside its doctrines of the Fall and original sin and total depravity, has a profoundly high view of mankind. Yes, we are mortal; yes, we are dead in trespasses and sins, sons of disobedience, by nature children of wrath; yes, our foolish hearts are darkened, and we suppress the truth in unrighteousness. We are, in short, a frightful piece of wreckage. But we *are wreckage*, not an amorphous mass "without form and void," as the world once was before the Spirit of God hovered over the face of the deep.

The Image of God in Man

We are not without a prior image. Instead, we are the wreckage of something gloriously magnificent, something that God Himself "crowned . . . with glory and honor." And in Christ we see perfectly revealed what we are destined to become through regeneration, sanctification, and glorification. As Calvin put it,

> [B]y the fall of Adam, all mankind fell from their primeval state of integrity, for by this the image of God was *almost* entirely effaced from us, and we were also divested of those distinguishing gifts by which we would have been, as it were, elevated to the condition of demigods; in short, from a state of the highest excellence, we were reduced to a condition of wretched and shameful destitution. . . . But as the heavenly Father hath bestowed upon his Son an immeasurable fulness of all blessings, that all of us may draw from this fountain, it follows that whatever God bestows upon us by him belongs of right to him in the highest degree; yea, he himself is the living image of God, according to which we must be renewed, upon which depends our participation in the invaluable blessings which are here spoken of.

Thus, in Calvin's words, "Christ is . . . the restorer of mankind."[15]

Now look back over a millennium earlier than Calvin, to Saint Athanasius. This great champion of orthodoxy wrote in his treatise *On the Incarnation of the Word* that Christ "was made man that we might be made God."[16] Now, Athanasius did not mean that man would become infinite, eternal, or immutable, capable of creation *ex nihilo*, or self-existent. He explained what he meant, in part, by his next words: "For He was made man that we might be made God; and He manifested Himself by a body that we might receive the idea of the unseen Father; and He endured the insolence of men *that we might inherit immortality.*" But he thought not only of immortality but also of man's participation in the moral nature of God and in His glorious dominion over creation:

> [Christ] is . . . *the Deliverer of all flesh and of all creation.* . . . For He has become Man, that He might deify us *in Himself,* and He has been born of a woman . . . in order to transfer to Himself our erring generation, and that we may become henceforth a holy race, and 'partakers of the Divine nature,' as blessed Peter wrote.[17]

What did Athanasius mean by saying that Christ became "the Deliverer of all flesh *and of all creation*"? Surely he had in mind the Fall, God's judgment on the Serpent, Eve, and Adam, and God's curse on the earth; surely he had in mind Paul's great affirmation that God had subjected the creation to corruption "in hope; because the creation itself also will be delivered from the bondage of corruption into the glorious liberty of the children of God" (Rom. 8:20–21). Athanasius, like Paul, saw that the redeeming and delivering work of Christ was not restricted to the salvation of the souls of the elect but included the restoration of mankind to his original glory and of the physical universe as well.[18]

What is it that is being restored in mankind through Christ's redeeming work? The image of God. And what is that? In the Reformed faith, we think of something like the words of the *Westminster Confession,* that God created people "with reasonable and immortal souls, endued with knowledge, righteousness, and true holiness, after his own image" (IV.ii). The Reformed faith has long and rightly emphasized man's rational and moral nature in considering the image of God. Unfortunately, however, this emphasis can obscure other aspects of the image of God in man that are equally important and, in the context of Genesis 1:26, much more immediately recognizable. Consider that the proof texts offered for these clauses in the *Confession* are Colossians 3:10 (which tells of knowledge) and Ephesians 4:24 (which tells of true righteousness and holiness). Granted, these verses address the subject. But they are far from the immediate context of Genesis 1:26, where we are first told that God created man in His image. What would the novice reader of Scripture think of as the image of God in man if he attended carefully to the immediate context?

Imagine yourself in his place. You have just read this startling statement: "And God said, 'Let Us make man in Our image, according to Our likeness.'"

What would you already know about God that would help you to understand the meaning of the phrase "in Our image"?

Well, you would know what you had read in Genesis 1:1–25. "In the beginning God *created* the heavens and the earth"—so the image of God includes creativity. "Then God said, 'Let there be"—and behold! look at the list! Light, a firmament, and oceans, and dry land, and grass, and herbs, and trees, and stars, and sun, and moon, and birds, and sea creatures, and land creatures! An astonishing variety of things living and non-living! And He instructed all the living things to multiply and fill their various niches in the world. So the image of God includes a wonderful love of variety and life and fruitfulness.

So, if you were just starting out reading the Bible, what would you think God's image is? Principally, creativity. No wonder Dorothy Sayers considered man's capacity to make things a crucial part of the image of God in man.[19] And that is the first great distinction between the environmentalist and Biblical views of man and his relationship to the world. Environmentalism— in non-Christian circles at least, but all too often even among evangelicals— starts off on the wrong foot, denigrating mankind, denying the *imago Dei*. It sees man chiefly as consumer, not producer. And because it does, it concludes that he is exhausting the resources of the earth.

Scripture has a different vision. It does not say, "Then God *cursed* them and said to them, 'Be fruitful and increase in number,'" but "Then God *blessed* them and said to them, 'Be fruitful and increase in number; fill the earth . . .'" (Gen. 1:28).[20] The human race is not the population explosion but the population blossom; not the population boom but the population bloom; not people pollution but the people solution; not cancer but an answer.

This different vision begets a different prediction: that people, because God made them in His image to be creative and productive, because He gave them *creative minds* like His, can bring order out of chaos, and higher order out of lower order, actually *making* more resources than we consume. So the Biblical view of man and the universe predicts that, as we apply our minds to raw materials, *scarcity of resources will decline*—in other words, the supply of resources will *increase* relative to the demand for them, causing *falling* labor-capital costs of resource production and *falling* inflation-adjusted resource prices. And that is precisely what we find when we look at history.[21]

But I risk running ahead of myself. Let us back up a little and consider more carefully what we have in mind by the *imago Dei* in mankind and, related to that, God's design for mankind on the earth. Scripture indicates three principal elements in the image of God in man. In Ephesians 4:24, Paul tells believers to "put on the new self, created to be like God in true righteousness and holiness." There is, then, a moral element to the image of God. In Colossians 3:10, Paul writes of this "new self" as "being renewed in knowledge in the image of its Creator." So rationality is another element of the image of God in man. And the context of Genesis 1:26 implies that creativity is a third element of the *imago Dei*.

The Cultural Mandate: Creation Stewardship

These three characteristics—holiness, knowledge, and creativity—ought all to be employed by man in fulfilling the vocation God gave us: to rule over the earth (Gen. 1:26). For while "The earth is the LORD's, and everything in it, . . . for he founded it . . . and established it . . ." (Ps. 24:1–2), God has entrusted the rule of the earth to mankind, for "The highest heavens belong to the LORD, but the earth he has given to man" (Ps. 115:16). Man is, of course, accountable to God for how he exercises this rule over the earth (Gen. 2:16–17). But we must not think that because we do not have supreme authority, we have no authority whatever—that we are no different from the earth itself and the other living creatures that God placed upon it. The tendency among some environmentalists to blur or erase the metaphysical and ethical hierarchy of man over other living creatures contradicts the Biblical teaching that God gave man a mandate to rule the earth.

What has often been called the cultural mandate may also be called the stewardship vocation: Man is to steward the earth as God's image/representative. The first two chapters of Genesis indicate that this vocation consists of four elements:

First, as there is eternal fellowship among Father, Son, and Holy Spirit in the Triune God, so that God says "Let us make man in *our* image," so there is to be fellowship among mankind, beginning with the fellowship of male and female (Gen. 1:27), between "the man and his wife" (Gen. 2:19–25).

Second, as God created life, so mankind is to generate life: "God blessed them and said to them, 'Be fruitful and increase in number; fill the earth . . .'" (Gen. 1:28).

Third, as God ruled over all creation, so man, as God's image, is to subdue and rule the earth and all living things in it: "God blessed them and said to them, '. . . subdue [the earth]. Rule over the fish of the sea and the birds of the air and over every living creature that moves on the ground'" (Gen. 1:28). The force of the Hebrew words translated *subdue* and *rule* here—both conveying strong, forceful subjugation—must not be ignored.[22] Although we should not read into them a harsh, careless oppression—which would be unlike God's rule over creation—we cannot escape the fact that they indicate subduing and ruling something whose spontaneous tendency is to resist dominion.

Fourth, as God initially planted a garden and commanded all the birds, fish, animals, and plants of the earth to be fruitful and multiply, so man is to *cultivate* and *guard*[23] the Garden (Gen. 2:15), enhancing and maximizing its fruitfulness for God's glory and man's benefit and protecting it from the wilderness (to the east of the Garden, Gen. 3:23–24) that otherwise would encroach on it.[24] Mankind was, then, to guide, aid, and increase the garden's productivity, and ultimately—by transforming all the earth into a garden—the earth's productivity, and he was to guard the garden against natural degradation that might result from neglect. Clearly the purpose of the cultivation was to enable the garden, and later the earth, to meet man's needs—and the needs of other creatures as well—more fully than it naturally would.[25]

The Fall and Its Effects

Man and woman, therefore—God's image bearers—were initially called to labor wisely, righteously, and creatively in loving fellowship to subdue and rule the earth and every living creature on it, whether in the sky, in the waters, or on the land, to cultivate and guard the Garden God initially planted, and to spread the garden over all the globe. But Scripture tells us that, rather than acting as a responsible, accountable steward, mankind rebelled against God's rule, hoping thereby to become supreme himself, "like God, knowing [i.e., defining] good and evil" (Gen. 3:1–7).

Every aspect of the image of God in man was corrupted by the Fall. What had been a sound mind full of the light of truth, full of the God who is the Truth, became unsound and darkened by falsehood (Rom. 1:21), futile, dark, and ignorant (Eph. 4:17–18). What had been a clear conscience, untainted by sin, became fouled with the stench of guilt and fear (Titus 1:15), so that, in the words of the Lutheran *Formula of Concord*, ". . . the understanding and reason of man in spiritual things are wholly blind, and can understand nothing by their proper powers . . . and . . . the yet unregenerate will of man is not only averse from God but has become even hostile to God, so that it only wishes and desires those things, and is delighted with them, which are evil and opposite to the divine will." The once living soul (Gen. 2:7) died (Gen. 2:17), becoming mere dust again (Gen. 3:19); he who had been alive in righteousness and holiness became "dead in trespasses and sins" (Eph. 2:1); the companion of God "followed the ways of . . . the ruler of the kingdom of the air, the spirit who is now at work in those who are disobedient" (Eph. 2:2); the child of God became a child of wrath (Eph. 2:3). His once fertile and creative brilliance ("for the fruit of the light consists in all goodness, righteousness and truth," Eph. 5:9) collapsed into "fruitless deeds of darkness" (Eph. 5:11).

The consequences were disastrous for man, other living creatures, and the earth itself. The corruption of man's knowledge, holiness, and creativity affected not only his own inward nature but also his dominion, cultivation, and guarding of the Garden and, ultimately, the whole earth. He was cast out of the Garden and barred from returning to it in his fallen condition, lest he eat of the Tree of Life and live forever in his rebellious state (Gen. 3:22–24). Since he refused to submit to God, he was no longer worthy of the earth's unreserved submission; hence God said, "Because you have . . . eaten from the tree about which I commanded you saying, 'You shall not eat from it'; cursed is the ground because of you; in toil you shall eat of it all the days of your life. Both thorns and thistles it shall grow for you; and you shall eat the plants of the field; by the sweat of your face you shall eat bread, till you return to the ground, because from it you were taken; for you are dust, and to dust you shall return" (Genesis 3:17–19).

Because of the Fall, with the breaking of fellowship with God (Gen. 3:24), human fellowship was broken (Gen. 3:7), with strife beginning between husband and wife (Gen. 3:16) and continuing between brother and brother (Gen. 4:1–8). Human fertility (Gen. 3:16) and creativity and dominion (Gen. 3:17–19) all were frustrated. By His curse on the ground (Gen. 3:17), God subjected the creation to futility (Rom. 8:20), so that "the whole creation has been groaning as in the pains of childbirth right up to the present time" (Rom. 8:22).

The Good News of Redemption

Indeed, man's wickedness increased through the generations following Adam and Eve, until at last "every inclination of the thoughts of his heart was only evil all the time," and "The LORD was grieved that he had made man on the earth, and his heart was filled with pain. So the LORD said, 'I will wipe mankind, whom I have created, from the face of the earth—men and animals, and creatures that move along the ground, and birds of the air—for I am grieved that I have made them'" (Gen. 6:5–7).

But there was a man—one man—who "was a righteous man, blameless among the people of his time, and he walked with God" (Gen. 6:9). Through Noah, whose life and calling prefigured Christ's, God saved the human race and all the rest of life on earth. "I am going to bring floodwaters on the earth to destroy all life under the heavens," God told Noah, "every creature that has the breath of life in it.[26] Everything on earth will perish. But I will establish my covenant with you, and you will enter the ark—you and your sons and your wife and your sons' wives with you. You are to bring into the ark two of all living creatures, male and female, to keep them alive with you" (Gen. 6:17–19). In the ark the world—human and subhuman alike—was saved, prefiguring the salvation of the world through Christ (1 Peter 3:20–22).

What happened through Noah was but a foretaste, a mere glimmer, of what God would later achieve through His Son, who, as we have already learned from Calvin and Athanasius, became "the restorer of mankind"[27] and "the Deliverer of all flesh and of all creation."[28] Christ, the "last Adam" (1 Cor. 15:45), "is the image of the invisible God, the firstborn [i.e., preeminent One] over all creation" (Col. 1:15), even "the radiance of God's glory and the exact representation of his being" (Heb. 1:3). In His life, He exercised a wise (Col. 2:3), righteous (1 John 2:2), and life–giving (1 Cor. 15:45) dominion over the earth itself (calming a storm, Mark 4:37–39), over plant and animal life (multiplying loaves and fishes, Matt. 14:13–21), and even over human life (healing the sick, Mark 5:25–34; raising the dead, Mark 5:21–24, 35–43). "While we were still sinners, Christ died for us" (Rom. 5:8), and by His death saved us from God's wrath, reconciled us to God, gave us the gift of righteousness (Rom. 5:9–11), and restored us to life (Rom. 5:19, 21), so that now those who are His are being restored in knowledge (Eph. 4:24) and righteousness and holiness (Col. 3:10). Having died for us, He rose again from the dead, so that for all who have died with Him, "just as Christ was raised from the dead through the glory of the Father, we too may live a new life" (Rom. 6:4), set free from slavery to sin and made again the servants of righteousness and of God Himself (Rom. 6:5–22).

In Christ the "incomparably great power" of God was displayed:

That power is like the working of his mighty strength, which he exerted in Christ when he raised him from the dead and seated him at his right hand in the heavenly realms, far above all rule and authority, power and dominion, and every title that can be given, not only in the present age but also in the one to come. And God placed all things under his feet and appointed him to be head over everything for the church, which is his body, the fullness of him who fills everything in every way. [Eph. 1:19–23]

Having risen from the dead, Christ now sits at God's right hand, from whence "he must reign until he has put all his enemies under his feet," including death, "the last enemy" (1 Cor. 15:25–26). "Then the end will come, when he hands over the kingdom to God the Father after he has destroyed all dominion, authority, and power" (1 Cor. 15:24). "For God was pleased to have all his fullness dwell in him, and through him to reconcile to himself all things, whether things on earth or things in heaven, by making peace through his blood, shed on the cross" (Col. 1:19–20).

The effects of the atoning death, victorious resurrection, and triumphant ascension of Christ, then, sweep over all of creation, including man, animals, plants, and even the ground itself. They include the restoration of the image of God in the redeemed and through them—and by common grace even through many who are not redeemed—the restoration of knowledge, holiness, and creativity in working out the cultural mandate, including human multiplication, subduing and ruling the earth, transforming the wilderness by cultivation into a garden, and guarding that garden against harm.

As the authors of *Earthkeeping in the Nineties* put it, "redeemed men and women are to be 'fellow heirs' with Christ—Christ, the sustaining *logos* of the world, in whom all things consist. The idea that humanity—redeemed humanity—is to share in that 'creatorly' task is clearly the implication of Romans 8:19. . . ."[29] Because of what Christ has accomplished, "The creation waits in eager expectation for the sons of God to be revealed. For the creation was subjected to frustration, not by its own choice, but by the will of the one who subjected it in hope that the creation itself will be liberated from its bondage to decay and brought into the glorious freedom of the children of God" (Rom. 8:19–21).

Imago Dei and the Population Debate

Such, then, is a Biblical vision of man, made in the image of God, fallen into sin and death, and now, in and by the last Adam, being restored to righteousness and life. This creature, "a little lower than God," "crowned with glory and honor," is what we have in mind when we talk about population growth and its effect on resources and the environment. While environmentalists fear that human population growth will strip the earth of its resources and strangle it with pollution, Biblical Christians—particularly those who are aware of the continuing growth of Christian faith around the world, with the transformation of culture that it brings[30]—can have confidence that, by the grace of God through the death, resurrection, and ascension of Christ and His present reign over all things, continued population growth will result not in the depletion but in the increased abundance of resources, and not in increased pollution of the earth but in its increased cleansing and transformation from wilderness to garden, "from its bondage to decay . . . into the glorious freedom of the children of God" (Rom. 8:21).

"What shall we say then? Shall we go on sinning so that grace may increase?" (Rom. 6:1) Shall we, presuming on the grace of God demonstrated
in the glorious redemption we have just described, turn our backs on the call
of creation stewardship, exchange a wise and righteous and creative dominion over the earth for a foolish and depraved and destructive tyranny? "By no
means! We died to sin; how can we live in it any longer?" (Rom. 6:2).

Far from justifying a careless attitude toward creation, the vision I have
sketched calls precisely for the pursuit of ever–improving care of creation—
care, however, that differs significantly from the subservience to nature that
characterizes much of the environmental movement. We are not the earth's
servants, but God's, and He has called us to serve Him, insofar as our relationship with the earth is concerned, by wise and righteous and creative dominion. This entails our fulfilling His command[31] to multiply and fill up the earth,[32]
to subdue and rule it (Gen. 1:28), and to cultivate and guard it (Gen. 2:15).

History tells us that mankind can do these things successfully—indeed,
that as human population has grown, we have done them increasingly successfully. I conclude, then, with a brief look at the history of man's ability to
produce more resources than he consumes and to improve rather than deterio-
rate the environment, and finally with some observations on why and how
man can do these things.

First, environmentalists, typically, are afraid that people are depleting the
earth's resources at an alarming rate, that increasing human population can
only advance this depletion, and that this is one of the two ways in which
population growth threatens the "carrying capacity" of the earth. But if the
history of resource supplies tells us anything, it tells us that resources are
becoming less scarce, not more; i.e., more abundant, not less. How do we
know that? By looking at the best measure of scarcity available: prices. The
long-term (and I mean centuries-long) trend of inflation-adjusted prices of
extractive resources (those we take out of the earth: minerals by mining,
crops—including wood—and livestock by harvesting, fish and some other
animals by hunting or fishing) is, almost without exception, downward, and it
has gotten more steeply downward precisely during the past hundred years or
so when human population has grown faster than at any time in history.[33] The
single exception appears to be wood, and there is a good theoretical/historical
explanation for that exception that predicts it will not remain so. Until very
recently in human history, wood has been so abundant in nature relative to
man's needs for it that, unlike food, man has seen little or no need to cultivate
it. In the last fifty years, however, rising prices for forest products have sig-
naled the opportunity for profit in plantation forestry. Not surprisingly, plan-

tation forestry has blossomed, and there is every reason to expect that in the reasonably near future the ratio of wood harvested from nature to wood harvested from plantations will resemble that of food harvested from nature to food harvested from farms.

Admittedly, the downward historical price trends of resources fly in the face of what seems like simple common sense, particularly for non-renewable resources like minerals. It is true that there is a finite amount of any given mineral in the earth.[34] It would seem logical, therefore, for a mineral's scarcity to increase—i.e., for its price to increase—with each unit consumed. But history tells us that human ingenuity, especially in the past two centuries, has devised increasingly efficient ways to extract, refine, and use resources—i.e., to reduce the cost and improve the productivity of mining and processing them and to increase both the usable quantity of them and the ratio of outputs to inputs in using them. In response to short-term price increases of some resources, we have also found ways to substitute other, more abundant resources to give us the same services, thus reducing the demand for the prior resources and therefore reducing their practical scarcity and so turning their price trend downward again.

Despite the counterintuitive character of this historical phenomenon, it is precisely what Christians, with a Biblical view of the image of God in man and particularly of the long-term impact of the redeeming work of Christ on humanity and culture, should predict. Think for a moment. When God created the heavens and the earth, what did He start with? Nothing. And what did He get? Everything! God created man in His image, to be creative like Him. Because we're finite, of course, we'll never make something from nothing, but the closer we get to it, the better we reflect, in that respect, the image of God. And because of what Scripture teaches about the impact of Christ's death, resurrection, and ascension on believing mankind through particular grace, mankind in general through common grace, and the creation at large, we should expect mankind to become better and better at making more and more from less and less as time goes on and the Church of Jesus Christ expands.

Second, many environmentalists also fear that, whatever might be true about resource availability, the pollution emitted by the growing human population and its growing economy threatens life itself—human and non-human alike. Again, however, I think history offers a different lesson, one into which space permits only the briefest glimpse here. I want to suggest looking at environmental history in three ways: (1) general trends in human life expectancy, which are the bottom line measurement of environmental quality; (2) two broad-brush comparisons between today's environment and the environments of the pre-industrial world by some leading historians; and (3) a general description of what I think is the dominant dynamic of pollution and environmental quality in the real world.

Worldwide trends in human life expectancy are, almost without exception, positive, and they have been throughout the roughly two hundred years since industrialization and modernization began. Around the mid-seventeenth century, life expectancy at birth everywhere in the world was about the same—somewhere in the late twenties. Today it is 66 years worldwide, 62 in low-income economies (66 in China and India, 55 in other low-income economies), 68 in middle-income economies, and 77 in high-income economies. The upward trend in life expectancy shows no sign of slowing; indeed, this sign of environmental improvement is the primary cause of the population growth that so many environmentalists fear threatens human well-being by damaging the environment.

Why do I point to human longevity as the "bottom line measurement of environmental quality"? Because in the final analysis, the environment is simply our surroundings, natural and manmade. It is not just mountains and forests and lakes and streams but also hospitals and schools and highways and cities and cars and telephones—literally everything that surrounds us. And the best test of its quality is how conducive it is to our survival. By that measure, the long-term news on the environment is clearly good—not unmixed, but good.

Not only life expectancy but more traditional methods of evaluating the environment yield the same conclusion: The environment is improving, not deteriorating. Just as a hospital patient might seem at first glance to be in horrible shape but turn out to be very much on the mend, so the environment is getting better, not worse, despite how bad it appears when we look at it without historical perspective. Historian Daniel Boorstin put the point well:

We sputter against The Polluted Environment—as if it was invented in the age of the automobile. We compare our smoggy air not with the odor of horsedung [sic] and the plague of flies and the smells of garbage and human excrement which filled cities in the past, but with the honey-suckle perfumes of some nonexistent City Beautiful. We forget that even if the water in many cities today is not as spring-pure nor as palatable as we would like, for most of history the water of the cities (and of the countryside) was undrinkable. We reproach ourselves for the ills of disease and malnourishment, and forget that until recently enteritis and measles and whooping cough, diphtheria and typhoid, were killing diseases of childhood, puerperal fever plagued mothers in childbirth, polio was a summer monster.[35]

Merely reading the description by French historian Fernand Braudel of the role famines and epidemics, especially the plague, played in shortening and making loathsome the lives of all people before the nineteenth century cannot fail to make us appreciate the healthier environment we enjoy today—an environment made that way largely by the introduction of chemicals that kill pests and germs and protect crops.[36] Is it sensible to consider these chemicals only as pollution?

What is the dominant dynamic driving this trend toward a better environment despite increasing population and growing economies? The answer is to challenge the question, for the question assumes that we *ought* to expect growing population and growing economies to cause increasing damage to the environment. But that assumption makes sense only from the perspective of the dominant vision of mankind held by environmentalists; it does not make sense from the perspective of the Biblical vision of mankind. Environmentalists assume that people are principally consumers and polluters; Biblical Christians assume that people are principally intelligent, well-meaning, creative producers and stewards, because that is what God made them to be and what He has been transforming them to be through the redeeming work of Christ. The dominant dynamic driving the trend toward environmental improvement is precisely growing human population and its growing economies. How so? Because a healthful, beautiful environment is itself a resource, something people can produce. Producing it requires wisdom and work and good will— all of these elements of the image of God in man, but more obviously, all of them elements of human nature and action. The more people there are to generate and refine ideas, the more knowledge there will be; the more people there are to value a healthful, beautiful environment, the more work will be done to produce one. And the more economies grow, the less people will have to worry about such basic things as putting food on the table, clothes on their backs, and roofs over their heads, and the more of their disposable income they will be able to devote to environmental stewardship. In other words, at the same time that we are learning to make more and more from less and less, we are also learning to do it while creating less and less pollution.

As societies make the transition from subsistence agriculture to industry, pollution increases, but the benefits to human life from the industrial activity clearly outweigh the costs to human life from the pollution—a fact attested to by declining death rates. Then, as they make the transition from largely industrial economies to largely service and technology oriented economies, pollution declines while material living standards continue to rise. The developed countries of the world, or what I call the first wave—mostly in Western Europe, Great Britain, and North America—went through both transitions before most of the rest of the world, and the last three decades of pollution statistics for these advanced countries show strong downward trends in almost every category, and almost every locale, of pollutants, in both emissions and ambient concentrations.[37] Many of the less-developed countries of the world—the second wave—are now going through the first transition, and so are experiencing the temporary increase in pollution associated with it (accompanied and, I hasten to add, outweighed by the benefits of the polluting activities); others are headed into the second transition and so are experiencing, or about to experience, the decline in pollution associated with it. What I predict with great confidence is that the second wave will go through both transitions more rapidly—and more cleanly—than the first wave did, because countries in it are exploiting technologies that did not exist when the first wave went through the transitions. As a result, people all over the world can expect a cleaner, safer, more healthful, more beautiful environment for our children's future. Not automatically. No, it will take lots of intelligent, hard work and lots of good, moral choices. But those are what God made people to do, and they are what Christ's redeeming work is enabling us to do despite our fall into sin.

Please don't misunderstand me. I am not saying that we should pave over the whole planet—which is hardly likely, anyway, granted that human settlements presently occupy only about 2 percent of the earth's land mass, excluding the continent of Antarctica.[38] We are to transform the earth into a garden, not an inner-city slum or a parking lot.

Neither am I predicting utopia. I *do* predict great material wealth and a healthful, beautiful environment for the vast majority of mankind everywhere, but we must not confuse quantity with quality. The world of the future will almost certainly be wealthier and environmentally cleaner than it is today—but it may also be vastly evil. Which it becomes depends on whether its people follow Jesus Christ, the Sun of Righteousness.

APPENDIX 1

🦎   🦎

The Garden and the Wilderness:
Toward a Biblical Foundation for Environmental Ethics

[The following is adapted from a guest lecture presented to the faculty and student body of Covenant College October 30, 1991.][1]

GENESIS 1:1 TELLS US, "IN THE BEGINNING GOD CREATED THE HEAVens and the earth." Verse 2 adds, "The earth was *without form, and void*; and darkness was on the face of the deep. And the Spirit of God was hovering over the face of the waters." Verses 3 through 30 then tell us how God went about giving form and content to what was once without form and void. Throughout the process, He brought increasing order out of chaos.

By speaking the word, He made light, and divided it from darkness, and gave each a name: He called the light Day and the darkness Night (vv. 4–5). By speaking the word, He made a firmament to divide the waters above from those below, and gave it a name: Heaven (vv. 6–8). By speaking the word, He separated the waters from the dry land, and gave each a name: He called the dry land Earth, and the waters Seas (vv. 9–10).

Then He turned His attention away from the Seas, toward the Earth, and brought order there. By speaking the word, He made grass, herbs, and fruit trees, each according to its kind—but He did not give them names (vv. 11–12). Then He turned His attention away from Earth, toward Heaven, and brought order there. By speaking the word, He made lights to divide Day from Night—a greater light to rule the Day and a lesser light to rule the Night—and stars for signs and seasons, for days and years, "to give light on the earth, and to rule over the day and over the night, and to divide the light from the darkness" (vv. 14–18). Then He turned His attention away from Heaven, to-

113

ward the Seas and the sky, and brought order there. By speaking the word, He made "an abundance of living creatures," each according to its kind (vv. 20–22). Then He turned His attention away from the Seas and the sky, toward the earth again, and brought order there. By speaking the word, He made "the living creature according to its kind" (vv. 24–25).

Now, notice that previously He had first made light and darkness, day and night, and later had made the greater and lesser lights to rule them. So also, having made sea creatures, air creatures, and land creatures, He now makes something to rule them, so bringing order to Earth and Seas and Sky alike: "Then God said, 'Let Us make man in Our image, according to Our likeness; let them have dominion over the fish of the sea, over the birds of the air, and over the cattle, over all the earth and over every creeping thing that creeps on the earth.' So God created man in His own image; in the image of God He created him; male and female He created them. Then God blessed them, and God said to them, 'Be fruitful and multiply; fill the earth and subdue it; have dominion over the fish of the sea, over the birds of the air, and over every living thing that moves on the earth'" (vv. 26–28). And just as God had given order to light and darkness by naming them Day and Night, and to dry land and water and sky by naming them Earth and Sea and Heaven, so God brought to Adam "every beast of the field and every bird of the air" so that Adam could begin His work of ruling over them by naming them, "And whatever Adam called each living creature, that was its name" (2:19).

My point should be clear. What began "without form and void" God immediately set about giving form and content; and He instructed man to pick up where He had left off, giving more form and content. I think, in fact, that the structure of the text is itself designed to drive home the point that bringing order out of chaos is an important focus. The phrase "Then God said" occurs nine times (Gen. 1:3, 6, 9, 11, 14, 20, 24, 26, 29), each time introducing an important new focus. Each day's work ends with a pronouncement: "So the evening and the morning were the first day," or "So the evening and the morning were the second day," or "So the evening and the morning were the third day," and so on, through the six creative days (vv. 5, 8, 13, 19, 23, 31), leading into the seventh day, the day of rest (2:2). Interestingly, God rested only after He had brought order to every part of creation: land, seas, sky, and heaven. Six times, at significant junctures in the narrative, the text tells us that God saw that what He had done was good (vv. 10, 12, 18, 21, 25, 31).

If anything should jump right out of the text at us, from both its content and its form, it is the coming of order, structure, system, rule. The climax of the text even comes when God makes someone to whom, unlike anything else

He has made, He speaks. And what does He say to this creature? "Have dominion." "Rule." Just as God has ordered things, so He wants man to continue
ordering things.

Now let us turn to chapter 2, where we find a repetition of the story of
creation, but with a new focus: the creation of man. And what happened in the
creation of man? "The LORD God *formed* man of the dust of the ground, and
breathed into his nostrils the breath of life; and man became a living being"
(v. 7). Just as the earth was once "without form and void," so man was once
mere "dust of the earth," formless and empty. And just as the Spirit of God
hovered over the face of the formless deep and gave it form and life, so also
the Spirit of God hovered over the formless dust and gave it form and life.
And later we learn, from words that should send shivers down our spines,
what it means to become "without form and void" again: "In the sweat of
your face you shall eat bread, till you return to the ground, for out of it you
were taken; for dust you are, and to dust you shall return" (3:19). It is as good
as God's saying "you shall become without form and void."

Where did God put the man when He first made him? In "a garden eastward in Eden" (v. 8). What was that Garden like? It had its own order, its own
design, just like everything else God had made. It was located "eastward in
Eden," toward the rising sun, on the verge of the wilderness. It had a middle,
where stood the Tree of Life and the Tree of the Knowledge of Good and Evil
(v. 9). Into it, through it, and out from it flowed a river that separated into four
rivers to water the whole land (vv. 10–14)—a pattern that we see reproduced
later in the Tabernacle and, ultimately, in the Bride of Christ, the holy city,
New Jerusalem, in which again we find the Tree of Life, the River of Life, and
the precious stones of the garden, all presented in a description of the most
orderly place imaginable (Rev. 21:9–22:5).[2] I don't want to get carried away
here into a discussion of the symbolism of the garden, the Tabernacle, and the
New Jerusalem. My point is simply to emphasize how important *order* is in
God's economy.

Now I want to set the orderliness of the Garden, the Tabernacle, and the
New Jerusalem in contrast with the disorder described in Genesis 1:2, which
says that immediately after God created the heavens and the earth, "The earth
was *without form* and *void*." The words *without form* translate the single Hebrew word *tôhûw*, which is derived from a root meaning "to lie waste." It
denotes a desolation, a worthless thing, confusion, vanity, waste, or wilderness. Just how intense a desolation the word denotes comes clear in some of
its other uses. In pointing out how God's greatness surpasses man's understanding, Job says, "He stretches out the north over *empty space* (*tôhûw*); He

hangs the earth on nothing" (Job 26:7). Comparing God's vastness with the minuscule size of all the nations, Isaiah wrote, "Behold, the nations are as a drop in a bucket, and are counted as the small dust on the scales; look, He lifts up the isles as a very little thing. And Lebanon"—Lebanon with forests so vast and game so abundant it was legendary—"Lebanon is not sufficient to burn, nor its beasts sufficient for a burnt offering. All nations before Him are as nothing, and they are counted by Him less than nothing and *worthless* (*tôhûw*)" (Isa. 40:17).

Tôhûw also connotes something contemptible in its emptiness, vanity, or confusion. God speaks with contempt of idols who can tell neither past nor future, who can control nothing, who can answer nothing. He concludes, "Indeed, they are all worthless; their works are nothing; their molded images are wind and *confusion* (*tôhûw*)" (Isa. 41:29). And when Moses describes the destitute situation of Israel when God first took it as His inheritance, he writes, "He found him in a desert land, and in the wa*ste* (*tôhûw*) howling wilderness" (Deut. 32:10); from there He delivered Jacob and "made him ride in the heights of the earth, that he might eat the produce of the fields; He made him draw honey from the rock, and oil from the flinty rock; curds from the cattle, and milk from the flock, with fat of lambs; and rams of the breed of Bashan, and goats, with the choicest wheat; and you drank wine, the blood of grapes" (vv. 13–14). He took him, we might say, from the formless wilderness into the formed garden.

The word *void* in Genesis 1:2 translates a Hebrew word that is, if possible, even more intense than *tôhûw*, a word that rhymes with it: *bôhûw*, derived from a root meaning "to be empty." What is *bôhûw* is a vacuity, an undistinguishable ruin, emptiness. The word is used only three times in the Hebrew text of the Old Testament, and in all three instances it is used in conjunction with *tôhûw*—always following it, always intensifying it. We have looked already at Genesis 1:1. The two other passages are Isaiah 34:11 and Jeremiah 4:23. Let's look at them.

First we must set Isaiah 34 in its context. Isaiah has just prophesied the *restoration* of Zion, a prophecy that comes to full fruition in the new Jerusalem, the Church of God. Consider his glowing description of her:

Look upon Zion, the city of our appointed feasts;
Your eyes will see Jerusalem, a quiet home,
A tabernacle that will not be taken down;
not one of its stakes will ever be removed,
nor will any of its cords be broken.

But there the majestic LORD will be for us
A place of broad rivers and streams,
In which no galley with oars will sail,
Nor majestic ships pass by
(For the LORD is our Judge,
The LORD is our Lawgiver,
The LORD is our King;
He will save us). . . .

Isaiah 33:20–22

The description is of a city quiet and peaceful, perfectly ordered and stable.
But immediately, in chapter 34, Isaiah shifts to a vision of God's judgment on
the nations, and he singles out Edom. Contemplate the description, in which
Isaiah uses the language of de-creation:

Come near, you nations, to hear;
And heed, you people!
Let the earth hear, and all that is in it,
The world and all things that come forth from it.
For the indignation of the LORD is against all nations,
And His fury against all their armies;
He has utterly destroyed them,
He has given them over to the slaughter.
Also their slain shall be thrown out;
Their stench shall rise from their corpses,
And *the mountains shall be dissolved,*
And *the heavens shall be rolled up like a scroll*;
All their host shall fall down
As the leaf falls from the vine,
And as fruit falling from a fig tree.
For My sword shall be bathed in heaven;
Indeed it shall come down on Edom,
And on the people of My curse, for judgment.
The sword of the LORD is filled with blood,
It is made overflowing with fatness,
With the blood of lambs and goats,
With the fat of the kidneys of rams.
For the LORD has a sacrifice in Bozrah [the capital of Edom],
And a great slaughter in the land of Edom.

Isaiah 34:1–6

And now ponder God's description of *how* He will bring about the slaughter.
He will do it by overrunning Bozrah and all of Edom with wild beasts and

turning the once civilized, ordered land into an uncivilized, chaotic wilderness—reversing the dominion of man over nature in judgment of Edom's crimes:

> The wild oxen shall come down with them,
> And the young bulls with the mighty bulls;
> Their land shall be soaked with blood,
> And their dust saturated with fatness.
> For it is the day of the LORD's vengeance,
> The year of recompense for the cause of Zion.
> [Edom's] streams shall be turned into pitch,
> And its dust into brimstone;
> Its land shall become burning pitch.
> It shall not be quenched night or day;
> Its smoke shall ascend forever.
> From generation to generation it shall lie waste;
> No one shall pass through it forever and ever.
> But the pelican and the porcupine shall possess it,
> Also the owl and the raven shall dwell in it.
> And He shall stretch out over it
> The line of *confusion* (*tôhûw*) and the stones of *emptiness* (*bôhûw*).
> They shall call its nobles to the kingdom,
> But none shall be there, and all its princes shall be nothing.
> And thorns shall come up in its palaces,
> Nettles and brambles in its fortresses;
> It shall be a habitation of jackals,
> A courtyard for ostriches.
> The wild beasts of the desert shall also meet with the jackals,
> And the wild goat shall bleat to its companion;
> Also the night creature shall rest there,
> And find for herself a place of rest.
> There the arrow snake shall make her nest and lay eggs
> And hatch, and gather them under her shadow;
> There also shall the hawks be gathered,
> Every one with her mate.

Isaiah 34:7–15

Jeremiah makes the same use of the language of de-creation when he prophecies God's judgment on apostate Jerusalem:

> At that time it will be said
> To this people and to Jerusalem,
> "A dry wind of the desolate heights blows in the wilderness

Toward the daughter of My people—
Not to fan or to cleanse—
A wind too strong for these will come from Me;
Now I will also speak judgment against them."
"Behold, he shall come up like clouds,
And his chariots like a whirlwind.
His horses are swifter than eagles.
Woe to us, for we are plundered!"
O Jerusalem, wash your heart from wickedness,
That you may be saved.
How long shall your evil thoughts lodge within you?
For a voice declares from Dan
And proclaims affliction from Mount Ephraim:
"Make mention to the nations,
Yes, proclaim against Jerusalem,
That watchers come from a far country
And raise their voice against the cities of Judah.
Like keepers of a field they are against her all around,
Because she has been rebellious against Me," says the LORD.
"Your ways and your doings
Have procured these things for you.
This is your wickedness,
Because it is bitter,
Because it reaches to your heart."

And then Jeremiah truly laments at what he foresees:

O my soul, my soul!
I am pained in my very heart!
My heart makes a noise in me;
I cannot hold my peace,
Because you have heard, O my soul,
The sound of the trumpet,
The alarm of war.
Destruction upon destruction is cried,
For the whole land is plundered.
Suddenly my tents are plundered,
and my curtains in a moment.
How long will I see the standard,
And hear the sound of the trumpet? . . .
I beheld the [land], and indeed it was *without form* (*tôhûw*), and *void* (*bôhûw*);
And the heavens, they had no light.
I beheld the mountains, and indeed they trembled,

And all the hills moved back and forth.
I beheld, and indeed there was no man,
And all the birds of the heavens had fled.
I beheld, and indeed the fruitful land was a wilderness,
And all its cities were broken down
At the presence of the LORD,
By His fierce anger.

Jeremiah 4:11–26

What Isaiah and Jeremiah both described as the most catastrophic, devastating judgment on any people was God's de-creating their land—returning it to a state "without form and void," making it a formless, empty wilderness under the dominion of the birds of the air and the beasts of the field instead of under the dominion of man. Just so, when Jeremiah foretells the destruction of Babylon, he says, "And the land will tremble and sorrow; for every purpose of the LORD shall be performed against Babylon, to make the land of Babylon *a desolation without inhabitant. . . .* The sea has come up over Babylon; she is covered with the multitude of the waves. Her cities are a desolation, a dry land and *a wilderness, a land where no one dwells, through which no son of man passes*" (Jer. 51:29, 42–43). And when Isaiah laments God's judgment on Zion, he prays, "Do not be furious, O Lord, nor remember iniquity forever; indeed, please look—we all are Your people! *Your holy cities are a wilderness, Zion is a wilderness, Jerusalem a desolation*" (Isa. 64:9–10).

Yet what Scripture consistently treats as a curse is the romantic dream of much of the environmentalist movement. Think of the description of the desolation of the land of Edom under God's judgment in Isaiah 34:10–15: "no one shall pass through it forever and ever. But the pelican and the porcupine shall possess it, also the owl and the raven shall dwell in it. And he shall stretch out over it the line of confusion and the stones of emptiness. . . . And thorns shall come up in its palaces, nettles and brambles in its fortresses; it shall be a habitation of jackals, a courtyard for ostriches. The wild beasts of the desert shall also meet with the jackals, and the wild goat shall bleat to its companion; also the night creature shall rest there, and find for herself a place of rest. There the arrow snake shall make her nest and lay eggs and hatch, and gather them under her shadow; there also shall the hawks be gathered, every one with her mate." That language is enough to make leaders of the Sierra Club, or the Wilderness Society, or the National Wildlife Foundation, or the World Wildlife Fund, or Earth First!, or any of a score of other environmentalist organizations wax rhapsodic in wistful longing.

If the language of de-creation is the language of judgment and curse, the language of re-creation is that of blessing and restoration. We saw in the description of Zion under the rule of King Messiah in Isaiah 33:20–22 that this blessing entailed order and stability. In Isaiah 35:1–2, we see that it includes the transformation of the wilderness into the garden: "The wilderness and the wasteland shall be glad for them, and the desert shall rejoice and blossom as the rose; it shall blossom abundantly and rejoice, even with joy and singing. The glory of Lebanon shall be given to it, the excellence of Carmel and Sharon. They shall see the glory of the LORD, the excellency of our God."

The themes of wilderness and garden are set in direct contrast in Psalm 107:33–38, which tells of what God does with the land of the wicked and the land of the righteous. With the land of the wicked, "He turns rivers into a wilderness, and the watersprings into dry ground; a fruitful land into barrenness, for the wickedness of those who dwell in it." But with the land of the righteous, "He turns a wilderness into pools of water, and dry land into watersprings. There He makes the hungry dwell, that they may establish a city for a dwelling place, and sow fields and plant vineyards, that they may yield a fruitful harvest. He also blesses them, and they multiply greatly; and He does not let their cattle decrease."

Notice carefully what the psalmist connects with God's blessing on the land of the righteous. He brings water to the desert, makes the hungry establish a city there and sow fields and plant vineyards and reap a fruitful harvest, and He "blesses them, and they multiply greatly; and He does not let their cattle decrease." Quite simply, among the signs of God's blessing on people are the transformation and development of their land and the growth of their population—and with it, their food supply. When God curses a land, He empties it of human population and domestic animals, returning it to the wild beasts. But when He blesses it, He multiplies its human population and builds up its herds.

This is no accident. It is rooted in the very nature of man and beast and in God's creative order. To mankind alone, among earthly creatures, did God give the capacity of reason, of wisdom, of *Logos*. Mankind alone, among earthly creatures, has the ability to bring proper order to the world. Just as He made the greater light to rule the day and the lesser light to rule the night, so also God made man to rule the sea, the sky, and the earth. And man exercises that rule by possession, occupation, and rational ordering.[3] So the parts of the command in Genesis 1:28 are not independent of each other; they are dependent: "Be fruitful and multiply; fill the earth and subdue it; have dominion over the fish of the sea, over the birds of the air, and over every living thing that moves on the earth." Fruitful multiplication is a necessary prerequisite to filling the earth; and filling the earth is a necessary prerequisite to subduing it and having dominion over it.

The connection between populating a region and subduing it is significant elsewhere in Scripture, too. One of the reasons Pharaoh ordered the oppression of the Israelites was that their population was growing large enough that he considered them a threat to his dominion:

> Now there arose a new king over Egypt, who did not know Joseph. And he said to his people, "Look, the people of the children of Israel are more and mightier than we; come, let us deal shrewdly with them, lest they multiply, and it happen, in the event of war, that they also join our enemies and fight against us, and so go up out of the land." Therefore they set taskmasters over them to afflict them with their burdens. And they built for Pharaoh supply cities, Pithom and Raamses. But the more the afflicted them, the more they multiplied and grew. And they were in dread of the children of Israel. So the Egyptians made the children of Israel serve with rigor. And they made their lives bitter with hard bondage—in mortar, in brick, and in all manner of service in the field. All their service in which they made them serve was with rigor.
>
> Then the king of Egypt spoke to the Hebrew midwives, of whom the name of one was Shiphrah and the name of the other Puah; and he said, "When you do the duties of a midwife for the Hebrew women, and see them on the birthstools, if it is a son, then you shall kill him; but if it is a daughter, then she shall live." But the midwives feared God, and did not do as the king of Egypt commanded them, but saved the male children alive. So the king of Egypt called for the midwives and said to them, "Why have you done this thing, and saved the male children alive?" And the midwives said to Pharaoh, "Because the Hebrew women are not like the Egyptian women; for they are lively and give birth before the midwives come to them." Therefore God dealt well with the midwives, and the people multiplied and grew very mighty.
>
> Exodus 1:8–20

No wonder Proverbs 14:28 says, "In a multitude of people is a king's honor, but in the lack of people is the downfall of a prince"!

A particularly striking illustration of this lesson comes in Exodus 23:20–30, with God's preparing Israel to leave the Wilderness of Wandering and enter the Promised Land. In close connection God assures His people (1) that they will have dominion in the Land; (2) that He will ensure adequate food and water for them there; (3) that they will suffer no sickness, miscarriage, or barrenness—i.e., that their population will be healthy, long-lived, and fruitful; and (4) that He will drive out before them the present inhabitants of the Land, whose tally of sin at last is full:

> "Behold, I send an Angel before you to keep you in the way and to bring you into the place which I have prepared. Beware of Him and obey His voice; do not provoke Him, for He will not pardon your transgressions; for My name is in Him. But if you indeed obey His voice and do all that I speak, then I will be an enemy to your enemies and an adversary to your adversaries. For My Angel will go before you and bring you in to the Amorites and the Hittites and the Perizzites and the Canaanites and the Hivites and the Jebusites; and I will cut them off. You shall not bow down to their gods, nor serve them, nor do according to their works; but you shall utterly overthrow them and completely break down their sacred pillars. [Words, by the way, that would not go over well with the champions of cultural relativism or of preserving the products of various cultures!] So you shall serve the LORD your God, and He will bless your bread and your water. And I will take sickness away from the midst of you. No one shall suffer miscarriage or be barren in your land; I will fulfill the number of your days.
>
> "I will send My fear before you, I will cause confusion among all the people to whom you come, and will make your enemies turn their back to you. And I will send hornets before you, which shall drive out the Hivite, the Canaanite, and the Hittite from before you."

And now listen to this fascinating promise:

> *"I will not drive them out from before you in one year, lest the land become desolate and the beasts of the field become too numerous for you. Little by little I will drive them out from before you, until you have increased, and you inherit the land."*

God actually promises Israel that He will leave the abominable pagans in control of the Land long enough for Israel to come in and occupy it all, lest something even worse occur: the land returns to wilderness and the wild beasts become so numerous as to be uncontrollable.

I will never forget a time in the mid-1970s, when I lived in Southern California. The sprawling megalopolis of Los Angeles had spread to cover many areas that even recently had been wild desert—as, in fact, all of that land once had been. But little pockets of the wild remained here and there in and around the city. In those pockets, wild animals persisted—and still do. Among them were coyotes, which normally eat mostly rodents, snakes, and an occasional small bird. As the city grew, the carnivorous coyotes began to run short of their normal fare. And then, little by little, reports began trickling in of coyotes coming up out of flood control channels into people's back yards and snatching infants left momentarily unattended. I doubt that even the Hillside Strangler or the Freeway Rapist, though they probably killed more people, ever managed to provoke so much fear in that city as did those coyotes. Why? Because, I believe, the coyotes were *wild*. They reminded people of what life would be like if they *didn't* subdue the wilderness.

What God promised Israel was that He would ensure, by driving out the pagans only incrementally, that Israel would have time to take control of the land before it reverted to a howling wilderness—the only thing worse than its being under the dominion of pagans.

In this, as in so many other ways, the deliverance of Israel foreshadowed the wider deliverance to come under Christ. After pointing out that part of the Curse on Adam's sin was that animals became wild and threatened mankind, David Chilton remarks,

> In Christ, however, man's dominion has been restored (Ps. 8:5–8 with Heb. 2:6–9). Thus, when God saved His people, this effect of the Curse began to be reversed. He led them through a dangerous wilderness, protecting them from the snakes and scorpions (Deut. 8:15), and He promised them that their life in the Promised Land would be Eden-like in its freedom from the ravages of wild animals: "I shall also grant peace in the land, so that you may lie down with no one making you tremble. I shall also eliminate harmful beasts from the land" (Lev. 26:6). In fact, this is why God did not allow Israel to exterminate the Canaanites all at once: *the heathen served as a buffer between the covenant people and the wild animals* (Ex. 23:29–30; Deut. 7:22).
>
> Accordingly, when the prophets foretold the coming salvation in Christ, they described it in the same terms of Edenic blessing: "I will make a covenant of peace with them and eliminate harmful beasts from the land, so that they may live securely in the wilderness and sleep in the woods" (Ezek. 34:25). "No lion will be there, nor will any vicious beast go up on it; these will not be found there. But the redeemed will walk there" (Isa. 35:9). In fact, the Bible goes so far as to say that through the Gospel's permeation of the world the wild nature of the animals will be transformed into its original, Edenic condition:
> The wolf will dwell with the lamb,
> And the leopard will lie down with the kid,
> And the calf and the young lion and the fatling together;
> And a little boy will lead them.
> Also the cow and the bear will graze;
> Their young will lie down together;

And the lion will eat straw like the ox.
And the nursing child will play by the hole of the cobra,
And the weaned child will put his hand on the viper's den.
They will not hurt or destroy in all My Holy Mountain,
For the earth will be full of the knowledge of the LORD
As the waters cover the sea.   (Isa. 11:6–9; cf. Isa. 65:25)[4]

To what extent should Isaiah's language be taken literally? Will lions, with their fangs just made for tearing meat, one day eat nothing but straw, and be as content with that as oxen are? I don't know. But I would suggest that perhaps we go too far in reading this as figurative if we forget, first, that apparently in the Garden of Eden before the Fall no animal constituted the least threat to man; second, that God certainly intended the Israelites to take Him literally when He promised to drive the pagan inhabitants out of the Promised Land slowly so that the wild beasts would not take over and threaten Israel's safety there; and third, that God spoke literally when He threatened that if Israel disobeyed His commandments He would punish it with the ministration of wild beasts: "I will also send wild beasts among you, which shall rob you of your children, destroy your livestock, and make you few in number; and your highways shall be desolate" (Lev. 26:22)—a threat fulfilled by the plague of fiery serpents (Num. 21:6), reinforced in the curses of Deuteronomy 28, where He said, "Your carcasses shall be food for all the birds of the air and the beasts of the earth, and no one shall frighten them away" (Deut. 28:26), and reflected in the incident when two female bears "came out of the woods and mauled forty-two" youths who had mocked Elisha (2 Kings 2:24) and when "the Lord sent lions among [the newly arrived re–settlers of Samaria who did not fear Him], which killed some of them" (2 Kings 17:25).

I don't want to belabor the point. It is simply this: that human multiplication, coupled with the incremental transformation of wilderness into garden, bringing the whole earth under human dominion, taming the wild beasts, and building order out of chaos is a good thing. Man's work is to follow the example set by God in creation: to constantly increase the orderliness of creation—a process that began with his naming the animals. That is why the orderly music of Johann Sebastian Bach and Wolfgang Amadeus Mozart and Thomas Luis de Victoria is *more authentic music* than the cacophony of modern rock by 2 Live Crew, Slayer, and Stryper; it is why the art of Michelangelo and Titian, of Rembrandt and Rubens, of John Singer Sargent and Thomas Eakins, is *more authentic art* than the chaotic modern art of Pablo Picasso and Salvador Dali and Theodor Roszak; and it is why "a well-tended garden is better than a neglected woodlot"[5] or a desert or a swamp.

What am I saying? That the whole surface of the earth should be transformed into Wal-Mart stores, freeways, skyscrapers, and industrial factories? That we should ignore the extinction of species, the destruction of rain forests, and the paving over of migratory birds' nesting grounds? Certainly not. Of all people, I would be the most hypocritical to say so. After all, I consciously moved out of cities into a rural farm setting. But I must admit that when my wife and I, living on an isolated ranch in northwest Arkansas, used to hear a pack of coyotes and wild dogs—abandoned by their owners—howling across the pastures, we were thankful that we could listen to that wild sound with the excitement of romance instead of the trembling of fear.

You see, it is possible for mankind to tame and even settle a region without robbing it of its beauty. It is possible for us even to develop an area's resources without destroying either its magnificence—as well-managed selective cutting in the lumber business can show—or its suitability as habitat for wild creatures.

I have a feeling that what most people really have in mind when they say they want to preserve the wilderness is that they want to preserve natural beauty and grandeur. That can be done—it has been done throughout much of the world—without excluding human occupation and even use of the land. But quite frankly, the desire to keep large tracts of land—millions of square miles—in the wild, natural state, unchanged by humanity, is both unbiblical, in that it contradicts the dominion mandate, and elitist. Only the privileged few can afford to travel long distances with the special supplies and equipment necessary for safety and survival in the real *wilderness*. What is implied in their saying that we should keep such regions isolated and largely inaccessible is, "Keep out of them yourself, but let us go into them to enjoy them as we wish."

Since I wrote this essay in mid-1991, some environmentalists have promoted a new plan, called the North American Wilderness Recovery (a.k.a. Wildlands) Project, that would entail a vast system of connected wilderness areas crisscrossing the continent, covering at least half of the lower forty-eight states with core reserves in which all trace of human habitation would be removed and where no humans would even be permitted to enter, all surrounded by buffer zones in which only limited human activity would be permitted. "Ultimately, inhabited land would exist as islands surrounded by this wilderness network." Originally thought too radical for serious consideration by mainstream environmentalists, the plan has picked up increasing support. Michael Soule, conservation biologist at the University of California, Santa Cruz, and creator of the plan, explains that the intent would be not merely to preserve species or ecosystems or habitats, but to preserve "wildness," which, he insists, entails "fierceness." When Soule, Earth First! founder Dave Foreman, and conservation biologist Reed F. Noss presented the proposal at the annual meeting of the Society for Conservation Biology in June 1993, it drew strong applause, and Mark Shaffer, vice president of resource planning and economics at the Wilderness Society—presumably a more mainstream environmentalist organization—commented on the proposal, "It's the right vision, it's the vision we have to pursue or say good-bye to Mother Nature."[6]

Should we protect nature from wanton destruction? Yes, of course we should. "The earth is the LORD's, and all its fullness, the world and those who dwell therein" (Ps. 24:1). We are called in Genesis 2:15 not only to cultivate the Garden (that is, to increase its productive potential) but also to guard it. But let me point out one important thing about that instruction. Look at what the text says, and look at it carefully in light of the distinction I have made this evening between the garden and the wilderness: "Then the LORD God took the man and put him *in the **garden** of Eden to tend and keep it*." God didn't tell man to protect the wilderness against the encroaching garden. He told man to protect the *garden* against the encroaching *wilderness*. God told Adam to protect the *Garden*; He did not tell Adam to *protect* all the rest of the earth. Rather, He told Adam to *subdue* and *rule* the rest of the earth. Indeed, we may infer from this and the general garden-versus-wilderness theme of Scripture that an implicit part of the cultural mandate was the gradual transformation of the rest of the earth into the garden.

Does this imply that we are to despoil the earth, to treat it with wanton disregard? Certainly not. But it does imply that we must take seriously the broad and deep implications of God's Curse on the ground, of the distinction between garden and wilderness, between order and chaos, between land under man's godly (or ungodly) dominion and land unsubdued and unruled. It implies that our goal should be not to sustain wilderness wherever it exists but to transform wilderness into garden. It implies that we must recognize that nature untouched by human hand is not necessarily to be preferred, theologically or morally (or aesthetically), to nature transformed by the hand of man; renewed and delivered, albeit in part, from the Curse; recovered from wilderness and made into garden again. It might at least tell us that we see with distorted vision when we mourn and protest the deaths of a few hundred or even a few thousand birds and fish and mammals because of an oil spill off the coast of Alaska or California while we ignore the deaths of hundreds of millions of them off the western coast of Latin America every time El Niño, a natural warm Pacific current, shifts northward, as it does regularly, robbing those creatures—naturally—of their usual rich forage.

I do not pretend to have worked out many implications of this garden-versus-wilderness theme in Scripture. At this point my use of it is mainly negative: as a fulcrum on which to rest a lever of criticism against what I consider the unbiblical and anti-human environmentalist worldview. More difficult will be the task of translating this into a positive picture of what we *ought* to be doing with the world. For the present, I will venture to suggest that what we ought to be doing includes sustaining or even improving the beauty of much of the world, bringing more and more of it under human control, and making it serve human needs and aspirations more readily to the end that human beings live longer, live healthier, live happier, and, most important, live holier than at present.

APPENDIX 2

🐾　　🐾

A Christian Perspective on Biodiversity:
Anthropocentric, Biocentric, and Theocentric Approaches to Bio-Stewardship

[The following is adapted from an address to the South Carolina Division of the Society of American Foresters, annual meeting, June 1994.]

Maintaining Biodiversity: A Generally Good End

Whatever our assumptions, I think all of us here would agree that, in general, maintaining biodiversity is a good end. None of us would favor the willy-nilly elimination of species, subspecies, varieties, or even distinct populations of varieties of life. Yet I say that maintaining biodiversity is a good end "in general" because there are some limits to this end. Although there are others, I mention here just three.

First, I trust that no one here would shed a tear if HIV, the AIDS virus, were to become extinct, even though that would constitute some reduction of biodiversity. Presumably the same would hold true for botulism, diphtheria, polio, smallpox (which now continues to exist only in a laboratory test tube where, for some macabre reason, it is preserved—not, one hopes, for posterity), and other such viruses. But this conclusion can be held only on the assumption that there is some qualitative distinction among life forms that make some worth preserving and others not merely not worth preserving but even worth eliminating intentionally, and this in turn implies that biological hierarchicalism—the belief in varying levels of value for different forms of life—is unavoidable.

Second, sometimes there are tradeoffs in our efforts to maintain biodiversity. Protecting one species in one location might entail reducing or even eliminating another species there, whether intentionally or as an indirect

129

effect, or might consume resources that otherwise could be used to protect a different species in a different location that, without them, will go extinct. As economists put it, there is no such thing as a free lunch; opportunity costs are inescapable. It is not self-evident what should be done in the face of such tradeoffs, but the tradeoffs are unavoidable, and clearly the biological heirarchicalism noted under the prior point must affect our choices.

Third, we cannot avoid opportunity costs of species protection that go beyond missed opportunities to protect other species. This is not to say that species should not be protected, but that we must not naively pretend that directing some resources to protecting species has no impact on the rest of our lives. A million dollars spent to preserve a local population of one bird species along the South Carolina coast cannot be spent to feed hungry children in Ethiopia, protect innocent victims in Rwanda or Bosnia, conduct research for a cure for cancer or heart disease, or engineer an efficient replacement for CFCs to protect stratospheric ozone or improve solar energy cells to reduce the burning of fossil fuels and so reduce the enhanced greenhouse effect.[1] To say this is not to prejudge which of these ends ought to get the million dollars. Such judgments rest on moral *a priorii* and scientific theories and data that are distinct from the recognition of cost. But it is to insist, first, that we cannot act as if the opportunity costs did not exist, and second, that choosing among these competing claims on our spending requires not only empirical analysis but also value judgments that rest on underlying assumptions of an unavoidably religious nature. It is precisely on such underlying assumptions that I wish to focus now.

The Unavoidability and Importance of Religious Assumptions

In our secular milieu, some people insist that fundamental religious questions are either simply irrelevant or so personal and subjective as to have no legitimate bearing on public policy decisions. But such a secular view is itself a fundamentally religious perspective. The word *secular* derives from the Latin word *sæcularis*, meaning "worldly" or "temporal," something belonging to an age. The secular worldview values the world and the present age over spiritual reality and eternity, and such a value is inherently religious. If to value spiritual reality and eternity over worldly reality and the present age is religious, to embrace the opposite position is equally religious. For secularists to rule out "religion" as irrelevant or too inherently subjective for intrusion in public policy is clearly a case of special pleading. By so doing they reserve for themselves a liberty that they deny to everyone else: the liberty to bring their religious convictions to bear in public debate. It should be no surprise, then, that American courts have repeatedly found Secular Humanism to be a variety of religion—a finding quite in keeping with the claims of Secular Humanists themselves.

The case that religious assumptions are not only unavoidable but also fundamentally important to our attitudes toward ecology—including toward biodiversity—was made by the historian Lynn White Jr. in his famous article, "The Historical Roots of Our Ecologic Crisis," first published in *Science* in 1967 reprinted in many places since then.[2] "What people do about their ecology depends on what they think about themselves in relation to things around them," White wrote. "Human ecology is deeply conditioned by beliefs about our nature and destiny—that is, by religion."[3]

White argued that many of our ecologic problems derive from the wedding of science and technology in the eighteenth and nineteenth centuries, and that these endeavors in turn were profoundly shaped by a world view inherited from medieval Christianity. For almost all Western scientists up through the early eighteenth century, science had meant "thinking God's thoughts after Him," and when this was wedded with technology—the application of scientific knowledge to specific methods by which to manipulate the world—it gave rise to what White called "the Baconian creed that scientific knowledge means technological power over nature," a creed whose "acceptance as a normal pattern of action may mark the greatest event in human history since the invention of agriculture, and perhaps in nonhuman terrestrial history as well."[4]

Particularly important to Western Christianity's impact on ecology, White asserts, has been its anthropocentrism.[5] In Western Christianity, according to White, "Man shares, in great measure, God's transcendence of nature."[6] Also important was Christianity's denial of animism, according to which every *locus* in nature has its own spirit or *geni*. "By destroying pagan animism," White says, "Christianity made it possible to exploit nature in a mood of indifference to the feelings of natural objects."[7]

The fruit of these Christian attitudes about science, man, and nature, according to White, has been a triumphalist attitude toward nature: "We are superior to nature, contemptuous of it, willing to use it for our slightest whim."[8] As a result, our wedding of science and technology has given "mankind powers which, to judge by many of the ecologic effects, are out of control. If so, Christianity bears a huge burden of guilt."[9]

Before I respond to White's thoughts, I should point out that White was himself a Christian, and that his criticisms of Christianity's impact on ecology were intended not to condemn Christianity but to call it to reformation. Unfortunately, many people have thought they amounted to a prescription for rejecting Christianity. On the contrary, his article hinted that other religions—including a secularist dependence on more science and technology[10]—offered no promising solutions to the problem. Instead, White proposed substituting for what has been the dominant view of mankind's relation to nature in Christianity another view promoted by St. Francis of Assisi, whom he proposed as "a patron saint for ecologists."[11]

Like White, I approach these issues as a Christian. Also like White, I recognize that to some extent Western Christianity has fostered an exploitative attitude toward nature. I would nuance this criticism in a couple of ways, however. First, it is much easier for us, protected as we are from the elements of nature by two centuries' worth of technological buildup, to think of nature as a friend than it was for our ancestors to do so. The man-against-nature perspective that dominated much of Western history (and still dominates the day-to-day life of many pre-industrial peoples of the world) was rather understandable in an agrarian society dependent almost wholly on weather and in which people were extremely vulnerable to storms, earthquakes, and infectious diseases. The Baconian mindset—however mistakenly so called—has afforded us the luxury of thinking now of a truce, or better yet, of an alliance, that our ancestors could hardly consider. Second, I believe the exploitative attitude toward nature is not inherently Christian but is much more deeply rooted in the growth of Renaissance and Enlightenment humanism, which progressively excluded God and divinized man, ultimately making man autonomous. It is mankind's accountability to God that civilizes and limits us, that makes us not autonomous, self-ruled, but theonomous, God-ruled. "If you will not have God," wrote T. S. Eliot, "—and He is a jealous God—then you must pay your respects to Hitler or Stalin." Or as Dostoyevsky put it, "Without God, anything is permissible."

Truly Biblical Christianity denies precisely what White attributed to Christianity: the view that "God planned all of [creation] explicitly for man's benefit and rule: no item in the physical creation had any purpose save to serve man's purposes."[12] Indeed, rather than being "the most anthropocentric religion the world has seen," as White charged,[13] Biblical Christianity is God-centered. For Biblical Christianity tells us that God created all things for His pleasure (Rev. 4:11) and that the heavens declare not the glory of man but the glory of God (Ps. 19:1). Biblical Christianity teaches that man, although created in God's image and likeness and instructed to "rule over the fish of the sea and over the birds of the sky and over the cattle and over all the earth, and over every creeping thing that creeps on the earth" (Gen. 1:26), is accountable to God for how he exercises that rule, for God expressly told him "to cultivate and to keep" the Garden of Eden (Gen. 2:15), and it may be argued that one aspect of man's failure in the first sin was not protecting the Garden from the encroachment of Satan (Gen. 3:1–6). Indeed, we can go farther yet. The Bible says that God cursed the earth as a judgment on human sin (Gen. 3:17), subjecting the creation to "futility" and "slavery to corruption" (Rom. 8:20–21). Yet it also says that the creation will be delivered from its "slavery to corruption" through the redeeming work of Christ and the transforming power of His resurrection working through those who believe in Him (Rom. 8:18–25). Thus truly Biblical Christianity teaches that mankind has a triple responsibility toward the earth as a steward of God: to guard it against degradation, to cultivate it to increase its fruitfulness, and to restore its beauty and fruitfulness where these have been damaged by sin and the Curse.

Such notions should be welcome to those who care about ecology and the maintenance of biological diversity. But they come with a price. While a steward is necessarily accountable and therefore not autonomous, he necessarily also exercises some authority over whatever it is that he stewards. Stewardship without authority is impossible. And the Bible expressly affirms, as we have already seen, that God gave man authority over everything on the earth (Gen. 1:26–28). Indeed, while Psalm 24:1, a favorite verse among Christian ecologists, tells us, "The earth is the LORD's, and all it contains," Psalm 115:16 tells us, "The heavens are the heavens of the LORD; but the earth He has given to the sons of men." And Psalm 8:3–6 says, "When I consider Thy heavens, the work of Thy fingers, the moon and the stars, which Thou hast ordained; what is man, that Thou dost take thought of him? And the son of man, that Thou dost care for him? Yet Thou hast made him a little lower than God, and dost crown him with glory and majesty. Thou dost make him to rule over the works of Thy hands; thou hast put all things under his feet. . . ."

To be theocentric, as Biblical Christianity is, does not imply putting all created life on the same level. I spoke earlier about "biological hierarchicalism," an order of value and priority among life forms, as necessarily underlying our recognition that such life forms as HIV and botulism are not necessarily worth preserving. A better way of picturing things might be to say that there are concentric circles of priority, with God at the very center, man in the next circle outward, and other life forms in concentric circles radiating outward from there. In this perspective, animal life would be closer to the center than plant life, and more intelligent animals would be more central than less intelligent animals—intelligence being one of the marks (along with moral character—in humans, of course) of likeness to God.

Alternative World Views' Attitudes toward Man and Nature

This view of man and the world stands in stark contrast to views that have become increasingly influential among ecologists and other environmentalists. Although the Christian view sees man as fallen in sin, it still sees him as bearing the image of God and therefore the highest—or most central—of all *created* things. Such respect for human beings is in short supply among some leading environmentalists.

Among these are the Deep Ecologists. Often pantheists—who believe that God is everything—and sometimes explicitly embracing such Eastern religions as Hinduism and Buddhism,[14] the Deep Ecologists are spiritual and religious in their attitudes toward environmental issues. Some actively seek to revive such pagan ways as Druidism, witchcraft, Native American religions, and—among feminists—goddess worship. Drawing from both the Eastern religions and Darwinian science, they tend to find man's identity with the rest of nature in his ascent through the evolutionary chain of being. Thus, "One itinerant environmentalist conducts 'workshops' in which participants are urged to remember their alleged evolutionary history by rolling on the ground and imagining what their lives were like as dead leaves, slugs, and lichens."[15]

The Deep Ecologists derive their views from mysticism and intuition. Arne Naess, a Norwegian philosopher, is one of the chief framers of the Deep Ecology worldview and the coiner of the phrase *deep ecology*.[16] He specified that his work consists not "of philosophical or logical argumentation" but is "primarily intuitions."[17] Just how intuitive this worldview—which Naess calls "ecosophy"—is may be illustrated by his student and translator David Rothenberg's description of one of Naess's lectures in Oslo: "After an hour he suddenly stops, glances quickly around the stage, and suddenly leaves the podium and approaches a potted plant to his left. He quickly pulls off a leaf, scurries back to the microphone, and gazes sincerely at the audience as he holds the leaf in the light so all can see. 'You can spend a lifetime contemplating this', he comments. 'It is enough. Thank you.'"[18]

The focus on intuition in the Deep Ecology movement explains, in part, why feminism allies itself with environmentalism, particularly with Deep Ecology and animal rights. Contemporary feminism rejects science outright—or redefines it—because science operates in a manner not sufficiently sensitive to "feminine thought patterns" because it is a fundamentally "masculine" discipline. "Science's insistence on being tough, rigorous, rational, impersonal, and unemotional is intertwined with men's gender identities," says feminist theologian and animal rights theorist Carol Adams, author of *The Sexual*

Politics of Meat: A Feminist-Vegetarian Critical Theory.[19]

At Deep Ecology's root is the insistence that "all life is fundamentally one." From this principle flows a new vision of Self-realization—with a capital *S*: "a bold attempt to connect the general statement that 'all life is fundamentally one' with our individual needs and desires." Here all distinction between God and the world collapses in the vision of the one Self that encompasses not only all of life but all of everything.[20]

Deep Ecology explicitly rejects any distinction between man and nature. Naess complains that while "Shallow Ecology"—his term—does fight "against pollution and resource depletion," its central objective is "the health and affluence of *people*. . . ." In contrast, Deep Ecology involves "Rejection of the man-in-environment image in favour of *the relational, total-field image.*"[21] In other words, man's needs and desires are not to be considered as in any sense higher than those of the rest of nature, for man is nothing more than a part of nature.

Naess sees and embraces the logical implication of his views: "*Biospherical egalitarianism—in principle*. . . . To the ecological field worker, *the equal right to live and blossom* is an intuitively clear and obvious value axiom. Its restriction to humans is an anthropocentrism with detrimental effects upon the life quality of humans themselves."[22] Or as Earth First! founder David Foreman puts it, ". . . man is no more important than any other species. . . . It may well take our extinction to set things straight."[23]

A second important element of the modern environmentalist movement is the animal rights movement. If "all life is fundamentally one," as Naess insists—in concert with scientific naturalism and the other evolutionary religions: Hinduism, Buddhism, and the contemporary New Age Movement— then no one part of life has any greater claim on life and health than any other. Consequently, as animal rights philosophers John Harris and Stanley and Roslind Godlovitch put it, ". . . there can be no rational excuse left for killing animals, be they killed for food, science or sheer personal indulgence."[24]

The logic is inescapable. But it is also unlivable, for without consuming life, human life cannot continue. Naess stepped back from the abyss when he proclaimed "*Biospherical egalitarianism—in principle*," adding, "The 'in principle' clause is inserted because any realistic praxis [i.e., staying alive] necessitates some killing, exploitation, and suppression."[25] So Naess permits killing and eating animals.

That won't do for the animal rights crowd. To them, such inconsistency is mere "human chauvinism," as David Greanville puts it.[26] The more common label is *speciesism*, a word coined in 1973 and made popular by philosopher

Peter Singer's book *Animal Liberation* in 1975. What is speciesism? It is, according to Singer, "a prejudice or attitude of bias toward the interests of members of one's own species and against those of members of other species." For proponents of animal rights, speciesism is so self-evidently wrong that "it should be obvious that the fundamental objections to racism . . . made by Thomas Jefferson . . . apply equally to speciesism. If possessing a higher degree of intelligence does not entitle one human to use another for his own ends, how can it entitle humans to exploit nonhumans for the same purpose?"[27] Speciesism is to animals what racism is to racial minorities, sexism to members of the opposite sex, and anti-Semitism to Jews: an unjustifiable prejudice against those unlike oneself.

Singer builds his whole argument for animal rights and against speciesism on the assumption of essential equality between human and other animal life forms, an equality as morally significant as the equality of Blacks and Whites and of men and women. If the fundamental equality of Blacks and Whites makes racism immoral, and the fundamental equality of men and women makes sexism immoral, then the fundamental equality of humans and other animals makes speciesism immoral.

There is grave danger in this line of argument. The assumption that biological equality necessitates *equal* treatment does not define *right* treatment. While Singer argues from biological equality to the conclusion that we should treat animals as we treat humans, one could as readily argue from biological equality that we should treat humans as we treat animals. Animal rights philosopher Patrick Corbett asks, "Is it not perverse to prefer the lives of mice and guinea pigs to the lives of men and women?" No, he answers, because "if we stand back from the scientific and technological rat race for a moment, we realize that, since animals are in many respects superior to ourselves, the argument collapses."[28] What Corbett neglects is that "animals are in many respects superior to ourselves" means the same as "people are in many respects inferior to animals," and if that is so then there is no reason to expect people to behave differently from—or better than—animals.

Paradoxically, biological egalitarianism—the belief that all animals are equal because all are part of the evolutionary continuum—lies at the root of racism, which sees certain races as lower on the evolutionary scale than others and therefore properly to be treated more like animals than the higher races. Never forget that the full title of Charles Darwin's *The Origin of Species* was *The Origin of Species By Means of Natural Selection, Or the Preservation of Favored **Races** in the Struggle for Life*. Richard Hofstadter, in *Social Darwinism in American Thought*, showed conclusively "that Darwinism was one of the chief sources of racism and of a belligerent ideology which characterized the last half of the 19th century in Europe and America. . . ."[29] When Adolf Hitler applied Darwinism to morality, he concluded, "There is absolutely no other revolution but a *racial* revolution. There is no economic, no social, no political revolution. There is only the struggle of *lower races* against the *higher races*."[30] Karl Marx considered Darwin's *Origin of Species* a scientific basis for his theory of the class struggle and wanted to dedicate an edition of *Das Kapital* to Darwin. Evolutionary biology applied to ethics has led historically not to humane treatment of beasts but to beastly treatment of humans.

Perhaps this explains why Earth First! activists pound spikes into trees to discourage loggers from cutting them down and sawmill operators from milling them: When the power blades hit the hidden spikes, the blades can explode, threatening serious injury or death to operators. Perhaps it explains why Sea Shepherds activists boast of sinking twelve whaling ships—at considerable risk to the ships' crews.[31] Perhaps it explains why one animal rights activist—a woman—was convicted for attempting to murder, with two pipe bombs filled with nails, the president of U.S. Surgical Corporation, which uses animals to teach doctors surgical procedures.[32]

This perspective trivializes racism by putting speciesism on the same level with it. If I were a Black, I'd be worried about anyone who said that speciesism was as bad as racism.

Alas, the animal rights movement is blind to this sinister flip side of the coin of evolutionary ethics. The assumption that man's treatment of man, not animals' treatment of animals, should be the standard of man's treatment of animals is at least as anthropocentric as the insistence that people have rights that animals don't. And it is more condemnable because it is so hypocritical. At the bottom of the contents page of every issue, *The Animals' Agenda* proudly asserts that it "makes every effort to ensure that products and services advertised herein are consistent with the *humane* ethic" (emphasis added). And on the last page of *The Animal Contract*, a popular book based on a controversial television series of the same title, Desmond Morris has written, "It is dishonourable to break a contract and that is what we have done with our animal friends. They are our relatives and we too are animals. To be brutal to them is to become brutalised in all our dealings, with humans as well as with other species."[33] Here is anthropocentric speciesism with a vengeance! Why should we favor "the *humane* ethic" over "the *beastly* ethic" if human beings are essentially equal to animals? Why decry "brutal" behavior? After all, a brute is by definition "a beast; any animal."[34]

The practical implication of the animal rights movement is that human beings, who alone respect anybody's rights, must become extinct, while all other species continue feasting merrily on each other. Bidinotto draws the inference clearly:

> Any intelligible theory of rights must presuppose entities capable of defining and respecting moral boundary lines. But animals are by nature incapable of this. And since they are unable to know, respect, or exercise rights, the principle of rights simply can't be applied to, or by, animals. Rights are, by their nature, based on a homocentric (man-centered) view of the world.
>
> Practically, the notion of animal rights entails an absurd moral double standard. It declares that animals have the "inherent right" to survive as *their* nature demands, but that man doesn't. It declares that man, the only entity capable of recognizing moral boundaries, is to sacrifice his interests to entities that can't. Ultimately, it means that *only* animals have rights: since nature consists entirely of animals, their food, and their habitats, to recognize "animal rights" man must logically cede to them the entire planet.[35]

The Deep Ecologists' and animal rights movement's equating people with animals might actually seem mild compared with the attitudes toward humanity among some leaders in the population control movement. In 1970, Kingsley Davis wrote contemptuously, "In subsequent history the Twentieth Century may be called either the century of world wars or the century of the population plague,"[36] an attitude that fueled his suggesting, seven years later, that population be reduced by promoting the breakdown of the family, "very high divorce rates, homosexuality, pornography, and free sexual unions"—with easy access to abortion.[37]

Davis is not alone in hating people. In an article in *The Animals' Agenda*, a magazine published by the Animal Rights Network and portraying itself as moderate, Sydney Singer writes, "For an animal rights activist, it's easy to become disgusted with humankind. Humans are exploiters and destroyers, self-appointed world autocrats around whom the universe seems to revolve." Condemning the use of animals in medical research that has contributed to cures or effective treatments for once fatal diseases, he adds, "It is often hard to feel compassion for humans in their pain and fear as they brutalize other animals. . . . In the face of speciesist rationalizations for animal exploitation, which frame the issue in terms of animal suffering or human suffering, it's hard not [to] take sides and fight for the animals." And no wonder; Singer, like most other animal rights advocates, equates human beings with animals: "When the ethical issue of active euthanasia arises concerning a terminal patient who is asking to be killed, I find myself thinking about the millions of dogs and cats 'euthanized' each year in pounds."[38] Singer was a medical student when he wrote the article. You might pray for his patients. But Singer can hardly compete with Ingrid Newkirk, of People for the Ethical Treatment of Animals (PETA), who was cited in *The Washington Post* as saying, "Six million people died in concentration camps, *but six billion broiler chickens will die this year in slaughter houses*"![39]

If putting people on the level of animals isn't bad enough, how about putting them on the level of trees? The West German Green Party's Carl Amery said in 1983, "We, in the Green movement, aspire to a cultural model in which the killing of a forest will be considered more contemptible and more criminal than the sale of 6-year-old children to Asian brothels."[40] Michael W. Fox, one of the chief gurus of the radical environmentalist and animal rights movements, writes in his book *Returning to Eden* that man "is the most dangerous, destructive, selfish and unethical animal on earth."[41]

David Brower, of Friends of the Earth, considers "other people's children" pollution and therefore an environmental concern. Said he, "Childbearing [should be] a punishable crime against society, unless the parents hold a government license. . . . All potential parents [should be] required to use contraceptive chemicals, the government issuing antidotes to citizens chosen for childbearing."[42]

Not to be left behind in this attack on reproductive freedom, Paul Ehrlich, author of *The Population Bomb* and *The Population Explosion*, writes, "Several coercive [methods of birth control] deserve serious consideration, mainly because we will ultimately have to resort to them, unless current trends in birth rates are revised." He suggests deindustrialization (since the wealth made by industries makes providing for children easier), liberalized abortion, and tax breaks for sterilized couples.[43]

Amery, Brower, and Ehrlich are mild compared with Les Knight, founder of VHEMT (pronounced "vehement")—the Voluntary Human Extinction Movement. "The hopeful alternative to the extinction of millions of species of plants and animals," he says, "is the voluntary extinction of one species: *Homo sapiens*—us. When every human makes the moral choice to live long and die out, Earth will be allowed to return to its former glory. Each time one of us decides not to add another of us to the burgeoning billions already squatting on this ravaged planet, another ray of hope shines through the gloom. . . . A baby condor may not be as cute as a baby human, but we must choose to forgo one if the others are to survive."[44]

If restraints on reproduction don't work, we can always turn to killing people outright. Norwegian philosopher of ecology Arne Naess, founder of Deep Ecology, suggested an ideal world population of 100 million.[45] One wonders what he would do with the other 5 billion of us! In reviewing Bill McKibben's *The End of Nature*, National Park Service biologist David Graber wrote,

> Human happiness, and certainly human fecundity, are not as important as a wild and healthy planet. I know social scientists who remind me that people are part of nature, but it isn't true. Somewhere along the line—at about a million years ago, maybe half that—we quit the contract and became a cancer. We have become a plague upon ourselves and upon the Earth. . . . Until such time as Homo Sapiens should decide to rejoin nature, some of us can only hope for the right virus to come along.[46]

Graber didn't need to wait long. The Earth First! newsletter suggests, "If radical environmentalists were to invent a disease to bring human populations back to sanity, it would probably be something like AIDS. It has the potential to end industrialism, which is the main force behind the environmental crises."[47]

No wonder population controllers choose destructive terminology to describe humanity and the growth of its population. To them we are the population bomb, the population explosion, the population boom, the population plague, a cancer, or people pollution.[48]

But Biblical Christianity has a different view of people. Created in the image of God, who Himself is creative, we, too, should be—and can be—creative and productive, not destroying but restoring the earth. This view of mankind is borne out in the historic decline in resource scarcity demonstrated by falling money prices (the only practical measure of scarcity) and labor/capital costs for resources throughout the last few centuries, the very time during which human population has grown so rapidly.[49] Thus, the human race is not the population explosion but the population blossom; not the population boom but the population bloom; not people pollution but the people solution; not cancer but an answer.

Conclusion

Let me conclude with a few comments specifically on the application of this Christian understanding of humanity and its relationship with the rest of creation to questions related to biodiversity.

First, this hierarchical, or concentric-circles, view justifies putting man's needs ahead of the needs of other life forms. This doesn't mean people should run rampant over other species. God has made us stewards, responsible to Him for restoring, cultivating, and guarding the earth. Biblical law includes laws specifically requiring care for non-human life. Deuteronomy 25:4, for instance, forbids muzzling an ox while it treads out grain, implying the principle that animals must be adequately cared for while they are in the service of human beings. Deuteronomy 22:6 indicates a care for the preservation of animal populations in specific places: "If you happen to come upon a bird's nest along the way, in any tree or on the ground, with young ones or eggs, and the mother sitting on the young or on the eggs, you shall not take the mother with the young; you shall certainly let the mother go, but the young you may take for yourself;" but notice the motive: it is for man's benefit, "in order that it may be well with you, and that you may prolong your days." Deuteronomy 20:19 forbids a "scorched earth" policy of warfare: "When you besiege a city a long time, to make war against it in order to capture it, you shall not destroy its trees. . . ."

Second, Biblical ethics, which in the Ninth Commandment forbids false witness, finds no more room for false or misleading information about ecology than about anything else. Rather, it requires that we be up front and open about facts. For instance, most laymen are under the impression that when an animal or plant is put on the endangered species list, that means there is a real risk that its whole species may become extinct. They are not aware that the Endangered Species Act defines a species, for the purposes of the law, as either a species or a local or regional population of that species. Some of the "species" listed as endangered are in no danger whatever of becoming extinct; they are listed only because local populations may be threatened, even though those local populations may be genetically indistinguishable from populations found elsewhere.

Another example of the need for better truth-telling in the biodiversity debate is the matter of just how rapidly species are becoming extinct. Few people realize that claims of scores, hundreds, or thousands of extinctions per year, like those found in Vice President Al Gore's *Earth in the Balance*, lack any basis in empirical field studies—a fact admitted repeatedly by the authors of *Tropical Deforestation and Species Extinction*,[50] even though the book was written to provide empirical evidence for high extinction rates.[51] As illustration, and as time permits, let me share with you a few representative quotations from that volume:

[Martin W. Holdgate, director-general of the IUCN, in the foreword:] The coastal forests of Brazil have been reduced in area as severely as any tropical forest type in the world. According to calculation, this should have led to considerable species loss. Yet no known species of its old, largely endemic, fauna can be regarded as extinct. Genetic erosion has undoubtedly taken place, and the reduced, remnant populations may be much more vulnerable to future change, but the study illustrates the need for very careful field documentation to compare with calculation in this and other situations.

[W. V. Reid:] . . . 60 birds and mammals are known to have become extinct between 1900 and 1950. [p. 55]

[D. Simberloff:] It is a commonplace that forests of the eastern United States were reduced over two centuries to fragments totalling 1-2% of their original extent, and that during this destruction, only three forest birds went extinct—the Carolina parakeet (Conuropsis carolinensis), the ivory-billed woodpecker (Campephilus principalis principalis), and the passenger pigeon (Ectopistes migratorius). Although deforestation certainly contributed to the decline of all three species, it was probably not critical for the pigeon or the parakeet (Greenway, 1967). Why, then, would one predict massive extinction from similar destruction of tropical forest? [p. 85. Yet, Simberloff makes such predictions.]

[V. H. Heywood and S. N. Stuart:] IUCN, together with the World Conservation Monitoring Centre, has amassed large volumes of data from specialists around the world relating to species decline [worldwide], and it would seem sensible to compare these more empirical data with the global extinction estimates. In fact, these and other data indicate that the number of recorded extinctions for both plants and animals is very small. . . . [p. 93]

[Same:] Known extinction rates [worldwide] are very low. Reasonably good data exist only for mammals and birds, and the current rate of extinction is about one species per year (Reid and Miller, 1989). If other taxa were to exhibit the same liability to extinction as mammals and birds (as some authors suggest, although others would dispute this), then, if the total number of species in the world is, say, 30 million, the annual rate of extinction would be some 2300 species per year. This is a very significant and disturbing number, but it is much less than most estimates given over the last decade. [p. 94]

[Same:] . . . if we assume that today's tropical forests occupy only about 80% of the area they did in the 1830s, it must be assumed that during this contraction, very large numbers of species have been lost in some areas. Yet surprisingly there is no clear-cut evidence for this. . . .[52] Despite extensive enquiries we have been unable to obtain conclusive evidence to support the suggestion that massive extinctions have taken place in recent times, as Myers and others have suggested. On the contrary, work on projects such as Flora Meso-Americana has, at least in some cases, revealed an increase in abundance in many species (Blackmore, pers. comm. 1991). An exceptional and much quoted situation is described by Gentry (1986) who reports the quite dramatic level of evolution in situ in the Centinela ridge in the foothills of the Ecuadorian Andes where he found that at least 38 and probably as many as 90 species (10% of the total flora of the ridge) were endemic to the 'unprepossessing ridge'. However, the last patches of forest were cleared subsequent to his last visit and 'its prospective 90 new species have already passed into botanical history', or so it was assumed. Subsequently, Dodson and Gentry (1991) modified this to say that an undetermined number of species at Centinela are apparently extinct, following brief visits to other areas such as Lita where up to 11 of the species previously considered extinct were refound, and at Poza Honda near La Mana where six were rediscovered. [p. 96]

[Same:] . . . actual extinctions [in the Mediterranean region] remain low. . . . As Greuter (1991) aptly comments, 'Many endangered species appear to have either an almost miraculous capacity for survival, or a guardian angel is watching over their destiny! This means that it is not too late to attempt to protect the Mediterranean flora as a whole, while still identifying appropriate priorities with regard to the goals and means of conservation.' [p. 102.]

[K. S. Brown and G. G. Brown:] . . . the group of zoologists could not find a single known animal species which could be properly declared as extinct [in the Brazilian tropical forest area], in spite of the massive reduction in area and fragmentation of their habitats in the past decades and centuries of intensive human activity. A second list of over 120 lesser-known animal species, some of which may later be included as threatened, show no species considered extinct; and the older Brazilian list of threatened plants, presently under revision, also indicated no species as extinct (Cavalcanti, 1981). [p. 127]

[Same:] Closer examination of the existing data on both well- and little-known groups, however, supports the affirmation that little or no species extinction has yet occurred (though some may be in very fragile persistence) in the Atlantic [Brazilian] forests. Indeed, an appreciable number of species considered extinct 20 years ago, including several birds and six butterflies, have been rediscovered more recently. [p. 128]

The authors of this volume also acknowledge the lack of sound empirical basis for estimating species extinction rates:

[Whitmore and Sayer:] Estimates of plant and invertebrate extinctions are inevitably largely a matter of speculation. Consequences for species survival of the degradation, partial clearance and fragmentation of large forest areas are simply not known though biologists have begun to think about the problem (e.g. Simberloff, chapter 4). [p. 9]

[Whitemore and Sayer:] . . . the relationship between forest loss and species loss is not arithmetic. To extrapolate upon such a relationship presents an excessively pessimistic view. [p. 11]

[Reid:] . . . How large is the loss of species [worldwide] like to be? Although the loss of species may rank among the most significant environmental problems of our time, relatively few attempts have been made to rigorously assess its likely magnitude. [p. 55]

[Heywood and Stuart:] It is impossible to estimate even approximately how many unrecorded species may have become extinct. [p. 95]

[Reid:] While better knowledge of extinction rates can clearly improve the design of public policies, it is equally apparent that estimates of global extinction rates are fraught with imprecision. We do not yet know how many species exist, even to within an order of magnitude. [p. 56]

[Reid:] The best tool available to estimate species extinction rates is the use of species-area curves. . . . This approach has formed the basis for almost all current estimates of species extinction rates. [p. 57]

[Heywood and Stuart:] There are many reasons why recorded extinctions do not match the predictions and extrapolations that are frequently published. . . . [p. 93]

The comment of the volume's editors in the preface sums matters up rather nicely—and candidly:

Many people have asked IUCN to comment on the numerous conflicting estimates of species extinction and some would like us to come up with a firm and definitive figure for the number of species which are being lost in a given period of time. The data available would not enable this to be done with any reasonable degree of scientific credibility and we have not attempted to do so in this book. [p. xi]

These authors are not alone in these assessments of the dismal lack of solid empirical grounds for any claims of species extinction rates. Norman Myers, who has made some of the strongest claims about very high rates,[53] now writes, "Regrettably we have no way of knowing the actual current rate of extinction in tropical forests, nor can we even make an accurate guess."[54] As Simon and Wildavsky put it,

> One would think that this state of affairs would make anyone leery about estimating future extinctions. Nevertheless Myers continues, "But we can make substantive assessments by looking at species numbers before deforestation and then applying the analytical techniques of biogeography. . . . According to the theory of island biogeography, we can realistically reckon that when a habitat has lost 90% of its extent, it has lost half of its species" (1989, p. 43). But this is mere speculation. And Lugo finds that in Puerto Rico, the "massive forest conversion did not lead to a correspondingly massive species extinction, certainly nowhere near the 50% alluded to by Myers" (1989, p. 28).[55]
>
> Confirmation of the absence of scientific evidence for rapid species extinction is implicit in the nature of the "evidence" cited by, for example, Edward O. Wilson. He says that "the extinction problem" is "absolutely undeniable." But all he cites are "literally hundreds of anecdotal reports" (Charles C. Mann, "Extinction: Are Ecologists Crying Wolf?" *Science* 253 (August 16, 1991), 736–38). The very reason for the scientific method in estimating rates is that anecdotal reports are of little or no value, and often mislead the public and policymakers; that's why expensive censuses and other data-gathering instruments are mounted.[56]

The purpose of pointing to the lack of sound scientific evidence regarding the rate of species extinction is not to belittle or ignore what might be a significant problem but to remind ourselves that sound policy must be based on sound information. Presently there is next to none in regard to overall rates of species extinction worldwide, by continent, or even within much smaller regions and locales. Without that information, wise policy cannot be crafted.

Third, granted the principles of Biblical stewardship, which involve a free market within the moral restraints of God's law,[57] we should recognize that, when acting wisely, human beings can and should be viewed not as enemies but friends of endangered species. One of the most important ways to ensure that this friendship occurs is to seek ways to turn protection of species to people's advantage. We do not, after all, worry about chickens becoming extinct, although we slaughter billions every year in the United States alone. Instead, we worry about rhinoceroses becoming extinct. If there were adequate market rewards for raising rhinos, that worry would quickly disappear. Instead, our present Endangered Species Act, by requiring harsh penalties for anyone who destroys a member of an endangered species, creates the opposite incentive for landowners: to destroy members of endangered species that they find on their lands before bureaucrats or environmentalists discover that they are there, in order to avoid the likelihood of penalties or severe restrictions on land use in the future. Thus the punitive nature of the ESA works against the ends for which the legislation was crafted. Reward landowners for protecting endangered species on their property and they will do it. Find ways to reward the preservation and cultivation of species through the market, and you will find ways to remove them from the danger of extinction.

APPENDIX 3

❧ ❧

Anomalies, the Good News,
and the Debate Over Population and Development:
A Review of Susan Power Bratton's *Six Billion and More*

[The following is adapted from *Stewardship Journal*, vol. 3, no. 3 (Summer 1993), 44–53.]

IN *SIX BILLION AND MORE: HUMAN POPULATION REGULATION & CHRIStian Ethics*, Susan Power Bratton tackles a subject that few evangelicals have confronted in any but the most simplistic way. In trying "to develop a Christian ethical framework for determining 'rights and wrongs' in dealing with human population regulation" (18), Bratton asks difficult questions about population regulation at both personal and societal levels, and her discussions are thought provoking, particularly regarding ethical principles.

Summary

Bratton's view of the present state of the world's population (chapter 1), more negative than I believe the facts warrant, is still less alarmist than views promoted by many anti-population growth organizations. Her discussion of why populations rise and fall (chapter 2) is competent and includes a good description of demographic transition, albeit giving economic development too little weight in indirectly influencing fertility rates.

Her discussion of Biblical themes related to reproduction and population (chapter 3) is both interesting and helpful, although she commits some exegetical/hermeneutical fallacies from time to time (e.g., "Although set in the imperative, 'be fruitful and increase' is actually, as the Genesis texts clearly indicate, a blessing . . . [and] is therefore not an ethical imperative . . ." [43]— the fallacy of false choice; it could be *both* blessing *and* imperative, and the

147

imperative verbs, coupled with the context, indicate that it is both) and assumes greater discontinuity between the testaments (64–65) than Reformed theologians grant (hence her insistence that the Old Testament's highly favorable attitude toward childbearing and large families is not normative because it is not explicitly repeated in the New Testament).

For me, chapter 4, on the history of both Christian teaching and social behavior in the West regarding childbearing and population regulation, was the most interesting in the book, containing fascinating descriptions of how past generations shaped their own choices, and the consequences of those choices. Particularly enlightening—and humbling—was her description of how far short Christian practice has fallen from Christian ideals, with many practicing abandonment and infanticide throughout history.

In chapter 5 Bratton accurately but uncritically describes the fears of environmentalists related to population growth. Sadly, she perpetuates myths like declining quality of farm soil under high-tech agricultural methods,[1] increasing scarcity of non-renewable resources,[2] a direct and linear correlation between population growth and rising levels of pollution,[3] massive rainforest depletion and consequent species extinction,[4] destruction of the ozone layer by man-made chemical pollutants,[5] acid rain as a major killer of forests and aquatic life,[6] and deleterious global warming.[7]

Bratton squarely opposes secular approaches to population control like Garrett Hardin's "lifeboat ethics" and Paul Ehrlich's "triage" in chapter 6, arguing rightly that these are inconsistent with Christian principles like justice and the preference for life. In chapter 7 she sensibly rebuts what she calls the ethnocentric fears of writers like Ben Wattenberg that the United States and other developed countries are being transformed by immigration and losing their dominance in the world because their populations are nearing stability while less-developed nations' populations are growing rapidly.

She paints a picture of "The Exploding Third World" in chapter 8 in a manner that will feed many people's fears of "overpopulation" and consequent poverty and famine. I will return to this issue in more detail below. Chapter 9, on population regulation and justice, sets the stage for a largely voluntarist ethic of reproductive choices, and chapter 10 argues against coercion except under extreme circumstances. In refreshing contrast with secular writers like Paul Ehrlich and many officials in national and international population regulation agencies, Bratton favors narrow limits on coercive methods of population regulation:

Coercive methods . . . potentially represent a collision between two competing sets of values: the integrity of the individual and the safety of the community. Following contemporary ideals that consider the rights of the individual inalienable, we could only consider violating the right of privacy when, as in the case of war, the community is really under a life-or-death threat. This is a "lesser of two evils" argument which requires that several criteria be met before coercive means of regulating population can be considered. First, coercive methods [of population regulation] should only be employed where famine is a serious threat or mortality due to *widespread* [emphasis original] malnutrition is occurring, and the crisis is directly related to population levels and not to some other factor such as lack of land for peasant farming.[8] In other words, some restriction of individual reproductive options is appropriate where mortality or great suffering will result if populations continue to expand. The threat must be proven—the projections of environmental alarmists are not by themselves adequate to justify coercion. Second, food, health care, educational opportunities, and other resources are relatively equitably distributed within the society. Coercion is not appropriate where malnutrition is strongly related to social class, where a majority of the populace is well fed, or where socioeconomic problems independent of population growth are causing shortages. In the latter case, just distribution of resources would be the first step in relieving famine. Third, an attempt has already been made to make family planning services widely available, and people have not been willing to use them or have been unwilling to reduce family size. Fourth and last, other methods of encouraging reduced birthrates have already been seriously attempted and have failed. [181]

"Very few societies worldwide presently meet these criteria," she adds. Indeed, in light of empirical and theoretical studies of the relationship between population density and growth, on the one hand, and economic development, nutrition, health, and mortality, on the other, I think *no* society meets these criteria.

Bratton recognizes the potential for abuse in coercive methods of population planning, noting that they "pose dangers of racism, sexism, classism, and culturism" (182). Recent renewed emphasis on coercive population control in China, reported in the Western press in the spring of 1993, led to forced abortions and infanticide, often dictated by sex selection, so that, for instance, about 8 percent of girls conceived appear to become victims of abortion or infanticide (about 900,000 each year).[9]

On the whole, *Six Billion and More* is a serious attempt to address a critical current issue from a Christian perspective, and Bratton is to be commended for her contribution to ongoing debate. Nonetheless, the book also has some serious weaknesses.

Critical Response

In the past two centuries, while the world's population has roughly quintupled, infant mortality has plunged from around 400 per thousand to around 50, life expectancy at birth has risen from around 30 to around 65, and the average material standard of living (measured in things like the quality, abundance, and affordability of food, clothing, shelter, transportation, communication, education, health care, recreation, and so on) has multiplied many times over. Some countries began rapid upward trends in population, health and longevity (which generally coincide), and living standards slightly over two hundred years ago, some less than fifty years ago, and a handful have hardly started. Nonetheless, the overwhelming dominance of these trends is undeniable.

These trends seem like obviously good news to anyone who values humanity. How can one help rejoicing that, worldwide, only about one in twenty[10] newborns will die before its first birthday instead of eight in twenty?[11] That, worldwide, the average person born today can expect to live more than twice as long as the average person born two centuries ago? That, worldwide, the average person has many times more and better clothing, housing, amenities such as electricity and indoor plumbing, and all the many other material things that help him to enjoy a long, safe, and healthy life, than the average person born in 1790? That the low-income economies of the world experienced a 20 percent increase in daily calorie supply per capita between 1965 and 1989,[12] significantly boosting their inhabitants' health and energy available for doing the work they need to do to create added wealth?[13]

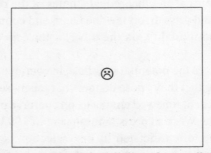

Figure 1. The high visibility of anomalies.

Yet many people read even good news as bad. Consider the contents of figure 1. What do you see? A frowning face? True, but not the whole truth. You see about 1.97 square inches of white paper and less than .03 square inch of ink. The frowning face represents less than 1.5 percent of the total space within the figure.

Sometimes anomalies are important. If you're feeling chest pains and you go to the doctor, you really don't care that she sees that your bones are intact, your digestive tract is working properly, and your brain waves are normal. You want to know the cause of your chest pains, and you don't want her to overlook the tiny blood clot—the anomaly—in one small artery of your heart. But you also don't want her to do a quadruple bypass if only one artery is restricted and the rest are all healthy.

Unfortunately, many people writing in the complex field of the economics of demography act like the doctor who sees nothing but anomalies and treats the patient as if every internal organ were failing when all he has is a headache caused by an infected root canal. This problem is one of several that mar Bratton's understanding of the dynamic interrelationships of population, culture, economic growth, resource availability, and environmental quality. Three examples from *Six Billion and More* illustrate this problem.

Focusing on the Negative

Nowhere in the book does Bratton acknowledge the positive phenomena, plain in economic history and dominant in the vast majority of the world, summarized in the first two paragraphs of this section of this review. To paint a fair and accurate picture of the world, she should have painted this overwhelmingly positive picture first; then, if she had wanted to focus on certain alarming anomalies, she could have done so without stacking the deck.

Selecting Unrepresentative Data

Bratton focuses only on unrepresentative data, and frequently she misunderstands them. For instance, she writes, "In Africa many countries have both declining income per capita and perhaps more critically, declining grain supplies. Between 1980 and 1986 income per person declined 28 percent in Nigeria and 8 percent in Kenya. Between the early 1970s and 1985, grain production per person fell 7 percent for Nigeria, 11 percent for Ethiopia, 19 percent for Kenya, 25 percent for Zambia, and a worrisome 52 percent for Angola"[14] (138–39).

Before questioning the significance and accuracy of the picture she paints, it would be well to notice a fundamental mistake in economics in surmising that declining grain supplies (by which she apparently means domestic grain production) are more baneful than declining income per capita. International trade makes the amount of food any given nation produces practically irrelevant. Rising per capita incomes and falling real food prices permit nations to import food, and the fact that sub-Saharan African countries, whose per capita incomes rose an anemic 5 percent from 1965 to 1990 (but at least they did rise!), imported 86 percent more cereals in 1990 than in 1974 (not including international food aid in cereals, which increased 194 percent [in *weight*, not monetary value]) reflects this.[15]

Now for the data. Bratton focuses on sub-Saharan Africa—the part of the continent south of the Sahara desert, excluding South Africa. Her descriptions fit neither South Africa nor the north African countries, let alone the vast majority of the world, where this region's negative trends are almost everywhere reversed and its positive trends are magnified. Sub-Saharan Africa has been the focus of much international development attention in the last twenty years, and rightly so, because of recurring food shortages and other economic

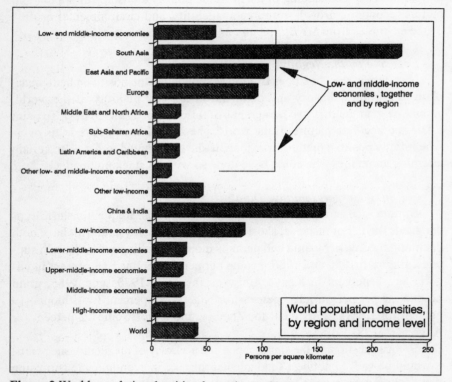

Figure 2. World population densities, by region and income level, 1990. *Source:* The World Bank, *World Development Report 1992* (New York: Oxford University Press, 1992), 218–219.

problems (most brought on by incompetent governments and civil strife). But to make it the model on which to base discussion of population's relationship to economic development and environmental quality is to make the anomaly the rule.

Even in looking just at sub-Saharan Africa, Bratton's time frames and country samples are suspicious—more significant data would take in more of the countries and a longer time frame—and her rooting the problems in population is mistaken.

There are thirty-eight countries in sub-Saharan Africa (excluding South Africa).[16] A convenient time frame is 1965-1990, a period for which data are fairly complete for all these countries in sources published by the World Bank.[17] The data show that 3 of the countries had higher food production per capita in 1990 than in 1965, and 35 lower—a situation that, at first glance, sounds ominous but was mitigated by a variety of factors, including higher incomes that permitted these countries to import more food, resulting in a slight increase in daily calorie supply per capita.[18] In 13 countries, real gross domestic product growth exceeded population growth; in 13, the opposite occurred; and for 9 countries, data were inadequate to plot a trend. In 35 countries, gross national product *per capita*, measured in constant dollars, rose; in only 2 (Mozambique and Zaire) it fell; and for 1, adequate data were unavailable.

More important, Bratton's assumption that sub-Saharan Africa's deplorable economic condition is tied to overpopulation does not fit the facts. First, its density in 1990, even after more than doubling in the previous 25 years, was 21 persons per square kilometer, 46 percent lower than the density for the world as a whole and lower than the average densities of the high-, middle-, and low-income economies of the world, as shown in figure 2.

Second, sub-Saharan Africa's population growth rate, while high, was lower than that of the Middle East and North Africa, a region that, with almost identical population density but far poorer natural resources (particularly for agriculture), experienced much higher rates of growth of agricultural output, gross domestic product, and daily calorie supply per capita (see figure 3, "Middle East and North Africa vs. Sub-Saharan Africa: Comparative performance, 1965–1990"). Rapid population growth does not condemn countries to poverty or hunger, and it is not the real explanation of the difficulties of sub-Saharan Africa.

Third, the one region of the world with 1990 gross national product per capita roughly equal to sub-Saharan Africa's, South Asia, experienced 50 percent higher growth in gross domestic product, 45 percent higher growth in agricultural output, and 450 percent higher growth in daily calorie supply per capita, despite a population density over ten times higher, and while sub-Saharan Africa's growth in agricultural production lagged 36 percent behind its growth in population, South Asia's ran ahead by 25 percent (see figure 4, "South Asia vs. Sub-Saharan Africa: Comparative performance, 1965–1990"). High population density does not condemn countries to poverty or hunger, and even if sub-Saharan Africa had a high population density (it does not), that would not explain its problems.

Contrary to what one would surmise from reading Bratton's discussion, population growth and density do not cause sub-Saharan Africa's problems. Socialist economic policies embraced by the region's governments, particularly their high subsidies to industry at the expense of high taxes on agriculture,[19] combined with religio-cultural factors that impede human productivity

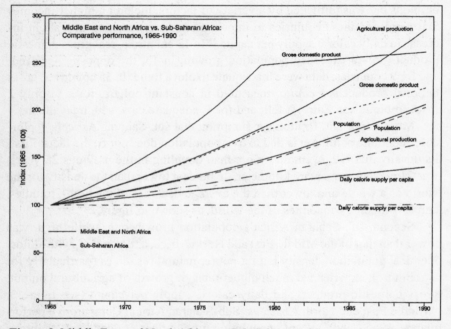

Figure 3. Middle East and North Africa vs. Sub-Saharan Africa: Comparative performance, 1965–1990. *Note:* Indexes for agricultural production, gross domestic product, and population are calculated from average annual growth rates for the periods 1965–1980 and 1980–1990; indexes for daily calorie supply per capita are a straight line drawn from the beginning figure (1965) to the ending figure (1989). *Source:* The World Bank, *World Development Report 1992* (New York: Oxford University Press, 1992), 220–221, 268–269, and 272–273.

(e.g., the cultural preference for males to leave most heavy work to females, intertribal warfare, a continuing infra-continental slave trade, a property rights system that is primitive at best), do.

Snapshots, or Moving Pictures?

Bratton frequently provides snapshots of data that appear horrible to us but lack historical perspective. This is the case in the paragraph immediately following the one quoted above: ". . . infant mortality [in sub-Saharan Africa] is still high, averaging 100 infants per thousand born, or about one child in ten." Yet for sub-Saharan Africa as a whole, infant mortality fell by 32 percent in the twenty-five years from 1965 to 1990 (from 157 per thousand to 107 per thousand); all of the seven countries she mentioned in the previous paragraph as examples of disaster shared in that happy decline—Angola down 27 percent, Ethiopia down 20 percent, Kenya and Nigeria down 40 percent, Rwanda down 15 percent, Uganda down a meager 2 percent (by far the smallest decline in the region), and Zambia down 32 percent; and not a single country in

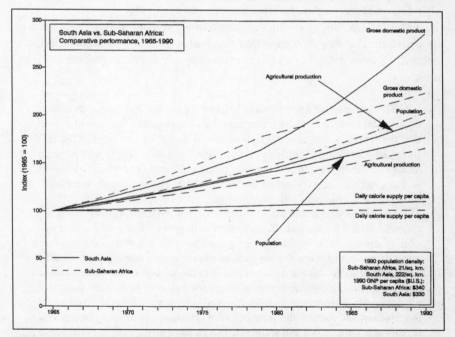

Figure 4. South Asia vs. Sub-Saharan Africa:Comparative performance, 1965–1990. *Note:* See note to figure 3. *Source:* The World Bank, *World Development Report 1992* (New York: Oxford University Press, 1992), 220–221, 268–269, and 272–273.

the region had a stable or rising infant mortality rate.[20] Although the improvement began later than it did in the United States, this achievement exceeds that of Massachusetts, which took forty years (from the late 1870s to the late 1910s) to reduce infant mortality from 156 to 100 per thousand.[21]

The lack of historical perspective is one of the most serious weaknesses in much writing about inequalities of wealth in the world. (It mars studies of many other subjects as well, such as pollution, in which people don't notice that air and water pollution emissions and concentrations have been falling for at least the last twenty years in the industrialized world—outside communist countries.) It leads people to embrace utopian schemes for instant equalization rather than recognizing the long-term, difficult, but realistic measures that have brought about real growth in nations that have advanced or are advancing rapidly. It is right to be saddened by the still high rates of infant mortality, malnutrition, hunger, and other evils associated with low degrees of economic development, but it is destructive of sound policy analysis and prescription to let that sadness blind us to history's lessons about what activities have actually lifted nations out of poverty.

Futurist Max Singer wisely suggests that we substitute a dynamic view of the world for the snapshot view that dominates most media reports and, unfortunately, even many books about economic development and the environment:

> This perspective can help us to balance the normal static, snapshot view of the world with a broader understanding. For example, we are often told that the world is divided into rich countries and poor countries. This is a little like describing a family as being divided into little people who have no money and have to go to bed at nine o'clock and big people who are allowed to drive the car and stay out as late as they like. The big people were once little, and the little ones will become big. . . .
>
> If we look [sic] at the world with the kind of dynamic, historic perspective with which we look at a family, we would give a more realistic description by saying: "The world is passing from poor to rich. All countries were poor, some countries are already rich, others are nearly there, and others still have farther to go." Because we are now in the middle of the development process that is responsible for our passage from poor to rich, some countries are now widely separated from others. And since we are barely conscious of the process, the current distance between countries seems permanent, and therefore highly unfair and immoral. But to have a reasonable perspective on the moral question, the world, like a family, should be seen as a dynamic process in which today is only a long moment.[22]

One reason the static view is dangerous is that it prompts people to ignore long-term solutions and look for quick fixes. But as Singer points out, "It is not possible to jump to the end. Each country, like each person—although for different reasons—has to go through a learning process, step by step. At each point one can only learn to take the next step, not how to jump up to the final level."[23] Bratton's book would have been much improved by applying this lesson.

Conclusion

Other weaknesses impair the usefulness of *Six Billion and More*. Bratton thinks Paul Ehrlich's predictions of famine and other disasters in *The Population Bomb* (1968) were right (19); history proved them wrong. She thinks in terms of earth's supporting people (19), not of people's supporting people—a fundamental mistake that fails to recognize the implications of the image of God in man, which point toward people's producing more than they consume. This is the theoretical explanation of the long-term downward real price trend of nearly every extractive resource (mineral, vegetable, and animal), showing decreasing scarcity, while the price of people (labor) trends upward, showing increasing scarcity.[24] Consistent with this, she neglects to look forward to the changing economic impact of today's rapid population growth two or three decades down the line. The bias toward economically non-productive children and youth caused by today's rapid growth becomes a bias toward economically productive adults later (as fertility rates decline in response to declining infant and child mortality rates), resulting in delayed but greater economic growth.[25]

Bratton also mistakenly thinks Thomas Robert Malthus "correctly identified a principle of population growth: Human and animal populations increase geometrically . . . as compared to the slower, often arithmetical, increase of vital food resources" (89). Actually, long-term trends in food supply and affordability, nutrition, and resulting measurements of health, stature, and longevity prove that food resources have grown more rapidly than human population—and this has occurred because people produce both the food and the capital and organizational resources that multiply agricultural productivity. It has also occurred despite the shift of larger and larger proportions of populations out of agriculture and into industry and services—or more precisely, increased agricultural productivity has made it possible for a few people to meet all the food needs of the world.

She consistently uses terms like *justice* and *fairness* without adequately defining them, particularly along Biblical lines. Her usage suggests an entitlement/distributivist rather than a desert-based definition, contrary to Biblical usage.[26] Both her failure to define these terms and her unbiblical use of them vitiate what is, granted her purpose of providing *ethical* grounds for population regulation, the most important chapter in the book—chapter 9, "Population Regulation and Justice," which assumes an entitlement (positive rights) theory of justice in which desiderata ("A mother should be able to safely bear and raise a child to maturity. . . . Everyone should have access to the basic necessities of life including food, water, clothing, housing, and health care. . . . Couples should be able to have children if they so desire. . . . Children should grow up having the opportunity for an education, a job or other socially productive role, marriage, and a family." [155–56]) substitute for the nonaggression (negative) rights entailed in, for example, the Ten Commandments.

Frequently Bratton lapses into vague generalizations that are worse than useless policy guidance because, by their very ambiguity, they provide justification for nearly any conceivable intrusion into private life: "Societal response to population processes is necessary when individual couples, desiring to attain [the desiderata cited in the previous paragraph here], behave in ways that prevent the above conditions from being met in the society at large. This could happen if the couples are only considering their own self-interest, if they have family goals that are not appropriate to current economic conditions, or if they do not have the societal support or the physical resources necessary to change their behavior" (156). She naively idealizes "democratic processes" as guarantees against statist oppression: "In order to preserve democratic processes and protect human rights, we can add a further criterion to the implementation of coercive methods and negative incentives: The implementation of coercive methods should not depart from democratic processes. The populace should favor and support any social sanctions or negative incentives . . ." (182). The twentieth century has witnessed the adoption of policies that have sacrificed millions on the alter of "democracy" in the totalitarian communist nations. Why, one such nation, now mercifully deceased, called itself the German *Democratic* Republic![27]

In discussions of ethics, Bratton shifts conveniently back and forth between highly principled and crudely utilitarian argumentation as need suits. She argues on utilitarian grounds that anti-abortion groups should not oppose government funding of family planning activities merely because those activities promote abortion, since "Stopping abortion funding saves fetuses, [but] that is all. It does not protect the newborn infants or their mothers and siblings from food shortages and disease outbreaks" (192). Four pages later, shifting to principled ground, she promotes as the ultimate cure for the world's ills "the completely pro-life position," which "requires that all activities that threaten human life, such as the development of nuclear weapons and the international arms race, be replaced by peaceful alternatives . . ." (196). Would the West's capitulation to Soviet hegemony have saved human lives? (Keep in mind that estimates of the numbers of their own people killed intentionally by Soviet governments in this century range from 15 million to 125 million.) Or might our production of nuclear and other high-technology weapons have deterred aggression and so saved lives? And granted that abortion has claimed nearly 30 million lives in the United States alone since 1973, and scores of millions more around the world, does failure to oppose policies that promote abortion comport with a "completely pro-life position"?

Sometimes she uses her utilitarian arguments in myopic ways: "Many anti-abortion activists from the developed world expect child survivorship patterns in the developing world to be similar to those in their own environments and assume that if a fetus is saved, a child is also saved. This is not the case" (193). In abortion, fetal mortality is essentially 100 percent; when children are born, infant and childhood mortality, even in the lowest-income nations of the world, averages less than 20 percent. That means stopping all abortions would instantaneously cause an improvement of over 80 percent in child survival. Sounds pretty "completely pro-life" to me. And this is not even to mention the morally significant difference between intentionally killing people and not being able to keep some living.

In short, *Six Billion and More*, while an *important* contribution to debate, suffers such serious moral, theoretical, and empirical flaws that it should not be embraced by thoughtful Christians as a truly *positive* contribution.

APPENDIX 4

     ❧   ❧

A Critique of the
Evangelical Declaration on the Care of Creation

[Following is the text—omitting illustrations and the editor's introduction—of my article "Are God's resources finite?" published in *World*, November 27, 1993, pp. 10–13.]

WHAT, ACCORDING TO THE DECLARATION, IS THE STATE OF THE ENVIronment? In a nutshell, "We and our children face a growing crisis in the health of the creation. . . . Yet we continue to degrade that creation." And the Christian's responsibility? ". . . to work for godly, just, and sustainable economies which reflect God's sovereign economy and enable men, women and children to flourish along with all the diversity of creation." In addition, Christians are "to work for responsible public policies which embody the principles of biblical stewardship of creation."

The vagueness of both points permeates the Declaration, shielding it from specific criticisms. Nonetheless, there is enough substance, in light of an earlier draft and relevant work by Calvin DeWitt, one of its chief authors, to reveal the underlying perspective.

Central to their document is the assertion that the "growing crisis in the health of the creation" consists of seven "degradations of creation": "(1) land degradation; (2) deforestation; (3) species extinction; (4) water degradation; (5) global toxification; (6) the alteration of atmosphere; (7) human and cultural degradation." The lack of specificity hinders attempts to test the Declaration for empirical veracity. The terms lend themselves to no direct empirical measurement. Only identifying specific concerns permits testing them.

Land Degradation: What is "land degradation"? Chief in the minds of

161

the authors was probably the belief, as the earlier draft put it, that "we continue to degrade the soil through unsustainable practices of agriculture and animal husbandry, leading to abandonment or decline in productivity of agricultural land." Not much here is open to direct empirical measurement. But the claim that we are experiencing a "decline in productivity of agricultural land" is measurable—and it is false. Cereal grain is the most important agricultural product. Worldwide, average world cereal grain yields per acre and production per person both rose steeply from 1950 to 1990. (Similar trends hold true not only for the world as a whole but for every major region and regardless of income level of the nations involved.) There is no reason to expect these trends to reverse.

Deforestation: The prior draft claimed: "In both tropical and temperate regions we are rapidly destroying forests. . . ." No quantification here, but perhaps the claim is based on annual deforestation data published in the World Bank's *World Development Report, 1993*, which reported, among others, annual deforestation of 13,800 square kilometers in Brazil's legal Amazon for 1990. But such numbers are meaningful only as proportions of total forest (in this case, about a fourth of 1 percent), in the context of long-term trends (in this case, the annual rate fell 23 percent from 1989 to 1990, and it has fallen consistently since the early 1980s), and in the context of overall numbers for the world and its major regions.

Although there has been significant net deforestation in some tropical rainforests in the past decade (especially in Brazil, Indonesia, and Mexico), worldwide data published by the United Nations Food and Agriculture Organization indicate that total forested area in both the temperate regions and the world as a whole was higher by the mid-1980s than it had been at the end of the 1940s—and rising.

The rainforest deforestation data can be deceptive also because they apply only to *natural* growth, and in the past decade *plantation* forests have contributed increasing amounts to total forested area, significantly reducing net deforestation.

Species Extinction: Neither the present version nor the earlier draft of the declaration specifies a rate or a long-term trend in species extinction, so we cannot know just what the authors claim is happening. Perhaps, however, they have in mind a claim like that of Calvin DeWitt, director of the evangelical Au Sable Institute of Environmental Studies, one of the Declaration's main authors and the only one with specific expertise in environmental science, in his introduction to *The Environment and the Christian*: "Three species of creatures are extinguished *daily*" (p. 15, emphasis original). That comes to about

1,100 species per year. At least DeWitt's claim is far lower than several numbers offered by Vice President Al Gore (with whom members of the Evangelical Environmental Network met before their October drafting conference) in his *Earth in the Balance*.[1]

However, there simply are no empirical data to back up *any* claims of specific rates of species extinction. Even such leading prophets of species extinction as Norman Myers and Thomas Lovejoy frankly admit this. The numbers are based on dubious extrapolations from presumed relationships between deforestation rates and species extinction. Until observational data are forthcoming—and they do not appear on the horizon—there is no good reason to believe that species extinctions are occurring much more rapidly today than they have for thousands of years of human history—that is, perhaps one per century.[2]

Water Degradation: Again, without specifics we can't be sure what the authors mean by "water degradation." The prior draft claimed, "We have used surface water carelessly, resulting both in depletion which threatens food production, and pollution which affects human health. In oceans, we have fished many stocks to the point of collapse, and diminish its productivity by using it as a sink for our wastes."

Consider freshwater. First, water is a renewable resource. Water consumed does not disappear; it reenters the ecosystem to be used again and again.

Second, according to World Bank data, most countries presently withdraw (temporarily for use before returning to the cycle) only a few percent of total domestic natural water resources (from rainfall and river flow) each year. There is, in fact, such abundance of fresh water relative to human use that one of the chief reasons for its abuse is its very low cost.

Third, additional supplies of fresh water, if needed, would be available anywhere in the world affordably by transport and desalination.

Fourth, if water pollution were an *increasing* threat to human health, data should reveal a downward trend in the availability of safe water. But worldwide access to safe water is increasing. (The slight downward curve [in an accompanying graph] for high-income nations from 1985 to 1990 appears to result from statistical sample anomalies, not from actual decreased access to safe water.)

Fifth, if water depletion were threatening food production, agricultural yields should be falling or costs rising, or both—the opposite is true.

There simply is no evidence that freshwater resources are significantly endangered. Local water pollution is a genuine problem, sometimes severe; but on a global scale, water pollution is insignificant and, in advanced economies, declining, as it will do as other economies grow to afford cleaner technologies.

Is pollution reducing marine fish populations? Not according to the best indicator we have—worldwide fisheries landings. United National Food and Agricultural Organization data show a steady increase not only in total landings from 1938 to 1990 (from about 20 to about 100 million metric tons) but also in landings per capita (from about 8 to about 18 kilograms per person). There is no indication that this trend has reached its peak and is about to reverse.

Global Toxification: Judging by its use in DeWitt's *The Environment and the Christian*, this term appears to refer to pollution with chemical like DDT. But no data support major worldwide damage done by such chemicals—indeed, DDT appears to have done little of the damage earlier attributed to it (and it paid great benefits by reducing populations of disease-bearing insects like mosquitos, which spread malaria in tropical regions). Indeed, biochemist Bruce Ames of the University of California at Berkeley has pointed out that over 99.9 percent of all chemical pesticide residues in the food supply are produced by plants and other organisms, not by man, and that natural pesticides tend to be more powerful and more broad-spectrum than manmade pesticides, which are genetically targeted and thus effective at much lower doses while posing little or no risk to man.

Alteration of Atmosphere: Apparently, granted the background both of the prior draft and of DeWitt's *The Environment and the Christian*, this vague term refers to alleged global warming and ozone depletion. But hard data do not support the claim either that global warming and long-term ozone depletion are occurring or that there is a significant correlation between human activity and global temperature and ozone trends.

Robert C. Balling, in *The Heated Debate*, a comprehensive book on the global warming controversy, points out that of the approximately 0.45 degrees-C century-long rise in global average temperatures, at most one-third might be attributable to human activity, and there are serious statistical, theoretical, and methodological reasons to question even that connection. (For instance, most of the increase occurred *before* human production of greenhouse gases began its strong rise in the middle of this century; it slowed significantly afterward.)

No one knows what is a "normal" concentration of stratospheric ozone. Our data stretch back only to the 1950s, and during that time fluctuations up and down have been about equally large; there is no discernible long-term downward trend. Furthermore, fluctuations in ozone concentration correlate better with fluctuations in energy output from the sun than with human emissions of alleged ozone-depleting chemicals like chloro-fluorocarbons.

Human and Cultural Degradation: It is not clear either what this category includes or how it fits into an *environmental* declaration. If it is meant to say something about human health and longevity, it is flatly wrong. Average life expectancy worldwide has risen from around 30, two centuries ago, to about 65 today, with nearly 50 percent of that gain occurring in the last 40 years. This trend reflects improvements in the quantity and quality of food, clothing, shelter, hygiene, health care, and safety made possible by the astounding and unabated economic growth the world has been experiencing for over two centuries.

These are just a few examples of factual errors underlying the view of the environment portrayed by the Declaration. They illustrate a disturbing tendency among the Declaration's authors to mimic the claims of crisis current in the popular press and the secular environmental movement without checking the credibility of those claims. Evangelical leaders contemplating endorsing the Declaration or joining the Network should insist that these problems be addressed.

The Declaration is not all bad news. Refreshingly, it recognizes that poverty often causes environmental degradation, and so it supports the growth of "just, free economies" that create the wealth necessary to protect and restore the environment. It rightly calls Christians to the responsibility of stewardship (although it never specifies much about what actions that entails). It warns that many people are turning, in vain, to non-Christian religions for guidance in thinking about the environment. It firmly asserts the distinction between Creator and creature that has crumbled in the minds of many environmentalists West and East.

The Declaration suffers, however, not only from false factual assumptions like those examined above but also from some important problems in theory and worldview.

Take, for instance, the idea that we should work for "sustainable economies." Precisely what is a "sustainable economy"? The Declaration doesn't make it clear, but if the phrase here borrows anything from its use in the secular environmentalist movement, it probably excludes the productive economies of the West, despite the demonstrable fact that these economies do better at protecting and even improving the natural environment than do less-developed economies.

More important are the theological weaknesses of the document. First, like many other Christian writings on the environment, the Declaration prominently quotes Psalm 24:1, "The earth is the LORD's, and the fullness thereof." This is meant to remind us that we are only stewards, not absolute owners, of anything on the earth. The reminder is valid, so long as it is not pressed to the point of denying any true ownership by people. The Bible maintains a careful balance, recognizing God's ultimate ownership but also man's subordinate ownership. It not only says that the earth is the Lord's, but also in Psalm 115:16 that "the earth He has given to the sons of men"—a passage never cited in the Declaration.

Second, in its final words, the Declaration equates "God's good garden" with "our earthly home," mirroring a mistake common to many Christian writings on the environment. (I made the mistake myself four years ago in writing *Prospects for Growth: A Biblical View of Population, Resources, and the Future*.) The error here is failing to distinguish the garden into which God put Adam and Eve and which He instructed them to cultivate and guard (Gen. 2:15) from the surrounding earth, much of which was wilderness and which God instructed mankind to fill, subdue, and rule (Gen. 1:28). More important, the Declaration never mentions the curse God placed on the earth because of human sin (Gen. 3:17), by which He subjected the earth "to futility . . . in hope that the creation itself also will be set free from its slavery to corruption into the freedom of the glory of the children of God" (Rom. 8:20-21). It is simply wrong, Biblically, to assume that nature untouched by human hands is better than nature transformed by wise, godly human stewardship.

Third, and most important, the Declaration claims that many of the degradations discussed above "are signs that we are pressing against the finite limits God has set for creation." It adds, "With continued population growth, these degradations will become more severe." Underlying this notion is the idea that people are a burden rather than a blessing to the earth, that they are to be viewed chiefly as consumers and polluters rather than as producers and restorers. Hence, the common notion that growing population is stripping the earth of its resources and choking it with pollution.

But Scripture presents a very different picture of mankind—particularly in light of the image of God and of the particular and common effects of the redeeming work of Christ on the cross. Although some parts of the Bible lead us to emphasize true knowledge and holiness (rationality and morality) as chief elements of the image of God in man (Col. 3:10 and Eph. 4:24), the immediate context of Genesis 1:26–28, which tells us that God created us in His image, suggests another emphasis, albeit related to these. Before reading, "Then God said, 'Let Us make man in Our image,'" we read, "In the beginning God created the heavens and the earth" (Gen. 1:1), and we enjoy a glittering saga of the abundance and variety God made. The immediate context of Genesis 1:26, then, suggests that creativity is a central aspect of the image of God in man.

True, man fell into sin, and that fall has had serious consequences, physical and spiritual, causal and judgmental, for the whole human race. It plunged us and our world into decay and death. But it did not obliterate the image of God, and more important, the redeeming death and the resurrection of Christ have set in motion the reversal of the curse. We should expect, therefore, to see even in unredeemed mankind some glimmer of God-given creativity—and we do. We should also expect to see multiplying creativity as the gospel and Kingdom of Christ spread over the globe—and we do.

In today's economies, driven by rapidly expanding knowledge (itself reflecting the image of God), human creativity is multiplying. In advanced economies, the average person produces several times more resources than he consumes in a lifetime, leaving following generations with more, not less, wealth per capita than existed before. This is precisely what we should predict based on the Biblical revelation of the image of God in man, of the effects of wise and diligent work, and of the transforming effects of the gospel. It is also borne out in long-term economic data showing falling prices for extractive resources (mineral, vegetable, and animal) and rising prices for people (labor). Since price is a measure of scarcity, the falling resource prices demonstrate diminishing resource scarcity, while the rising labor prices demonstrate—contrary to intuition in light of our growing numbers—increasing scarcity of people!

The Declaration completely ignores this creative aspect of human beings. The closest it comes to it is saying that we should "sustain creation's fruitfulness." Frankly, under the curse, creation isn't particularly fruitful: "Thorns and thistles it shall grow for you," says Genesis 3:18. Mere hunting and gathering of what grows naturally can support only one or two people per square mile in the best natural habitats, not the over 100 people per square mile living worldwide; it is by hard work that mankind transforms the cursed earth—the wilderness—into a garden.

Do Christians have a responsibility for the environment? Certainly, and the Evangelical Environmental Network is right to remind us of that. But we also have a responsibility to think and act in regard to the environment in a manner that reflects the full spectrum of Biblical revelation and a prudent regard for truth in empirical issues. The Evangelical Declaration on the Care of Creation, sadly, falls seriously short of these two ideals.

APPENDIX 5

❧   ❧

Issues and Evidence, Not *Ad Hominem*, Should Characterize Environmental Debate; A Response to Richard Wright

[The following is adapted from an article submitted to *Perspectives on Science and Christian Faith*, the journal of the American Scientific Affiliation, and scheduled for publication in December 1995.]

IN "TEARING DOWN THE GREEN: ENVIRONMENTAL BACKLASH IN THE Evangelical Sub-Culture,"[1] Richard Wright censures my *World* magazine critique of the *Evangelical Declaration on the Care of Creation* (EDCC) and my *Prospects for Growth*.

His comment that my critique of the EDCC "concludes that there is no serious environmental problem in the world today" (p. 83) is verbally almost identical to the description of that critique by Gordon Aeschliman in his editorial in *Prism*; he said I had written that ". . . there is no substantial environmental problem in the world today." My article itself, however, said nothing of the sort. One wonders whether Wright read my article or only Aeschliman's misrepresentation of it. What I did say is that the sorts of crises emphasized in the EDCC (and its prior draft, the best evidence we have of the specifics lying behind the vague generalizations that dominate the *Declaration*) lacked sound empirical evidential basis.

There are indeed severe environmental problems. The worst ones are in developing countries and in present and former communist countries. Among them are unsafe drinking water (mostly because of contamination by untreated human and animal sewage and by natural bacteria, often also because of contamination by agricultural and industrial wastes); serious air pollution (lead, ozone, particulates, carbon monoxide, and other vehicular and industrial emis-

sions); deforestation and desertification (the two sometimes interrelated) ow-
ing largely to the gathering of fuel wood by poor people in marginal ecosystems; and the deterioration of agricultural soils because of primitive practices.
Such problems are directly implicated in the poor health and early mortality
of hundreds of millions of people in the developing world.

But these are not the sorts of things on which the EDCC, particularly
when understood in light of its penultimate draft, focuses: global warming[2] (a
still hypothetical danger that has not yet caused any deaths and may never,
even if it turns out real), acid rain[3] (which, even if one accepts claims about
harm to forests and lakes—which there is good reason to doubt, according to
the National Acid Precipitation Assessment Program—has certainly not killed
anyone), ozone depletion[4] (another hypothetical threat that has not yet led to
measurable non-natural increases in ground-level UV-B and may never, and
that certainly has not yet killed millions of people); massive species extinction[5] (another hypothetical danger for which there is at present no good empirical evidence, and that again has certainly not killed anyone); and so on.
My critique argued in part that the EDCC's promotion of the crisis mentality
on these still-hypothetical problems hazards Christian environmentalism's
credibility. Perhaps I should have added that it puts the focus—and invites the
lion's share of money and effort to be spent—on problems that, to whatever
extent they turn out real, are unlikely to be nearly so dangerous as such present
and actual problems, as unsafe drinking water in developing countries, which
are associated with a low degree of economic development.

My article also argued, as did *Prospects for Growth*, that in most of these
cases trends are either toward improvement already or can be predicted to be
such as economic development continues. There is a very strong statistical
correlation between level of economic development and reduction of pollution.[6] Long-term economic forces and trends lead me to believe that economic
improvement in developing countries will lead to improvements in all of the
areas mentioned in the previous paragraph; indeed, in many such countries,
for most of the factors, improvement has already been under way for from
one to three decades, as reflected in such statistical sources as the World Bank's
Social Indicators of Development on Diskette (annual). (An example of such
is the marked improvement in access to safe drinking water in low- and middle-
income countries from 1970 to 1990: up by about 63 percent in twenty years—
by 92 percent [from 28 to 54 percent] in rural areas and by 10 percent [from
75 to 83 percent] in urban areas.[7])

Wright pejoratively refers to some of my sources—specifically Julian L.
Simon, Herman Kahn, S. Fred Singer, and Dixy Lee Ray—as "scientific"

sources. But as Gregg Easterbrook wrote in *A Moment on the Earth: The Coming Age of Environmental Optimism,* "A rule of argument is that when opponents attack someone's qualifications or motives rather than rebutting the substance of arguments, this happens because they do not know how to rebut the substance. Increasingly in the 1990s, doctrinaire environmentalists have been impugning the qualifications or integrity of those who disagree with them."[8] Wright's placing quotation marks around *scientific* is just such a case of *argumentum ad hominem* abusive.

Wright refers in his article to scientific work as including "demographic" work (p. 87). Perhaps he is unaware that Simon, an economist at the University of Maryland, is one of the world's leading demographic scholars, which implies that he is a scientist.[9] (So why the quotation marks?) Many people know of him only from popular articles and his popular *The Ultimate Resource* (which, by the way, still contains a great deal of good science). But his *The Economics of Population Growth* (1977) is one of the most thorough and sophisticated analyses of the subject ever published; regardless whether one agrees with his conclusions, it must be acknowledged as scientific work. (Does writing popular articles and books disqualify one as a scientist? Then what happens to Carl Sagan, Paul Ehrlich, Lester Brown, and other heroes of environmentalism? Indeed, what happens to the many leaders of the evangelical environmental movement who have written popular articles or books?) Kahn was a physicist and applied mathematician with the Rand Corporation, long-time director of the Hudson Institute (a non-partisan scientific research institute), and a science advisor to the Air Force, the Atomic Energy Commission, the federal Office of Economic Planning, the Office of the Secretary of Defense, and the Department of State.[10] Singer is a distinguished geophysicist, former professor of environmental sciences at the University of Virginia, and one of the earliest (and continuing) researchers on stratospheric ozone (inventor, in fact, of the standard stratospheric ozone measuring instrument) under NASA, and presently director of the Science and Environmental Policy Project.[11] Ray was a long-time member of the zoology faculty at the University of Washington, chairman of the Atomic Energy Commission, and assistant secretary of state in the U.S. Bureau of Oceans.[12] To be qualified as a scientist, must one agree with Wright?

Furthermore, in *Prospects for Growth* I cited Simon only on the economics of demography—on which he is a recognized authority; I cited Singer only once, on stratospheric ozone—on which he is a recognized authority; I cited Ray only twice, once for her short and clear description of the *unenhanced* greenhouse effect and once for the rather pedestrian point that correlation doesn't prove causation in studies of the etiology of disease (Would Wright like to argue with her at either of these points?); and I never cited Kahn (as opposed to scientists who contributed chapters to a book of which he was co-editor). My only citations of these scientists, then, were entirely legitimate. And Wright completely ignored the dozens of other fully credentialed scientists I also cited.

Wright criticizes me for not having used standard statistical sources from the World Bank, the World Resources Institute, and the Worldwatch Institute (p. 83). I did use evidence from the World Bank's *World Development Report* (annual) in *Prospects for Growth*, as well as from various other standard statistical sources. (In fact, a whole appendix of the book was nothing but statistical tables [most adapted from *WDR*] that provided the statistical basis for lengthy discussion of the economics of demography in chapter 6.) I did not rely on information from either the World Resources Institute (compiler of the annual *Environmental Almanac*) or the Worldwatch Institute (producer of the annual *The State of the World*) because both are advocacy organizations whose reports time and again have contained unreliable data and horribly unreliable predictions. (One might, for an interesting exercise, look back through Worldwatch Institute President Lester Brown's track record as a prophet of trends in resource availability, agricultural productivity, poverty, hunger, famine, and so on. It's not a pretty sight.[13])

Rather than committing genetic and *ad hominem* fallacies, it would have been considerably more helpful for Wright actually to have interacted with some of the demographic and economic arguments in *Prospects for Growth*. But if he had, would I have been justified in writing off his arguments since, after all, his formal training is not in the economics of demography but in biology? For that matter, should I write off his arguments about ozone and global warming because he is neither a climatologist nor an atmospheric chemist but a biologist? (No. Logic and evidence, not credentials, should prevail.)

Nowhere in *Prospects for Growth* or in my critique of the EDCC did I ever say that the environment should be protected "*only* because it is important to man" (p. 88, emphasis added), and I don't believe that. It should be protected first and foremost because that is one of the tasks God has given to man (Gen. 2:15; a point I did make in *Prospects for Growth*, pp. 23–4, despite Wright's implying that somehow I had completely ignored the verse), and obedience to God is the most important motive for any act. In addition, it should be protected for God's pleasure and man's benefit, and finally it should be protected for the benefit of other creatures, independent of man's benefit. And by the way, I never wrote—and don't believe—that the rest of creation should be *enslaved* to mankind; that is Wright's word, not mine.

The Christian scientific community would be better served by arguments that stick to issues and evidences and avoid *ad hominem* and straw man attacks.

NOTES

CHAPTER 1: The Rise of Evangelical Environmentalism

1. Charles Rubin points out the difficulty of defining *environment* any more closely—and the totalitarian implications of this difficulty for environmental policy—in *The Green Crusade: Rethinking the Roots of Environmentalism* (New York: The Free Press, 1994), 242–4. The book is an outstanding discussion of the political and social aspects of the environmental movement.

2. "Everything has been visited, everything known, everything exploited. Now pleasant estates obliterate the famous wilderness areas of the past. Plowed fields have replaced forests, domesticated animals have dispersed wildlife. Beaches are plowed, mountains smoothed and swamps drained. There are as many cities as, in former years, there were dwellings. Islands do not frighten, nor cliffs deter. Everywhere there are buildings, everywhere people, everywhere communities, everywhere life. . . . Proof [of this crowding] is the density of human beings. We weigh upon the world; its *resources hardly suffice to support us.* As our needs grow larger, so do our protests, that already *nature does not sustain us.* In truth, plague, famine, wars and earthquakes must be regarded as a blessing to civilization, since they prune away the luxuriant growth of the human race." Emphasis added. From *Opera II: Opera monastica,* cited in David Herlihy, *Medieval Households* (Cambridge: Harvard University Press, 1985), 24, and—from Herlihy—in Susan Power Bratton, *Six Billion & More: Human Population Regulation and Christian Ethics* (Louisville, KY: Westminster/John Knox Press, 1992), 76. This citation is from Bratton.

3. Dave Foreman, *Confessions of an Eco-Warrior* (New York: Harmony Books, 1991), 11.

4. Aldo Leopold, *A Sand County Almanac, with Essays on Conservation from Round River* (New York: Ballantine Books, [1949] 1970).

175

5. Wesley Granberg-Michaelson, *Ecology and Life: Accepting Our Environmental Responsibility*, Issues of Christian Conscience, ed. Vernon Grounds (Waco, TX: Word Books, 1988), 69.

6. Undated press release by EEN/ESA received by the author as an enclosure with a letter dated November 17, 1993, from EEN Associate Allen Johnson.

7. This Society should be carefully distinguished from the International Green Cross, which is associated with former Soviet Premier Mikhail Gorbachev. The two are unrelated, and according to a notice in *Green Cross* (Winter 1995, p. 19), Gorbachev's group "has been making numerous erroneous statements in its public literature and . . . does not meet the standards for integrity [for] charitable groups" required by the New York Philanthropic Advisory Service. The notice adds, "Our understanding is that for legal reasons the Gorbachev group may not use the Green Cross name in the United States and its activities must take place under the name 'Global Green.'"

CHAPTER 2: Evangelical Environmental Worldview and Theology

1. Transcript taken from tape of "Chicago Talks," Friday, January 21, 1994.

2. Richard A. Young, *Healing the Earth: A Theocentric Perspective on Environmental Problems and Their Solutions* (Nashville: Broadman & Holman, 1994).

3. Loren Wilkinson, "New Age, New Consciousness, and the New Creation," in *Tending the Garden: Essays on the Gospel and the Earth*, edited by Wesley Granberg-Michaelson (Grand Rapids: Eerdmans, 1987), 6–29.

4. E.g., Loren Wilkinson, ed., *Earthkeeping in the Nineties: Stewardship of Creation*, rev. ed. (Grand Rapids: Eerdmans, 1991), 317; Young, *Healing the Earth*, 88; *Evangelical Declaration on the Care of Creation*, epigram.

5. Doing that is not the purpose of this book. I have taken steps toward it in *Prosperity and Poverty: The Compassionate Use of Resources in a World of Scarcity* (Westchester, IL: Crossway Books, 1988), chapters 11–13, *Prospects for Growth: A Biblical View of Population, Resources, and the Future* (Westchester, IL: Crossway Books, 1990), chapters 2–3, 9–10, and "Classical Problems in Politics," Introductory Lecture to the Politics Segment of Interdisciplinary Studies 116, Self in Society II (Lookout Mountain, GA: Covenant College, 1994, unpublished; available from the author).

6. Barry Commoner, *The Closing Circle: Nature, Man, and Technology* (New York: Alfred A. Knopf, 1971), 39; cited in Young, *Healing the Earth*, 52.

7. Vincent Rossi, "Theocentrism: The Cornerstone of Christian Ecology," in Wesley Granberg-Michaelson, *Ecology and Life: Accepting Our Environmental Responsibility*, Issues of Christian Conscience Series, ed. Vernon Grounds (Waco, TX: Word, 1988), 151–60: 158–9.

8. Lionel Basney, *An Earth-Careful Way of Life: Christian Stewardship and the Environmental Crisis* (Downers Grove, IL: InterVarsity, 1994), 39.

9. Basney, *Earth-Careful*, 46.

10. Various evangelical works on environmental ethics rightly point out that *nature* and *creation* have very different implications, the former secularizing and the latter reminding us of the world's origin and God's authority over it. Certainly a secularist notion of autonomous nature has no part in an evangelical environmental ethic. But not every use of *nature* implies secularism. More often the term simply denotes things as they occur apart from human intervention. That is how I use it here.

11. Beisner, *Prosperity and Poverty*, 28–9, and *Prospects for Growth*, 23–4.

12. Wilkinson, ed., *Earthkeeping*, 286–7. For similar equation of the earth and the Garden of Eden, see Young, *Healing the Earth*, 163; *Evangelical Declaration on the Care of Creation*, last sentence; William Dyrness, "Stewardship of the Earth in the Old Testament," in *Tending the Garden: Essays on the Gospel and the Earth*, edited by Wesley Granberg-Michaelson (Grand Rapids: Eerdmans, 1987), 54–55; Orin Gelderloos, *Eco-Theology: The Judeo-Christian Tradition and the Politics of Ecological Decision Making* (Glasgow: Wild Goose Publications, 1992), 13; Wesley Granberg-Michaelson, *Ecology and Life: Accepting Our Environmental Responsibility*, Issues of Christian Conscience, edited by Vernon Grounds (Waco, TX: Word Books, 1988), 57; Bruce C. Birch, "Nature, Humanity, and Biblical Theology: Observations Toward a Relational Theology of Nature," in Granberg-Michaelson, *Ecology and Life*, 143–50: 147–8; Evangelical Environmental Network, "Biblical Roots: Theological Foundations for Celebrating God's Creation," 11–12 (part of *A Starter Kit for Evangelical Churches to Care for God's Creation* distributed by the EEN and World Vision); Calvin B. DeWitt, ed., *The Environment and the Christian: What Can We Learn from the New Testament?* (Grand Rapids: Baker, 1991), 7.

13. The sense in which each of these environments—the earth, Eden, the Garden, the two special trees—was good may have differed in important ways. Perhaps one way in which the earth was good was as a domain in which Adam, God's image-bearer, would learn to exercise dominion; one way in which Eden was good was as an initial locale for man's transformational labors; one way in which the Garden was good was as an initial home and sanctuary for man, where he would commune with God; and one way in which the two trees were good was as tests of Adam's submission to God's rule.

14. James B. Jordan, *Through New Eyes: Developing a Biblical View of the World* (Brentwood, TN: Wolgemuth & Hyatt, 1988), 148. I am indebted to Jordan for the insights expressed here.

15. Jordan, *Through New Eyes*, chapter 12.

16. Basney, *Earth-Careful*, 31.

17. Calvin B. DeWitt, ed., *The Environment and the Christian: What Can We Learn from the New Testament?* (Grand Rapids: Baker, 1991), 114. It goes without saying that DeWitt is mistaken in saying that people have created our "social,

economic, and political structures" in "creation's garden." The Garden of Eden ceased to exist—and essentially the whole earth became wilderness—with the Flood.

18. Thomas Hobbes, *Leviathan* (I.13), edited by C. B. MacPherson (1651; New York: Penguin, 1978), 186.

19. See, e.g., Catharina J. M. Halkes, *New Creation: Christian Feminism and the Renewal of the Earth*, trans. Catherine Romanik (1989; Louisville, KY: Westminster/John Knox Press, 1991).

20. Wilkinson, ed., *Earthkeeping*, 286–7; Gelderloos, *Eco-Theology*, 13.

21. *Subdue* translates the Hebrew *kâbash*, to subdue, to bring into bondage, from a primitive root meaning to tread down or beat down, to make a path, to press or squeeze or knead, or to attack or assault; to bring into bondage; etc. (In addition to Genesis 1:28, see Numbers 32:20–22, 32:29, Joshua 18:1, and 1 Chronicles 22:17–19, the subduing of the land of Palestine, including the hostile nations in it, by Israel; 2 Chronicles 28:9–10, the subduing of Judah by Samaria to make them slaves; Nehemiah 5:5 and Jeremiah 34:11, 16, making slaves; Esther 7:8, to subdue or force a woman; Micah 7:19, subduing iniquities; Zechariah 9:15, subduing enemies in warfare.) *Rule* translates *râdâh*, to have dominion, chastise, tread, trample, or prevail against. (In addition to Genesis 1:26, 28, see Leviticus 25:39, 43, 46, Israelites are forbidden to rule fellow Israelite bondslaves with rigor; 26:17, if Israel rebels its enemies will reign over it; Numbers 24:19, Messiah will "have dominion, and shall destroy him that remaineth of the city"; Judges 5:13, Deborah had dominion over the mighty in battle; 1 Kings 4:24, Solomon had dominion over the land and kings from Tiphsah to Azzah; 5:16, 9:23, and 2 Chronicles 8:10, officers ruled over workers; Nehemiah 9:28, Israel's enemies had dominion over it; Psalm 49:14, the upright shall have dominion over fools; 68:27, Benjamin had dominion; 72:8, (Messiah) the king shall have dominion from sea to sea; 11:2, Messiah shall rule in the midst of His enemies; Isaiah 14:2, 6, restored Israel shall rule over its oppressors, who once ruled over it; 41:2, God subdues kings before the ruler from the east; Jeremiah 5:31, the priests bear rule in oppression over the people; Lamentations 1:13, Judah's conqueror prevailed against it; Ezekiel 29:15, humbled Egypt shall no more rule over the nations; 34:4, the shepherds of Israel ruled the people with cruelty.) In contrast, *till* translates *'âbad*, to labor, work, or do work; to work for another; to serve as subjects, while *keep* translates *shâmar*, to keep, watch, preserve, guard, wait for, or retain. Francis Brown, S. R. Driver, and Charles A. Briggs, edd., *A Hebrew and English Lexicon of the Old Testament*, trans. Edward Robinson (Oxford: Clarendon Press, [1907] 1978), 461, 712–13, 921–2, and 1036.

22. Gelderloos, *Eco-Theology*, 13.

23. Wilkinson, ed., *Earthkeeping*, 287.

24. Brown, Driver, and Briggs, *Hebrew and English Lexicon*, 1036.

25. C. F. Keil and F. Delitzsch, *Commentary on the Old Testament*, 10 vol-

umes, volume 1, *The Pentateuch*, 3 volumes in 1, translated by James Martin (Grand Rapids: Eerdmans, 1976 rpt.), 1:84.

26. Young, *Healing the Earth*, 163.

27. I do not, by using the word *theonomous*, identify with the school of thought known as theonomy associated with writers Greg Bahnsen, Rousas John Rushdoony, and Gary North. The word simply states well the opposition between autonomy (law of the self, in this case human law unrestricted by God's law) and theonomy (law of God). Although I respect much of their work, I am for very specific reasons not a theonomist in their sense of the term.

28. Wilkinson, ed., *Earthkeeping*, 294.

29. Putting a priority on human life must not be confused with anthropocentrism, a view with which many environmentalists have wrongly charged Christianity (see appendix 2). Christianity is neither anthropocentric nor biocentric nor even ecocentric but theocentric. It does, nonetheless, also promote a hierarchy of values: God, man, other sentient life, nonsentient life, and nonliving matter. See Young, *Healing the Earth*, chapter 10, and Vincent Rossi, "Theocentrism: The Cornerstone of Christian Ecology," in Wesley Granberg-Michaelson, *Ecology and Life: Accepting Our Environmental Responsibility*, Issues of Christian Conscience Series, edited by Vernon Grounds (Waco, TX: Word, 1988), 151–60.

30. Thus the following comment by Lionel Basney is simply fatuous: "'Is there such a thing,' Wendell Berry asks, 'as a Christian stripmine?' Obviously not. Its damage to the natural world, its expression of greed, dishonesty, waste and callousness make it one of the things you probably cannot do in the strength of Christ." Basney, *Earth-Careful*, 50.

31. E.g.: DeWitt, *Earth-Wise*, 50; *Evangelical Declaration on the Care of Creation*, "God declares all creation 'good' (Gen. 1:31); Wesley Granberg-Michaelson, *Ecology and Life: Accepting Our Environmental Responsibility*, Issues of Christian Conscience, ed. Vernon Grounds (Waco, TX: Word Books, 1988), 52; H. Paul Santmire, "God's Joyous Valuing of Nature," in Granberg-Michaelson, *Ecology and Life*, 178–81: 178.

32. "Chicago Talks," January 21, 1994, transcript. The propensity to confuse the Curse with the Fall is common in evangelical environmental writings. E.g.:

> We believe that the whole of God's creation is under the curse of sin and is suffering as a result of this condition. Sin affects the whole of human life, causing us to labor to eat, to fight disease and decay constantly, and to live governed by a self-centeredness that prompts us to take advantage of the rest of creation for our own selfish motives. Even nature suffers from disease, decay, and destruction.
>
> This state of affairs has resulted from and results in a severing of relationships—between God and God's creation, between human beings, and between humanity and the rest of creation. The universal need of all creation is thus to be

put back into right relationship with God (the Creator), with humanity, and with nature. [James W. Gustafson, "Integrated Holistic Development and the World Mission of the Church," in *Missionary Earthkeeping*, edited by Calvin B. DeWitt and Ghillean T. Prance (Macon, GA: Mercer University Press, 1992), 111–47: 114.]

The ground is cursed because we are set against it. Significantly, the word here translated "ground" is *adamah*, which suggests that the curse pronounced on *Adam* is in fact describing a division within himself. That division is his own inability to be at harmony with the earth—his tendency to regard his difference from nature as enmity with nature. In short, the curse describes not a quality in the earth itself, but human misuse of dominion. An accurate reading of the Hebrew would be: "cursed is the ground *to you*."
Because of this attitude of enmity between people and nature, humanity has lost its ability to be the "preserver" of the garden in which it was placed. This loss is poignantly implied in the statement that God "placed the cherubim, and a flaming sword which turned every way, to guard the way to the tree of life" (Gen. 3:24). [Note here the conflation of the tree of life with the whole garden, and in the broader context the conflation of the garden with the whole earth.] The word "guard" translates the same word, *shamar*, used to describe humanity's failed task in the garden. Their misunderstanding of dominion, a dominion that issues in enmity, makes humans unable to "guard" or "preserve" the life of the garden. It is an inability we still see manifested today. [Wilkinson, ed., *Earthkeeping*, 290.]

All of Scripture and history point to the fact that we cannot return to Eden. Our entire human condition is cursed by the Fall, and that includes creation, which, according to the Bible, groans in anticipation of its day of redemption. [Tony Campolo and Gordon Aeschliman, *50 Ways You Can Help Save the Planet* (Downers Grove, IL: InterVarsity Press, 1992), 10.]

33. DeWitt, *Earth-Wise*, 35.

34. Wilkinson, ed., *Earthkeeping*, 62.

35. Many environmental writers, evangelical and otherwise, lament the influence of Francis Bacon on modern science because Bacon saw nature as something to be conquered and science as a means of conquering it. (E.g., Wilkinson, ed., *Earthkeeping*, 157–66.) Perhaps the Baconian perspective is more belligerent toward nature than Scripture warrants, but at least it did take the Curse seriously and see applied science as one means of reasserting dominion.

36. DeWitt, *Earth-Wise*, 45.

37. *Evangelical Review of Theology* 17:2 (April 1993, special issue, "Evangelicals and the Environment: Theological Foundations for Christian Environmental Stewardship," edited by J. Mark Thomas), 124–5.

38. Rossi, "Theocentrism, 158–9.

39. Basney, *Earth-Careful*, 39.

40. Gregg Easterbrook, *A Moment on the Earth: The Coming Age of Environmental Optimism* (New York: Viking, 1995), chapters 4, 6, 8, and 10.

41. Young, *Healing the Earth*, 139–42.

42. Wilkinson, ed., *Earthkeeping*, 298–306; Granberg-Michaelson, *Ecology and Life*, 60–63, 116; Dennis E. Testerman, "Missionary Earthkeeping: Glimpses of the Past, Visions of the Future," in *Missionary Earthkeeping*, ed. Calvin B. DeWitt and Ghillean T. Prance (Macon, GA: Mercer University Press, 1992), 11–44: 12; Bruce C. Birch, "Nature, Humanity, and Biblical Theology: Observations Toward a Relational Theology of Nature," in Granberg-Michaelson, *Ecology and Life*, 143–50: 148–9; Ronald Manahan, "Christ as the Second Adam," and Raymond C. Van Leeuwen, "Christ's Resurrection and the Creation's Vindication," in *The Environment and the Christian: What Can We Learn from the New Testament?*, edited by Calvin B. DeWitt (Grand Rapids: Baker, 1991).

43. Wilkinson, ed., *Earthkeeping*, 298.

44. See E. Calvin Beisner, "A Little Lower Than the Angels," Lecture One of the Staley Distinguished Christian Scholar Lecture Series, Covenant College, October 29–31, 1991, published as *Man, Economy, and the Environment in Biblical Perspective* (Moscow, ID: Canon Press, 1994). I develop this point further in chapter 7 of the present work. For some discussion of how the Christian world view affected the development of science and market economies, see: Francis A. Schaeffer, *How Should We Then Live?* (Old Tappan, NJ: Revell, 1976; reprinted in *The Complete Works of Francis A. Schaeffer: A Christian Worldview*, 5 volumes (Westchester, IL: Crossway Books, 1982), 5:83–287, chapters 2–7; Nathan Rosenberg and L. E. Birdzell, Jr., *How the West Grew Rich: The Economic Transformation of the Industrial World* (New York: Basic Books, 1986), chapter 2; Stanley L. Jaki, *The Savior of Science* (Washington: Regnery Gateway, 1988) and *Scientist and Catholic: Pierre Duhem* (Front Royal, VA: Christendom Press, 1991).

45. See Robert Nisbet, *History of the Idea of Progress* (New Brunswick, NJ: Transaction, 1993).

46. This line of reasoning prompts serious questioning of the fashionable condemnations of Western culture and technology that occur frequently in evangelical and other environmentalists' literature. It is particularly ironic that evangelicals committed to the Reformed tradition of cultural transformation should be so quick to condemn Western culture and embrace other cultures. If the very culture that has been more heavily influenced by Christianity for two millennia, and by Protestant Christianity for four centuries, must consistently be condemned in comparison with Native American, Asian, African, and Latin American cultures, one wonders why Christians should bother trying to transform cultures. For examples of such thought, see Brian J. Walsh and J. Richard Middleton, *The Transforming Vision: Shaping a Christian World View* (Downers Grove, IL: InterVarsity Press, 1984); Wilkinson, ed., *Earthkeeping*, chapters 6–9; Stephen V. Monsma, ed., *Responsible Technology: A Christian Perspective* (Grand Rapids: Eerdmans, 1986).

47. The exception is wood. Why? Because until the last half century natural wood supplies have been so plentiful as to make plantation forestry barely competitive, if at all. Hence people have rarely intentionally cultivated wood, until recently. Now, however, with the expanding use of plantation forestry, we shall begin to see long-term downward trends in wood prices. In other words, wood is now undergoing the same economic process that food and other resources underwent long ago: a transition from declining supplies and consequently rising prices while people depended largely on natural supplies, to rising supplies and consequently declining prices as people turned from natural sources to intentionally produced sources.

48. Who mistakenly assert that entropy is an aspect of the Curse rather than of creation. As North points out, without entropy, Adam and Eve could not even have smelled the flowers in the Garden of Eden. Entropy, like everything else in creation, has come under the Curse, and therefore some of its effects are now destructive, but it is not itself part of the Curse.

49. Misconceptions of the Second Law of Thermodynamics abound. Here is a good definition of it:

> Closely associated with the concept of changes in entropy is **the second law of thermodynamics**. One statement of the second law is: *The total amount of entropy in nature is increasing.* Although we can pick out many natural processes that may involve increases in the degree of ordering (for example, the precipitation of salts in salt lakes or the growth of living organisms), other processes are taking places that decrease the order of nature (for example, the evaporation of water or the decay of organisms). The overall effects of the latter processes appear greater than of the former *in the part of the universe we observe* [emphasis added].
>
> Another way in which the second law is stated is: *In any spontaneous change the amount of free energy available decreases.* This is one way of saying that natural processes go downhill. A familiar example of the second law is that heat cannot pass from a colder to a hotter body without the action of some external agency. [Charles W. Keenan and Jesse H. Wood, *General College Chemistry*, 3d ed. (New York: Harper & Row, 1966), 420; emphases original except where noted.]

North comments on the authors' qualification, "in the part of the universe we observe":

> They do not explicitly argue that for every local decrease in disorder (decrease in entropy) there must be an even greater increase in disorder *for the universe as a whole*. They just state that in any part of the universe we observe, this is what we find. [Jeremy] Rifkin universalizes the process; so, for that matter, do most other scientists. They have done so ever since Rudolph Clausius first formulated the second law in 1850.

A textbook account informs the student that when a gas is in equilibrium, with its molecules randomly bouncing against the walls of a container—a container through which energy does not flow (a hypothetical condition that is never achieved in the real world)—the experimenter can draw some rigorously scientific conclusions. The second law officially applies only to this hypothetical *and impossible* condition: a perfectly closed system in equilibrium. This is why the main branch of the science of thermodynamics is called *equilibrium* thermodynamics. This is the thermodynamics of the textbooks. [Gary North, *Is the World Running Down? Crisis in the Christian Worldview* (Tyler, TX: Institute for Christian Economics, 1988), 50.]

It is not the thermodynamics of the real world.

50. E.g., Psalm 104:29–30: "When you hide your face, [the animals] are terrified; when you take away their breath, they die and return to the dust. When you send your Spirit, they are created, and you renew the face of the earth."

51. For this reason the insistently repeated calls among many evangelical thinkers for rejecting Platonic dualism need to be offset by the reminder that while Plato and the neo-Platonists were wrong in considering the material body a restricting prison of the soul, they were right in insisting that the soul was not dependent on the body for its existence (e.g., 2 Corinthians 5:8; James 2:26). While Platonic ethical dualism is false, metaphysical dualism is true.

52. It is alarming, therefore, that a psychology textbook commonly used in evangelical colleges explicitly embraces a metaphysical materialist view of the mind. See David G. Myers and Malcolm A. Jeeves, *Psychology Through the Eyes of Faith* (New York Harper and Row, 1987), 21–2. This unbiblical view has serious destructive implications for our understanding of man's role in the universe. According to this view, the mind is utterly dependent—even for its very existence—on the material world. This implies that the mind cannot effect a reversal of the entropy process. Hence, anyone who accepts the materialist psychology must reject the notion that the human mind, made in God's image to be creative, can reverse the entropy process. Anyone who thinks thus falls readily captive, therefore, to the notion that human beings inevitably are exhausting natural resources. For examples of such thinking, see Jeremy Rifkin (with Ted Howard), *The Emerging Order: God in the Age of Scarcity* (New York: Ballantine, [1979] 1983), and Rifkin (with Howard), *Entropy: A New World View* (New York: Bantam New Age Books, [1980] 1981). It should be no surprise that Rifkin, a Marxist, embraces this materialist psychology and its worldview implications; it is lamentable that some evangelicals (see, for another example, John White's ironically titled *Putting the Soul Back in Psychology: When Secular Values Ignore Spiritual Realities* [Downers Grove, IL: InterVarsity, 1987]) have embraced it.

53. C. S. Lewis, *Miracles: A Preliminary Study* (1946; New York: Macmillan, 1978), chapter 6: ". . . a supernatural event is present in every rational man. The presence of human rationality in the world is therefore a Miracle. . . ."

54. Adopting this perspective and the implications I have outlined would entail relinquishing some claims evangelical environmentalists have made regarding resource exhaustion. For instance, this perspective is not consistent, in my understanding, with the *Evangelical Declaration on the Care of Creation*'s insistence "that we are pressing against the finite limits God has set for creation" and that "With continued population growth, these degradations will become more severe."

CHAPTER 3: The Hazards of Developing an Ethic of Environmental Stewardship

1. Other evangelical environmentalists have also discussed environmental ethics, but it is both convenient and, I think, fruitful to carry on sustained interaction with one source, and the criteria suggested in *Earthkeeping* seem to me to be at least as sensible as those found elsewhere and are more systematic and comprehensive than most.

2. Loren Wilkinson, ed., *Earthkeeping in the Nineties: Stewardship of Creation*, rev. ed. (Grand Rapids: Eerdmans, 1991), 351.

3. Augustine, *Letters* cxiii. 3. 22 (MPL 33. 442); cited in John Calvin, *Institutes of the Christian Religion*, II.ii.11.

4. See E. Calvin Beisner, *Prosperity and Poverty: The Compassionate Use of Resources in a World of Scarcity* (Westchester, IL: Crossway Books, 1988), 144–45; Friedrich A. Hayek, "The Pretense of Knowledge," Acceptance Address for the Nobel Prize in Economics, 1975, in Hayek, *Unemployment and Monetary Policy: Government as Generator of the "Business Cycle"* (San Francisco: Cato Institute, 1979), 23–36: 36. Precisely such considerations led to Adam Smith's preference for an economics of personal freedom and underlie his doctrine of the "invisible hand" (by which he meant not some mechanical structure of the universe but the personal providence of God). See Adam Smith, *The Theory of Moral Sentiments*, IV.i.10; *History of Astronomy*, III.2; *History of Ancient Physics*, 9; *An Inquiry into the Nature and Causes of the Wealth of Nations*, IV.ii.2. For extended discussion of the role of humility in economic thought, see my "Stewardship in a Free Market," in *The Christian Vision: Morality and the Marketplace*, edited by Michael Bauman (Hillsdale, MI: Hillsdale College Press, 1994), 17–35.

In the narrowest sense, "the rule of law" is "the supremacy of law," a legal principle—or bundle of principles—that "provides that decisions should be made by the application of known principles or laws without the intervention of discretion in their application" (*Black's Law Dictionary*, 5th ed., 1196). More broadly, it is a synonym for justice: the impartial application to all people of transcendent law. It is to be distinguished from mere legislation or legality, positive (legislatively adopted) laws being themselves sometimes contrary to the rule of law. It may also be distinguished from mere legislation as formal laws from substantive rules. "The difference between the two kinds of rules is the same as that between laying down a Rule of the Road . . . and ordering people where to go; or, better still, between providing signposts and commanding people which road to take." (Friedrich A. Hayek, *The Road to Serfdom* [Chicago: University of Chicago Press, 1994], 74.) The rule of law "means that government in all its actions is bound by rules fixed and announced beforehand—rules which make it possible to foresee with fair certainty how the authority will use its coercive powers in given circumstances and to plan one's individual affairs on the basis of this knowledge" (ibid., 72). "General rules, genuine laws as distinguished from specific orders, must therefore be intended to operate in circumstances which cannot be foreseen in detail, and, therefore, their effect on particular ends or particular people cannot be known beforehand. It is in this sense alone that it is at all possible for the legislator to be impartial" (ibid., 76; see Leviticus 19:15: "Do not pervert justice; do not show partiality to the poor or favoritism to the great, but judge your neighbor fairly"; compare Exodus 23:2, 3, 6, 8; Deuteronomy 24:17). An implication of the rule of law is that even the highest governing authorities are themselves subject to the rule of law, not above it. Sad to say, this principle, once the cardinal postulate of jurisprudence, is little known even in law schools today. For explanation of the rule of law, see Hayek, The *Road to Serfdom*, chapter 6, "Planning and the Rule of Law"; Bruno Leoni, *Freedom and the Law*, 3d ed. (Indianapolis: Liberty Fund, 1991), chapter 3, "Freedom and the Rule of Law"; A. V. Dicey, *Introduction to the Study of the Law of the Constitution*, 8th ed. (Indianapolis: Liberty Fund, [1885; 1915] 1982), Part II, "The Rule of Law." For the specific principle that governing authorities are subject to the rule of law, see Samuel Rutherford, L*ex, Rex, or The Law and the Prince; A Dispute for the Just Prerogative of King and People* . . . (London: John Field, 1644; reprint edition, Harrisonburg, VA: Sprinkle Publications, 1982); Algernon Sidney, *Discourses Concerning Government* (London: J. Toland, 1698; new edition with introduction by E. G. West, Indianapolis: Liberty Fund, 1990).

5. See comments on the rule of law in the previous note.

6. Wilkinson, ed., *Earthkeeping*, 351.

7. See E. Calvin Beisner, "Justice and Poverty: Two Views Contrasted," in *Christianity and Economics in the Post-Cold War Era: The Oxford Declaration and Beyond*, edited by Herbert Schlossberg, Vinay Samuel, and Ronald J. Sider (Grand Rapids: Eerdmans, 1994), 57–80; Beisner, *Prosperity and Poverty: The Compassionate Use of Resources in a World of Scarcity* (Westchester, IL: Crossway Books, 1988), chapters 4–5; Walter Block, "Private Property and Wealth Creation," in *The Capitalist Spirit: Toward a Religious Ethic of Wealth Creation*, edited by Peter L. Berger (San Francisco: Institute for Contemporary Studies Press, 1990), 107–28. See also the discussion of the rule of law in note 4 above.

8. *The Oxford Declaration on Christian Faith and Economics*, paragraphs

38, 39, in *Christianity and Economics in the Post-Cold War Era*, edited by Schlossberg, Samuel, and Sider, 22. The *Declaration* inconsistently sets right alongside this impartiality-and-desert-based (negative rights) definition of justice a needs-based (positive rights) definition of justice that conflicts with it. The former is Biblical, the latter not. The point was a matter of intense debate during the Oxford Conference on Christian Faith and Economics in 1990 and led to the publication of papers defending both views: my "Justice and Poverty: Two Views Contrasted" and Stephen Charles Mott's "The Partiality of Biblical Justice: A Response to Calvin Beisner," both in Chr*istianity and Economics in the Post-Cold War Era*.

9. Wilkinson, ed., *Earthkeeping*, 352.

10. Wilkinson, ed., *Earthkeeping*, 352.

11. Julian L. Simon, *The Ultimate Resource* (Princeton, NJ: Princeton University Press, 1981), 93; emphasis original.

12. Wilkinson, ed., *Earthkeeping*, 352.

13. Gregg Easterbrook, *A Moment on the Earth: The Coming Age of Environmental Optimism* (New York: Viking, 1995), 644; emphasis original.

14. Wilkinson, ed., *Earthkeeping*, 352.

15. Many environmental writers urge us to adopt an old Iroquois custom of making no decision without first considering its effect on the next seven generations. How anyone in 1715 could have foreseen enough about us today—or how we could foresee enough about anyone in 2275—to apply that knowledge to decisions is beyond me.

16. Wilkinson, ed., *Earthkeeping*, 353.

17. Leonard E. Read, "I, Pencil: My Family Tree as Told to Leonard E. Read" (New York: Foundation for Economic Education, n.d.).

18. Hayek, "The Pretense of Knowledge," 24.

19. Wilkinson, ed., *Earthkeeping*, 353.

20. Wilkinson, ed., *Earthkeeping*, 353–54.

21. Wilkinson, ed., *Earthkeeping*, 354.

22. See George Grantham, "Agricultural Productivity Before the Green Revolution," and Dennis Avery, "Trends in Food Productivity," both in *The State of Humanity*, edited by Julian L. Simon (Oxford: Blackwell, 1995). In chapter 5 I discuss the claims (a) that vast amounts of American farmland are being converted to urban uses and (b) that the adequacy of American cropland is threatened by rapid topsoil loss through erosion.

23. Wilkinson, ed., *Earthkeeping*, 354.

24. For a serious attempt to discuss the ethics of population regulation, see Susan Power Bratton, *Six Billion and More: Human Population Regulation and Christian Ethics* (Louisville, KY: Westminster/John Knox Press, 1992). Much of Bratton's discussion of the ethical problems is commendable. For a critique of her book, however, see appendix 3.

25. Wilkinson, ed., *Earthkeeping*, 354–5.

26. We should be careful, however, to distinguish economic from technical efficiency. That a given energy technology is the most advanced or technically efficient does not necessarily mean that it is the most economically efficient at a given time or place. See Beisner, Pro*spects for Growth*, 36–37.

27. Wilkinson, ed., *Earthkeeping*, 355.

28. Wilkinson, ed., *Earthkeeping*, 355.

29. See Beisner, *Prospects for Growth*, 122–24, and Bernard Cohen, "The Risks of Nuclear Power," in *The State of Humanity*, edited by Julian L. Simon (Oxford: Blackwell, 1995).

30. Wilkinson, ed., *Earthkeeping*, 355–56.

31. Wilkinson, ed., *Earthkeeping*, 356.

32. Wilkinson, ed., *Earthkeeping*, 356.

33. Wilkinson, ed., *Earthkeeping*, 357.

34. See Beisner, *Prosperity and Poverty*, chapter 8; Ronald H. Nash, *Poverty and Wealth: The Christian Debate Over Capitalism* (Westchester, IL: Crossway Books, 1986), chapter 4; James D. Gwartney and Richard L. Stroup, *Economics: Private and Public Choice*, 4th ed. (San Diego: Harcourt Brace Jovanovich, 1987), 7–13; Eugen von Böhm-Bawerk, *Capital and Interest*, 3 volumes in 1, translated by George D. Huncke and Hans F. Sennholz (South Holland, IL: Libertarian Press, 1959), volume 2, *Positive Theory of Capital*, Book III: "Value and Price," 2:119–256.

35. Least of all economists. Of all people they ought to recognize the limits of their field. As Nobel Prize-winning economist James Buchanan put it in his essay "Methods and Morals in Economics," "The elementary fact is, of course, that *homo economicus* does exist in the human psyche, along with many other men, and that behavior is a product of the continuing internal struggle among these. . . . *Homo economicus* need not reign supreme over other men. . . ." James M. Buchanan, *What Should Economists Do?* (Indianapolis: Liberty Fund, 1979), 207.

36. Wilkinson, ed., *Earthkeeping*, 357–58.

37. Wilkinson, ed., *Earthkeeping*, 358.

38. Included in T. S. Eliot, *Christianity and Culture* (New York: Harcourt Brace Jovanovich, 1960).

39. See E. Calvin Beisner, "The Double-Edged Sword of Multiculturalism," *Occasional Paper of the National Association of Evangelicals*, September 1994, which was an abridged version of an article by the same title in *The Freeman*, vol. 44, no. 3 (March 1994), 104–112, which in turn was an abridged version of an unpublished paper presented to the faculty of Covenant College, Lookout Mountain, Georgia, December 1993.

40. Wilkinson, ed., *Earthkeeping*, 351–58.

41. See chapter 1, note 1.

42. One important exception, in my view, is their urging of small families and the pursuit of "zero population growth": ". . . those of us who would like to raise children ought to consider the size of the world population in determining how many children to bring into the world." (DeWitt, *Earthkeeping*, 366.) For why I oppose this counsel, see chapter 7 and *Prospects for Growth*, chapters 6 and 7.

43. Other helpful specific suggestions like these can be found, despite the book's unnecessary crisis mentality, in Tony Campolo and Gordon Aeschliman's *50 Ways You Can Help Save the Planet* (Downers Grove, IL: InterVarsity Press, 1992).

44. Wilkinson, ed., *Earthkeeping*, 381–82.

CHAPTER 4: The Use of Scripture by Evangelical Environmentalists

1. Orin Gelderloos, *Eco-Theology: The Judeo-Christian Tradition and the Politics of Ecological Decision Making* (Glasgow: Wild Goose Publications, 1992), 49.

2. Loren Wilkinson, ed., *Earthkeeping in the Nineties: Stewardship of Creation*, rev. ed. (Grand Rapids: Eerdmans, 1991), 51.

3. Calvin B. DeWitt, *Earth-Wise: A Biblical Response to Environmental Issues* (Grand Rapids: CRC Publications, 1994), 30. DeWitt uses the verse similarly in "Introduction" and "Seven Degradations of Creation" in *The Environment and the Christian: What Can We Learn from the New Testament?*, edited by DeWitt (Grand Rapids: Baker, 1991), 8 and 15; "Creation Watch Primer Sheet. 3. Deforestation and habitat destruction" (Mancelona, MI: Au Sable Institute, n.d.); "Seven Degradations of Creation: Responding in Worship," Degradation 3: "Deforestation and Habitat Destruction" (Mancelona: Au Sable Institute, n.d.; prepared for the Evangelical Lutheran Church in America).

4. Perhaps, however, Gelderloos means that dense populations reduce biodiversity *on the immediate land they occupy.* This is usually true, but it is (a) unavoidable if people are to live close enough together to benefit from proximity, (b) of doubtful significance since the reason for having cities is not to have wild species living in one's own yard but to enjoy the economic and social benefits of close association with other people, (c) probably beneficial to overall biodiversity because it reduces human intrusion on other land, and (d) at least in some respects not so damaging to biodiversity even within the cities as commonly thought. As an illustration of the last point, peregrine falcons, which in nature hunt pigeons and other small birds along cliff faces, have adapted well to city life, apparently finding skyscrapers and large urban pigeon flocks comfortable substitutes for cliffs and other prey.

5. This is a standard observation in commentaries. See, e.g., C. F. Keil and Franz Delitzsch, *Commentary on the Old Testament*, 10 volumes, translated by

James Martin (Grand Rapids: Eerdmans, 1976 rpt.), volume 7, *Isaiah*, 3 volumes in 1, by Franz Delitzsch, 1:166; Albert Barnes, *Notes on the Old Testament Explanatory and Practical*, 16 volumes, edited by Robert Frew (Grand Rapids: Baker, 1975 rpt.), *Isaiah*, 2 volumes, 1:122–23; Leslie C. Allen, *The Books of Joel, Obadiah, Jonah and Micah* (New International Commentary on the Old Testament; Grand Rapids: Eerdmans, 1976), 287–89; John Mauchline, *Isaiah 1–39* (London: SCM Press, 1962), 81–82; John N. Oswalt, *The Book of Isaiah: Chapters 1–39* (Grand Rapids: Eerdmans, 1986), 158–59.

6. I.e., "for any but these rich land purchasers," Gray, *The Book of Isaiah*, 91. Or for "the poor peasant between two wealthy landowners," I. W. Slotki, *Isaiah: Hebrew Text and English Translation with an Introduction and Commentary* (London, Jerusalem, and New York: Soncino Press, [1949] 1980), 23–24.

7. Oswalt, *The Book of Isaiah*, 158.

8. Francis Brown, S. R. Driver, and Charles A. Briggs, edd., *A Hebrew and English Lexicon of the Old Testament*, trans. Edward Robinson (Oxford: Clarendon Press, [1907] 1978), 109–10. Another possible solution would be to interpret Isaiah as referring to two different categories of property as defined by the Jubilee law. In the phrase "house to house," he would have in mind houses in unwalled villages, or the houses of Levites in walled cities, either of which were to be treated legally as agricultural fields, i.e., they must not be sold in perpetuity but must be returned at the Jubilee (Lev. 25:29–33). In the phrase "field to field," he would have in mind agricultural fields, which could not be sold in perpetuity (Lev. 25:23). Thus he covers both bases: some rich oppressors join house to house, others join field to field, but in either case it is not by building dwelling after dwelling on their own land that they sin but by purchasing—and through legal legerdemain permanently retaining—houses and lands previously owned by others who because of financial exigencies are forced to sell.

9. George Buchanan Gray, *A Critical and Exegetical Commentary on the Book of Isaiah* (International Critical Commentary; Edinburgh: T. & T. Clark, [1912] 1969), 1:90. Curiously, E. J. Young, while recognizing the Jubilee law foundation, applies Isaiah's woe to "wealthy landowners who buy up all the property that they can until their houses touch one another." (Edward J. Young, *The Book of Isaiah: The English Text, with Introduction, Exposition, and Notes*, 3 volumes [New International Commentary on the Old Testament; Grand Rapids: Eerdmans, (1965) 1978], 1:206.) But such an interpretation runs up against the sense of "you live alone in the land," which implies dwellings not densely packed together but widely separated, each surrounded by large fields and so isolated from other dwellings.

10. Wesley Granberg-Michaelson, *Ecology and Life: Accepting Our Environmental Responsibility*, Issues of Christian Conscience, ed. Vernon Grounds (Waco, TX: Word Books, 1988), 57, emphasis added.

11. Verse 18 explains what the "broken cisterns" represent: mutual defense

treaties with a pagan country (Egypt) that will not in fact protect Israel from its enemies.

12. See appendix 1 for a discussion of the ethical evaluation of wilderness, of the phrase *without form and void* in Scripture, and of the implication of these concepts for environmental ethics.

13. See chapter 3, note 4.

14. On all of these indexes of material progress, see Julian L. Simon, ed., *The State of Humanity* (Oxford: Blackwell, 1995).

15. On the influence of Christianity on Western culture, see E. Calvin Beisner, "The Double-edged Sword of Multiculturalism," *The Freeman*, vol. 44, no. 3 (March 1994), 104–112; Russell Kirk, *America's British Culture* (New Brunswick: Transaction Publishers, 1993) and *The Roots of American Order*, 3d ed. (Washington: Regnery Gateway, 1991), chapters 2, 5–8, 11–12; Christopher Dawson, *Progress and Religion: An Historical Enquiry* (New York: Sheed & Ward, 1938) and *Religion and the Rise of Western Culture* (Gifford Lectures, 1948–1949, University of Edinburgh; London: Sheed & Ward, 1950); T. S. Eliot, *Christianity and Culture: The Idea of a Christian Society and Notes Toward the Definition of Culture* (New York: Harcourt, Brace & World, 1940); Francis A. Schaeffer, *How Should We Then Live?* in *The Complete Works of Francis A. Schaeffer*, 5 volumes (Westchester, IL: Crossway Books, 1982), 5:83–277.

16. DeWitt, "Seven Degradations of Creation," in *The Environment and the Christian*, edited by DeWitt, 18–19; DeWitt, *Earth-Wise*, 33; and "Seven Degradations of Creation: Responding in Worship," 6, "Global Toxification."

17. DeWitt, *Earth-Wise*, 34; see also "Seven Degradations of Creation," 1, "Alteration of Earth's Energy Exchange," and *The Environment and the Christian*, 19–20.

18. DeWitt, ed., *The Environment and the Christian*, 22.

19. The same principle appears in Hosea 4:1–3, of which Granberg-Michaelson writes, "So the Bible clearly laments the deterioration of the environment" (*Ecology and Life*, 58–59). What Granberg-Michaelson does not mention is that "the deterioration of the environment" is caused not (in this instance) by what environmentalists would call poor ecological practices, but by God's judgment on other sorts of human sin ("There is no faithfulness, no love, no acknowledgment of God in the land. There is only cursing, lying and murder, stealing and adultery," verses 1b–2a).

20. The authors of *Earthkeeping in the Nineties* (p. 321), however, are much more reserved in their use of the Jubilee law.

21. Note here that Gelderloos is not saying merely that sabbath affects sustainability because of the requirement that the land lie fallow every seventh year. He insists rather that it is the Jubilee law's tendency to equalize wealth that enhances sustainability.

22. Gelderloos, *Eco-Theology*, 35 and 49.

23. That equality or some approximation of it is what Gelderloos has in mind by the phrase *equitable distribution* is implied by his saying immediately before that the Jubilee "deals with inequality." Properly used, despite their shared etymological root, *equity* (justice, impartiality, giving each his due, fairness, proper application of just rules) and *equality* (likeness in magnitude or dimensions, value, qualities, degree, and the like; evenness, uniformity, sameness) are not synonyms.

24. For the tribal census just before entry into Canaan, see Numbers 26. Sizes of tribal territories are rough estimates based on Barry J. Beitzel, *The Moody Atlas of Bible Lands* (Chicago: Moody Press, 1985), Map 31, "Tribal Distribution of Palestine."

25. That justice does not require equality, see E. Calvin Beisner, *Prosperity and Poverty: The Compassionate Use of Resources in a World of Scarcity* (Westchester, IL: Crossway Books, 1988), chapters 4–5, and "Justice and Poverty: Two Views Contrasted," in *Christianity and Economics in the Post-Cold War Era: The Oxford Declaration and Beyond*, edited by Herbert Schlossberg, Vinay Samuel, and Ronald J. Sider (Grand Rapids: Eerdmans, 1994), 57–80.

26. On the working of the Jubilee law, see Beisner, *Prosperity and Poverty*, chapter 5, and "A Closer Look at the Jubilee," *World*, vol. 3, no. 4 (April 25, 1988), p. 11.

27. Since income distribution data are notoriously unreliable both within countries and in cross-country comparisons, and since there is no single quantitative measure of environmental quality, it is extremely difficult—if not impossible with current data constraints—to quantify even an approximate relationship between income distribution and environmental quality. From the perspective of the overall healthfulness of the environment for human beings, two commonly used surrogates for environmental quality are life expectancy (higher is better) and child mortality rate (lower is better). A regression analysis I have done of ten-year averages of such statistics for 65 countries for which they are available from the World Bank's *Social Indicators of Development on Diskette, 1995* (Washington: World Bank, 1995) shows no statistically significant correlation between income distribution and either life expectancy or child mortality. There is, however, a moderately significant correlation between GNP per capita and both life expectancy (.34) and child mortality rate (.26).

28. Indur M. Goklany, "Richer Is Cleaner: Long-Term Trends in Global Air Quality," in *The True State of the Planet*, edited by Ronald Bailey (New York: Free Press, 1995), 339–77; The World Bank, *World Development Report, 1992* (Oxford and New York: Oxford University Press, 1992); G. Grossman and A. Krueger, *Environmental Impacts of a North American Free Trade Agreement*, Discussion Paper 158 (Princeton, NJ: Woodrow Wilson School, Princeton University, November 1991); N. Shafik and S. Bandyopadhyay, *Economic Growth and Environmental Quality: Time Series and Cross-Country Evidence*, Policy Research Working Papers (Washington: World Bank, June 1992); N. Shafik, *Eco-*

nomic Development and Patterns of Change, Oxford Economic Papers (forthcoming).

29. Vernon Visick, "Creation's Care and Keeping in the Life of Jesus," in *The Environment and the Christian: What Can We Learn from the New Testament?*, edited by Calvin B. DeWitt (Grand Rapids: Baker, 1991), 93–106: 96.

30. Jesus did imply, by teaching that we should take care of beasts of burden even on the sabbath (Luke 13:15; 14:5), that we should care for animals. His intent, however, was not to teach our duty to animals but to clarify the requirements of the sabbath law. In contrast, His clear intent in many other passages is to teach our duty to our fellow men (e.g., the Sermon on the Mount).

31. The late Presbyterian missionary to Asia, John M. L. Young, has written, "With the giving of the New Covenant we have the final proclamation for the fulfillment of God's purpose that men should serve him as stewards of his creation throughout the world. The 'cultural mandate' and the missionary mandate are thus vitally related." According to Young, the cultural mandate is "a basis for a real theology of missions," while the Great Commission "is basic to the fulfillment of God's purpose for the world—that men should serve him in every effort, bringing all things into subjection for his glory. Since the fall men themselves have to be brought into subjection first, made captives for Christ, in order to render his prescribed service. To achieve this end, the New Covenant, with its missionary mandate, the Great Commission, was given." John M. L. Young, "Theology of Missions, Covenant-centered," *Christianity Today*, 13:4 (November 22, 1968), 10–11, 12: 12.

32. E.g., Ghillean T. Prance, "The Ecological Awareness of the Amazon Indians," in *Missionary Earthkeeping*, ed. Calvin B. DeWitt and Ghillean T. Prance (Macon, GA: Mercer University Press, 1992), 45–61: 52, and Robert Clobus, "Ecofarming and Landownership in Ghana," in ibid., 63–89: 72. Prance allows that monoculture may work well in temperate climates, where winter freezes kill off pests, but not in the tropics. Yet the climate of Palestine is nearly tropical, and except at high altitudes winter temperatures rarely are low enough to kill pests.

33. There is some question as to the meaning of the Hebrew. It may instead denote Canaanite goddess-idols.

34. Dennis E. Testerman, "Missionary Earthkeeping: Glimpses of the Past, Visions of the Future," in *Missionary Earthkeeping*, ed. Calvin B. DeWitt and Ghillean T. Prance (Macon, GA: Mercer University Press, 1992), 11–44: 11–16.

CHAPTER 5: The Problem of Environmental Misinformation

1. Critiques of the scientific weaknesses of environmentalism include E. Calvin Beisner, *Prospects for Growth: A Biblical View of Population, Resources, and the Future* (Westchester, IL: Crossway Books, 1990) and *Man, Economy, and the Environment in Biblical Perspective* (Moscow, ID: Canon Press, 1994); Ronald

Bailey, ed., *The True State of the Planet* (New York: Free Press, 1995); and Julian L. Simon, ed., *The State of Humanity* (Oxford: Blackwell, 1995). Others are listed in the bibliography.

2. Claims of rapid conversion of agricultural land to urban and suburban use appear frequently in environmentalist literature. For example, Calvin B. DeWitt writes, "Of 400 million acres of cropland we have allotted for agriculture in the United States, three million are converted yearly to urban uses." ("Seven Degradations of Creation," in *The Environment and the Christian: What Can We Learn from the New Testament?*, edited by DeWitt [Grand Rapids: Baker, 1991], 15.) But the three-million acre figure—often repeated—derives from faulty comparisons of data between National Agricultural Lands Surveys done in 1967 and 1975, between which critically relevant definitions of land use changed. "'If you merged the surveys they seemed to produce a rapidly increasing level of conversion,' H. Thomas Frey, a Department of Agriculture geographer, says. 'If you adjusted for the changed definition there was almost no loss.' In 1984 the Soil Conservation Service issued a report effectively retracting the National Agricultural Lands Survey." Gregg Easterbrook, *A Moment on the Earth: The Coming Age of Environmental Optimism* (New York: Viking, 1995), 387. See also Julian L. Simon, "Are We Losing Our Farmland?" *The Public Interest* 67 (Spring 1982): 49–62; Simon, "The Phantom Farmland in Illinois," *The Champaign-Urbana News-Gazette*, May 17 and June 9, 1981; Simon, "The Farmer and the Mall: Are American Farmlands Disappearing?" *The American Spectator*, August 1982, 18–20, 40–41; all reprinted in Simon, *Population Matters: People, Resources, Environment, and Immigration* (New Brunswick: Transaction, 1990), 118–44.

3. Reductions in industrial sulfur dioxide emissions (because of improved pollution controls) may have caused a fictitious decline in total atmospheric ozone measurements large enough to eliminate the whole apparent downward trend since 1957. D. De Muer and H. De Backer, "Revision of 20 Years of Dobson Total Ozone Data at Uccle (Belgium): Fictitious Dobson Total Ozone Trends Induced by Sulfur Dioxide Trends," *Journal of Geophysical Research* 97:D5 (April 20, 1992), 5921–37.

4. Stuart Penkett, "Ultraviolet Levels Down, Not Up," *Nature*, September 28, 1989.

5. *Tropical Deforestation and Species Extinction*, edited by T. C. Whitmore and J. A. Sayer (London and New York: Chapman & Hall, 1992), xvii, 93, 96.

6. Richard Monastersky, "The Deforestation Debate," *Science News* 144(2) (July 10, 1993), 26–27; David Skole and Compton Tucker, "Tropical Deforestation and Habitat Fragmentation in the Amazon: Satellite Data from 1978 to 1988," *Science* 260 (June 25, 1993), 1905–10.

7. Loren Wilkinson, ed., *Earthkeeping in the Nineties: Stewardship of Creation*, rev. ed. (Grand Rapids: Eerdmans, 1991), 7.

8. Evangelical environmentalist Wesley Granberg-Michaelson, whose work

is well known to DeWitt and the other authors of *Earthkeeping*, offers yet another figure for annual worldwide loss of tropical rainforests: "the size of Scotland." (Wesley Granberg-Michaelson, *Ecology and Life: Accepting Our Environmental Responsibility*, Issues of Christian Conscience, ed. Vernon Grounds [Waco, TX: Word Books, 1988], 21.) But Scotland is only 78,768 square kilometers—two-thirds the size of Ohio and less than one-third the size of Michigan, and about 16 percent smaller than Indiana. And "An Open Letter to the Religious Community," signed by a group of scientists led by Carl Sagan in January 1990 and instrumental in launching the National Religious Partnership on the Environment, a branch of which is the Evangelical Environmental Network, decries "the obliteration of an acre of *forest* [emphasis added] every second"—which computes to 127,655 square kilometers annually, about half the size of Michigan, 7 percent larger than Ohio, and a third larger than Indiana. Whom shall we believe? And by the way, does the "Open Letter" claim refer to all forest types, or to tropical rainforests only? The Letter does not say. Neither does it point out that despite this rate of "obliteration," assuming it is true, total world forested area has held steady or increased slightly since the beginning of the twentieth century, which means that it would have been just as true to say "the regrowth of an acre of forest every second." But then that is not scary.

9. Calvin B. DeWitt, *Earth-Wise: A Biblical Response to Environmental Issues* (Grand Rapids: CRC Publications, 1994), 30.

10. Granberg-Michaelson, repeating a common claim in popular environmental literature, writes, "Scientists are estimating that as many as 1 million species of plant and animal life will become extinct, due to the human destruction of forests and ecosystems, by the end of the twentieth century." (*Ecology and Life*, 21.) Since his book was published in 1988, this implies 83,333 extinctions per year.

11. Wilkinson, ed., *Earthkeeping*, 28.

12. Calvin B. DeWitt, "Myth 2: It's Not Biblical to Be Green," *Christianity Today*, April 4, 1994, 27–31, 30. The claim appears also in DeWitt's Introduction to *The Environment and the Christian: What Can We Learn from the New Testament?*, which he edited (Grand Rapids: Baker, 1991), 16, and in DeWitt, *Earth-Wise*, 31.

13. DeWitt, *Earth-Wise*, 16.

14. Bruce Gardner, Letter to E. Calvin Beisner, April 20, 1994.

15. Earl R. Swanson and Earl O. Heady, "Soil Erosion in the United States," in *The Resourceful Earth: A Response to 'Global 2000'*, edited by Julian L. Simon and Herman Kahn (New York: Basil Blackwell, 1984), 202–23, 206.

16. *Prospects for Growth* and *Man, Economy, and the Environment in Biblical Perspective*.

17. Tony Campolo and Gordon Aeschliman rightly call contaminated water "the single largest death-inducing factor in the world today" (presumably other

than old age), but they are mistaken when they imply that "improper trash disposal, toxic waste, air pollution (brought down by the rain), runoff from pesticides and fertilizers, [and] underground fuel storage tanks" are the most common causes of lethal water pollution. (Tony Campolo and Gordon Aeschliman, *50 Ways You Can Help Save the Planet* [Downers Grove, IL: InterVarsity Press, 1992], 65.) Deaths from water pollution are almost unknown in the developed world. They happen by the millions in the developing world. And there the greatest hazard comes not from industrial pollution but from untreated sewage. Campolo and Aeschliman do mention sewage, but only as the last item on their list of causes, and they never hint that the causes have different levels of risk. Here, as elsewhere, an anti-industrial bias colors evangelical environmentalists' risk assessment.

18. Mikhail Bernstam, "The Wealth of Nations and the Environment," Institute for Economic Affairs, 1991; Gregg Easterbrook, *A Moment On the Earth: The Coming Age of Environmental Optimism* (New York: Viking, 1995), 330–31.

19. In a classic display of shortsightedness, Mutombo Mpanya laments the influence of missionaries on one African village's housing habits because "more mosquitoes could be found in modern homes than in the traditional ones since the smoke from fires in the latter repelled mosquitoes." ("The Environmental Impacts of a Church Project: A Zairian Village Case Study," in *Missionary Earthkeeping*, ed. Calvin B. DeWitt and Ghillean T. Prance [Macon, GA: Mercer University Press, 1992], 91–109: 107.) What he forgets is that the smoke in the traditional homes is also a major cause of respiratory ailments and deaths.

20. Easterbrook adds, "United States resource use is in fact too high." I think he's wrong, but that is beside the point here.

21. Easterbrook, *A Moment On the Earth*, 578–79, 582–83, 586, 587–88.

22. For representative examples see: Orin Gelderloos, a signer of the *Evangelical Declaration on the Care of Creation*: "The ecological changes with which we are concerned, e.g. carbon dioxide increase, pH changes, ozone destruction, loss of species diversity, and decreased levels of sustainability. . . ." (*Eco-Theology: The Judeo-Christian Tradition and the Politics of Ecological Decision Making* [Glasgow: Wild Goose Publications, 1992], 61, n. 4); J. Mark Thomas, "Introduction," in *Missionary Earthkeeping*, ed. Calvin B. DeWitt and Ghillean T. Prance (Macon, GA: Mercer University Press, 1992], 1–9), 2. There is some encouragement in the fact that an informational packet sent to churches by the Evangelical Environmental Network at least mentions lives lost to unsafe drinking water and frequently asserts the connectedness of environmental problems with poverty, sickness, and death in developing countries. ("Biblical Roots: Theological Foundations for Celebrating God's Creation" [Monrovia, CA: World Vision/Evangelical Environmental Network, n.d. (1994)], 9–10.) Nonetheless, the main focus of the EEN's most important document to date, the *Evangelical Declaration on the Care of Creation*, was on the hypothetical global and regional

problems, whose risks to human life are low, rather than on the indisputably real and deadly local problems discussed here.

23. Even Chernobyl, the worst nuclear power disaster in history, caused only about 400 immediate deaths, and estimates of long-term premature deaths from exposure to its radiation in the neighborhood of only 17,000. That is a tragedy, and the Soviet government bears full responsibility for the poor technology and sloppy operation of the Chernobyl reactor. The accidental radiation released at Windscale, a military reactor in England in 1957, may eventually have caused 300 premature deaths; to date, that is the worst nuclear power generating disaster in Western history. But the cost in lives of these disasters, tragic as it is, is minute compared with the daily cost in lives (about 11,000 children from impure waterborne diseases alone) of poor sanitation in the developing world. See Easterbrook, *A Moment On the Earth*, 503–12.

Many environmentalists mistakenly believe, like the authors of *Earthkeeping in the Nineties*, that each Western nuclear power plant is "a potential Chernobyl" (p. 11). But the Chernobyl reactor—and about eighteen others like it around the former Soviet bloc—used a technology significantly different from that used in Western reactors. In it,

> . . . the neutrons were moderated (slowed) by graphite instead of water. Perhaps more serious, the Chernobyl reactor had no containment shell.
>
> Chernobyl's graphite moderator system did not have the failsafe property of the Three Mile Island reactor. In the United States if water is cut off, the fission reaction stops because the moderator (water) is removed. With the Chernobyl reactor, water was used as a coolant and, along with graphite, as a partial moderator. When the reactor's core is deprived of water, the graphite continues to act as a moderator so the fission does not necessarily stop. Worse, with the coolant removed, the reactor may actually speed up. The reactor does not go to critical mass like a nuclear bomb, but it can blow itself apart because of chemical reactions (such as steam being generated when water falls on hot metal. [Ben Bolch and Harold Lyons, *Apocalypse Not: Science, Economics, and Environmentalism* (Washington: Cato Institute, 1993), 110.]

In other words, what happened at Chernobyl is physically impossible in Western reactors because of the design used.

Chapter 6: Observations on the Mind of the Evangelical Environmental Movement

1. Tony Campolo and Gordon Aeschliman, *50 Ways You Can Help Save the Planet* (Downers Grove, IL: InterVarsity Press, 1992), 9.

2. Gordon Aeschliman, "Somebody got shot in the head: *Creation after the fall,*" *Prism* 1:2 (December/January 1994), 7.

3. I have changed the wording at this point for clarity. Originally this had

read "just as it did in presently advanced countries (only probably faster)." That could have been understood to mean that the slowing of slash-and-burn would occur more slowly in the presently developing countries than it did in the presently advanced countries; my intent had been the opposite.

4. John Stott, *Involvement: Being a Responsible Christian In a Non-Christian Society* (Old Tappan, NJ: Fleming H. Revell, 1985), 160.

5. "The world is currently cropping or farming about 5.8 million square miles of land, roughly a land area the size of South America. . . . Humanity might already be farming three times that much land if farmers were still getting the low yields typical of the 1950s, before most of the world began using fertilizer and pesticides. That would have meant plowing down the land equivalent of North America in addition to South America. Thus, in a real sense, high-yield farming is saving 10 million square miles of wildlife habitat right now. . . .

"High-yield agriculture also deserves environmental credit for the big tracts of steep, rocky, drought-prone, and sandy soils that have been put back into grass and trees in the United States since farmers began boosting crop yields. . . . In 1880, there were 68 million acres of farmland in the Northeast. Today it has dropped by two-thirds, to 23 million acres. Fewer than 10 million acres are urbanized or used for transportation. The result has been a dramatic expansion of wildlife habitat in the region since the turn of the century." Dennis Avery, "Saving the Planet with Pesticides: Increasing Food Supplies While Preserving the Earth's Biodiversity," in *The True State of the Planet*, edited by Ronald Bailey (New York: Free Press, 1995), 49–82: 71–3.

6. Gregg Easterbrook, *A Moment on the Earth: The Coming Age of Environmental Optimism* (New York: Viking, 1995), 561.

7. Richard T. Wright, "Tearing Down the Green Environmental Backlash in the Evangelical Sub-Culture," *Perspectives on Science and Christian Faith* 47:2 (June 1995), 80–91: 83.

8. See appendix 5 for my complete response to Wright, including specifics on these scientists' credentials and accomplishments.

9. In "Another View," *World* 8:30 (January 8, 1994), 22, 24: 22 (his response to my critique of the EDCC), Sider specifies that Prance predicted "that by the turn of the century, over 1 million different kinds of animals, insects, and plants will be driven to extinction if current trends continue." This amounts to a rate of roughly 100,000 extinctions per year—at the high end of estimates found in environmentalist literature. For discussion of such, see chapter 5 and appendix 2.

10. T. C. Whitmore and J. A. Sayer, ed., *Tropical Deforestation and Species Extinction* (London and New York: Chapman & Hall, 1992).

11. "Chicago Talks," with Dick Staub, Friday, January 21, 1994; transcript from tape, on file.

12. Sider, "Another view," 22.

13. Edwin A. Olson, "A Response to Richard Wright's 'Tearing Down the

Green'," pre-publication draft submitted to *Perspectives on Science and Christian Faith*, 13.

14. At the time, a study by the Center for Media and Public Affairs of national media coverage from 1985 to late-1991 showed that most media accounts support the belief that global warming is real. But the Gallup poll, taken in October and November of 1991, found that: (a) while 60 percent of climatologists polled believed that global average temperatures had increased over the past century, only 19 percent believed human action was the cause, 44 percent believed it was not, and 37 percent were unsure; (b) despite the lack of consensus that any historic global warming was human induced, 66 percent believed that human-induced warming had begun to occur, but only 41 percent believed that "currently available scientific evidence substantiates its occurrence," while 21 percent believed that the evidence does not substantiate it; (c) 90 percent described the study of global climate change as an "emerging science" rather than a "mature science"; and (d) 70 percent rated the media's performance in informing the public about the scientific aspects of global warming as either fair (46 percent) or poor (24 percent), while only 30 percent rated the media's performance as good (26 percent) or excellent (4 percent). Washington: Center for Science, Technology & Media, press release, February 13, 1992.

Climatologist Patrick Michaels argues that "it is simply impossible to find any scientific consensus supporting the Popular Vision of climate disaster. Rather, the consensus [among professional climatologists and researchers on the greenhouse effect] is the opposite: the Popular Vision is unscientific." Patrick J. Michaels, *Sound and Fury: The Science and Politics of Global Warming* (Washington: Cato Institute, 1992), 185.

15. Calvin B. DeWitt, *Earth-Wise: A Biblical Response to Environmental Issues* (Grand Rapids: CRC Publications, 1994), 29.

16. A good example of this phenomenon is what happened to Robert Gentry, formerly a research scientist at the Oak Ridge National Laboratories and recognized as the world's leading researcher on polonium haloes (the microscopic striations left by the decay of the radioactive element polonium) in rocks. Although he had published a dozen scholarly articles in refereed science journals discussing these unusual phenomena, when he revealed in testimony during the trial of Arkansas's law requiring balanced treatment of scientific evidence for creation and evolution how some of his findings contradicted uniformitarian geological assumptions (an important aspect of conventional evolutionary thought), the federal grants that had underwritten his research were promptly canceled, he lost his research position at the Laboratories, and he became unable to have further articles on polonium haloes published in the refereed journals. See Robert V. Gentry, *Creation's Tiny Mystery* 3d. ed. (Knoxville, TN: Earth Science Associates, 1992). For other examples, see *Brief of the State in Opposition to ACLU Motion for Summary Judgment*, 2 volumes, in *Don Aguillard, et al.* vs. *Edwin W. Edwards,*

et al., U.S. District Court for the Eastern District of Louisiana, 81–4787, Section H, at 1:514–16. (The brief was later published as Wendell R. Bird, *The Origin of Species Revisited: The Theories of Evolution and of Abrupt Appearance*, 2 volumes [New York: Philosophical Library, 1987, 1988, 1989].)

17. See, e.g., Stanley L. Jaki, "Science and Censorship: Hélène Duhem and the Publication of the 'Système du monde'," *The Intercollegiate Review* 21:2 (Winter 1985–86), 41–9, for the story of how the ground-breaking researches of one great historian of science were held out of publication for some four decades because they challenged—indeed, demolished—a secularist belief that Christianity had been an obstacle to the development of science.

18. Julian L. Simon, "Resources, Population, Environment: An Oversupply of False Bad News," *Science* 208 (June 27, 1980); reprinted (without references) in Julian L. Simon, *Population Matters: People, Resources, Environment, and Immigration* (New Brunswick, NJ: Transaction, 1990), 39–54.

19. Julian L. Simon, "Adventures Getting Truth Published in the United States," in *Population Matters*, 494–505. In responding to letters from Carl Sagan and Edward O. Wilson about scientists engaging in advocacy regarding particular causes, in the "Letters" column of *Science* 260 (June 25, 1993), 1861, Koshland rightly observed "that even great scientists sometimes have to be assessed with a grain of salt when they become advocates." But his follow-up is chilling: "Let me state *Science*'s policy on covering scientist-advocates. We encourage our reporters to cover contentious issues of science and particularly to seek out protagonists who are scientists and who care about the policy implications of their research. Under no circumstances would we have a policy of failing to seek out the leaders in an area just because they are advocates, but we owe it to our readers to check their extrapolations or to interview proponents of alternative points of view *when we believe it desirable to present a balanced view of a controversial subject*" (emphasis added).

20. Krug's story was told on CBS's "60 Minutes," December 30, 1990. See Warren T. Brookes, "EPA Apologizes to Acid Rain Scientist," *Human Events* 51:20 (May 18, 1991): 11; Edward C. Krug, "Acid Rain: An example of environmental epistemology," *Mining Engineering* 44:12 (December 1992): 1431–4.

21. Thomas S. Kuhn, *The Structure of Scientific Revolutions*, Foundations of the Unity of Science Series, Volume 2, No. 2 (Chicago: University of Chicago Press, 1970); Kuhn, *The Essential Tension: Selected Studies in Scientific Tradition and Change* (University of Chicago Press, 1979); see also J. P. Moreland, *Christianity and the Nature of Science: A Philosophical Investigation* (Grand Rapids: Baker, 1989).

22. "Of the scores of scientists I interviewed for this book," wrote Ronald Bailey, "I could count on the fingers of one hand the number who did not mention funding and the scarcity of research monies. Lab directors are not only scientists; they are also public relations officers and politicians who must navigate the dark

byways of Congress and government agencies in search of the wherewithal to keep their organizations going. Consequently, they feel enormous institutional pressure to hype the work of their laboratories and to tie it to the solution of some looming mediagenic crisis." Ronald Bailey, *Eco-Scam: The False Prophets of Ecological Apocalypse* (New York: St. Martin's Press, 1993), 175.

"Why does this misuse of science continue? In any scientific discipline, there are only a few genuine apocalypse abusers. The motives are the usual ones—the quest for prestige and money. Harvard's Peter Rogers notes, 'Very rarely is the public informed that these predictions are based on elaborate research models that have not been fully validated and that the future funding of these model studies is subject to being cut off at any moment. This leads to the unconscious desire to present the model results in the best (i.e., most frightening) light to Congress and the federal government, which are ultimately the sole source of funding for this research.' Rogers adds, 'Because everyone else is crying "crisis," responsible scientists are forced to join the chorus or risk losing their research programs.'" Ibid., 166–7, citing Peter Rogers, "Climate Change and Global Warming," *Environment, Science & Technology* 24:4 (1990), 429.

23. Patrick J. Michaels, "Climate Change and Public Policy: Reaping the Whirlwind of Federal Monopoly," unpublished manuscript presented to the conference on "Creation at Risk? Religion, Science, and Environmentalism," sponsored by the Ethics and Public Policy Center, Washington, D.C., November 17–18, 1994.

24. Ben Bolch and Harold Lyons, *Apocalypse Not: Science, Economics, and Environmentalism* (Washington: Cato Institute, 1993), 119.

25. Loren Wilkinson, ed., *Earthkeeping in the Nineties: Stewardship of Creation*, rev. ed. (Grand Rapids: Eerdmans, 1991), 2.

26. Wilkinson, ed., *Earthkeeping*, 10.

Chapter 7: Imago Dei and the Population Debate

1. This chapter is adapted from a lecture presented at the Christianity Today Institute Conference on Population and Global Stewardship, Lisle, Illinois, April 21–23, 1994.

2. This date is about two hundred years later than common estimates, but there are good reasons—stemming from Paul's statement in Galatians 3:16–17 that the giving of the law at Sinai was 430 years after the establishment of God's covenant with Abram—to think conventional chronologies are mistaken. But the answer to this problem does not affect the subject of this book.

3. We can infer such fears from some earlier records, for example in the mention of a famine in Palestine in Genesis 12:10.

4. Estimates of Israel's population at the exodus vary. The one firm figure we have is that there were 603,550 males twenty years old and above (Numbers 1:46).

Some scholars extrapolate from this a total population of about 2 million (e.g., Ronald B. Allen and Kenneth L. Barker, notes to Numbers in Kenneth L. Barker, general editor, *The NIV Study Bible* [Grand Rapids: Zondervan, 1985], 190). This figure is based on the assumption of one wife and two children to every man twenty or older. However, demographics of less-developed agricultural peoples indicate that that assumption may be far from correct, leading to a serious under-estimate of Israel's population at the time. (Genealogical information from the Old Testament points in the same direction.) Marriage in such societies tends to come around the ages of fourteen to sixteen, and birth rates tend to be consider-ably higher than mere replacement rates. An assumption of four to six children to each man over twenty and his wife would not seem unlikely. This would yield a total population estimate for Israel of 3 million to 5 million at the time of the exodus.

As an aside, it is interesting to consider Israel's population density in Goshen (the region in Egypt in which they resided) prior to the exodus. At 2 million, their density would have been 800 to 1200 persons per square mile. (Goshen's specific area is not known. Rough estimates indicate that it was about forty to fifty miles square—i.e., 1,600 to 2,500 square miles.) At 3 million, their density would have been 1,200 to 1,875 per square mile. At 5 million, their density would have been 2,000 to 3,125 per square mile. Very few modern countries have such high popu-lation densities. (None but the city-states of Singapore [11,167 per square mile], Hong Kong [13,183 per square mile], and Macau [50,667 per square mile], plus the Gaza Strip [3,116 per square mile] exceeds 3,000 per square mile.) For com-parison, Japan's density in 1980 was roughly 830 per square mile, South Korea's was 1,088 per square mile, and that of Mauritius, in northern Africa, was about 1,200. (See U.S. Department of Commerce, Bureau of the Census, Sta*tistical Abstract of the United States, 1984* [Washington: Government Printing Office, 1984], 857–59, Table 1503.) The United States' population density in 1982 was about 65 per square mile; at that time the most densely populated state was New Jersey, with 996 persons per square mile. In 1980, average population density in U.S. urbanized areas was 2,675 persons per square mile; even in central cities, it was 3,551 per square mile. (See *Statistical Abstract . . . 1984*, 26, Table 24.) Whether Israel's population, then, was 2 million or 5 million when it left Goshen, certainly it is clear that at that time such an area, which was exceptionally fertile because of its location in the eastern part of the Nile delta, could support a very dense population, despite primitive methods of agriculture.

5. Emphasis added. From *Opera II: Opera monastica*, cited in David Herlihy, *Medieval Households* (Cambridge: Harvard University Press, 1985), 24, and— from Herlihy—in Susan Power Bratton, *Six Billion & More: Human Population Regulation and Christian Ethics* (Louisville, KY: Westminster/John Knox Press, 1992), 76. This citation is from Bratton.

6. Marcus and Karen Dean, letter to the editor, *Northwest Arkansas Morning*

News, Rogers, Arkansas, June 14, 1992. The Deans used their fears about over-population to support abortion as a means of population control.

7. Bratton, *Six Billion & More*, 97. The generally fearful view of human population growth is common among evangelical authors on population and the environment. See, for example, Loren Wilkinson, ed., *Earthkeeping in the Nineties: Stewardship of Creation*, rev. ed. (Grand Rapids: Eerdmans, 1991), 57, 59, 61–64, 366; Orin Gelderloos, *Eco-Theology: The Judeo-Christian Tradition and the Politics of Ecological Decision Making* (Glasgow: Wild Goose Publications, 1992), 48–49; Rosemary Radford Ruether, *Gaia & God: An Ecofeminist Theology of Earth Healing* (San Francisco: HarperCollins, [1992] 1994), 54, 92, 263.

8. Laurie Ann Mazur, "Beyond the Numbers: An Introduction and Overview," in *Beyond the Numbers: A Reader on Population, Consumption, and the Environment*, edited by Laurie Ann Mazur (Washington, D.C., and Covelo, CA: Island Press, 1994), 5.

9. Riane Eisler, *The Chalice and the Blade: Our History, Our Future* (San Francisco: Harper & Row Perennial Library, 1987), 174–75.

10. In *Six Billion & More*, a book particularly influential among evangelicals concerned about population and the environment, Bratton presents a slightly different breakdown of concerns: "One major environmental concern is that a growing human population needing more and more space will convert wildlands and the habitats of other species into developed property," threatening many species with extinction. "A second environmental problem is that rapidly expanding human populations, in the process of exceeding their food and land resources, usually damage what resources they have. . . . A third environmental problem is that an expanding human population consumes ever-greater quantities of nonrenewable natural resources. . . . A fourth environmental problem is that larger populations produce more pollution." (*Six Billion & More*, 97–8.) In terms of the analysis presented in the text of this chapter, Bratton's first and third problems would be listed under resource consumption, her fourth under pollution, and her third under either of the two, depending on how one wished to understand it.

11. See Paul R. Ehrlich, *The Population Bomb*, rev. ed. (original edition 1968; New York: Ballantine, 1986); Paul R. Ehrlich and Anne H. Ehrlich, *The Population Explosion* (New York: Simon and Schuster, 1990); Kingsley Davis, "The Climax of Population Growth," *California Medicine* 113 (November 1970), 33–9; Jacqueline Kasun, *The War Against Population: The Economics and Ideology of Population Control* (San Francisco: Ignatius, 1988), 196; David Brower, cited in Rael Jean Isaac and Erich Isaac, *The Coercive Utopians* (Washington: Regnery Gateway, 1985); also in Ray, *Trashing the Planet*, 169. For a more thorough discussion of the anti-human attitudes that dominate much of the environmentalist movement, see E. Calvin Beisner, "Imago Dei and Population Concerns," lecture 1 of The Staley Distinguished Christian Scholar Lectures, Covenant College, October 29–31, 1991 (Moscow, ID: Canon Press, 1994), 7–20.

12. Jerome Lejeune, testimony in *Junior L. Davis* v. *Mary Sue Davis* v. *Ray King, M.D., dba Fertility Center of East Tennessee*, Circuit Court for Blount County, Tennessee, Maryville, Equity Division, 1989. For Lejeune's full testimony and the judge's ruling, see *The Custody Dispute Over Seven Human Embryos: The Testimony of Professor Jerome Lejeune, M.D., Ph.D.* (Annandale, VA: Center for Law and Religious Freedom, 1990), 54, 57–58.

13. Ibid., 63.

14. John Calvin, *Commentary on the Book of Psalms*, trans. James Anderson, in *Calvin's Commentaries*, twenty-two volumes (Grand Rapids: Baker, 1984), 4(2):102–3. See also Alexander Maclaren, *The Psalms*, three volumes (New York: Hodder & Stoughton/George H. Doran, 1892), 1:73–4.

15. Calvin, *Psalms*, 4(2):104–5, emphasis added.

16. Athanasius, *On the Incarnation of the Word*, 54.3, in *A Select Library of the Nicene and Post-Nicene Fathers of the Christian Church*, second series, fourteen volumes, edited by Philip Schaff and Henry Wace, Volume IV, *St. Athanasius: Select Works and Letters*, translated by John Henry Cardinal Newman, edited by Archibald Robertson (Grand Rapids: Eerdmans, [1891] 1975), 65.

17. Athanasius, *Letters*, 60.4, to Bishop Adelphius, in ibid., 576, emphases added.

18. This must not be taken to imply universal salvation of all mankind. Nothing could be further from the truth. Scripture clearly affirms that those who reject the saving gospel of Christ will be forever lost, damned to eternity in torment (e.g., Matt. 25:46).

19. Basney, *Earth-Careful*, 79.

20. In every instance, the command to be fruitful, to multiply, to fill the earth and swarm in it (Gen. 1:22, 28; 8:17; 9:1, 7) comes in the context of God's blessing (Gen. 1:22, 28; 9:1, 7). A teeming population, then, should normally be thought of as a blessing, not a curse. This is the general principle in regard to all mankind, represented first in Adam and then in Noah. If anything, it is intensified in regard to the elect people of God, as we see in God's promises to Abraham: ". . . I will make you a great nation, and I will bless you . . ." (Gen. 12:2); "Now look toward the heavens, and count the stars, if you are able to count them. . . . So shall your descendants be" (Gen. 15:5); "I am God Almighty; walk before Me, and be blameless. And I will establish My covenant between Me and you, and I will multiply you exceedingly. . . . And you shall be the father of a multitude of nations. . . . And I will make you exceedingly fruitful, and I will make nations of you, and kings shall come forth from you" (Gen. 17:1–6). This promise was renewed to Isaac (Gen. 26:4, 24). So it was a sign of God's blessing on Israel that the nation, by the time of the Exodus, had grown to be "as numerous as the stars of heaven" (Deut. 10:22; cf. 1:10; cf. Gen. 47:27).

Growth didn't stop being a blessing after that. Instead, it was promised as a blessing on Israel's obedience: "And He will love you and bless you and multiply you; He will also bless the fruit of your womb and the fruit of your ground, your grain and your new wine and your oil, the increase of your herd and the young of your flock, in the land which He swore to your forefathers to give you. You shall be blessed above all peoples; there shall be no male or female barren among you or among your cattle" (Deut. 7:13, 14; cf. 30:5). In contrast, a decline in population was one form of curse God might send on His people if they rebelled (Deut. 28:62, 63; Lev. 26:22; Jer. 42:2; 5:6; 14:16; 15:3; 16:4; Ezek. 14:15).

Not only in mankind in the aggregate, but also in individual nations and families, population growth appears in the Bible as a blessing from God. "In a multitude of people is a king's glory, but in the dearth of people is a prince's ruin" (Prov. 14:28). As with nations, so with families: "Behold, children are a gift of the Lord; the fruit of the womb is a reward. Like arrows in the hand of a warrior, so are the children of one's youth. How blessed is the man whose quiver is full of them . . ." (Ps. 127:3–5). "How blessed is everyone who fears the LORD. . . . Your wife shall be like a fruitful vine, within your house, your children like olive plants around your table" (Ps. 128:1, 3). It is difficult to reconcile the present preference for small families—usually not more than two children per couple—with this Biblical view of children. Ordinarily, Christians should welcome, not try to avoid, additional children.

As we approach New Testament times, the promises of numerical growth to Israel broaden to include a prophesied extension of the people of God, the believing Gentiles who would be grafted into the olive tree (Rom. 11:17–21). For "it is not the children of the flesh who are children of God, but the children of the promise are regarded as descendants" (Rom. 9:8), and hence rightful heirs of the promises to Abraham (Rom. 4:13–16). This is how it comes about that "the number of the sons of Israel will be like the sand of the sea, which cannot be measured or numbered; and . . . that, in the place where it is said to them, 'You are not My people,' it will be said to them, 'You are the sons of the living God'" (Hos. 1:10; cf. Rom. 9:26). This new body, including believing Jews and Gentiles alike, will grow so large that, like "the host of heaven" and "the sand of the sea," it will be innumerable (Jer. 33:22).

God's original intention, then, was for man to multiply and fill the earth (Gen. 1:28). That intention was renewed in the covenant with Noah (Gen. 9:1, 7), and again with Abraham (Gen. 17:2) and Isaac (Gen. 26:4, 24), then with the nation of Israel (Deut. 7:13). Then it was renewed with all believers (Hos. 1:10; Rom. 9:26). And in the New Testament, the Apostle Paul tells us that God "made from one every nation of mankind to live on all the face of the earth, having determined their appointed times, and the boundaries of their habitation" (Acts 17:26, emphasis added). Clearly the Bible envisions, as part of God's purpose, a tremendous human population spread over the globe. (Beisner, *Prospects for Growth*, 50–52.)

21. E. Calvin Beisner, *Prospects for Growth: A Biblical View of Population,*

Resources, and the Future (Westchester, IL: Crossway Books, 1990), 114–17.

22. For *subdue* see Numbers 32:20–22; 32:29; Joshua 18:1; 1 Chronicles 22:17–19; 2 Chronicles 28:9–10; Nehemiah 5:5; Jeremiah 34:11, 16; Esther 7:8; Micah 7:19; Zechariah 9:15; for *rule* see Leviticus 25:39, 43, 46; 26:17; Numbers 24:19; Judges 5:13; 1 Kings 4:24; 5:16; 9:23; 2 Chronicles 8:10; Nehemiah 9:28; Psalm 49:14; 68:27; 72:8; 11:2; Isaiah 14:2, 6; 41:2; Jeremiah 5:31; Lamentations 1:13; Ezekiel 29:15; 34:4. See Francis Brown, S. R. Driver, and Charles A. Briggs, edd., *A Hebrew and English Lexicon of the Old Testament*, trans. Edward Robinson (Oxford: Clarendon Press, [1907] 1978), 461 and 921–22, respectively.

23. The Hebrew words so translated are *'âbad*, to work, and with the accusative of things, to till; and *shâmar*, to keep, watch, preserve, protect, or guard. See Brown, Driver, and Briggs, *Lexicon*, 713 and 1036.

24. Various writers—myself included—have mistakenly used Genesis 2:15 as if it told man to cultivate and guard the whole earth. See Beisner, *Prospects for Growth*, 131; Brian J. Walsh and J. Richard Middleton, *The Transforming Vision: Shaping a Christian World View* (Downers Grove, IL: InterVarsity Press, 1984), 54. Attention to the geographical information in Genesis 1–3, however, makes it clear that the garden was different from the rest of the world, and attention to the themes of garden (a symbol of life and blessing) and wilderness (a symbol of death and curse) in the rest of Scripture indicates that an important aspect of the cultural mandate was the call to transform the rest of the earth—which at the end of the events described in Genesis 3 was wilderness—into a garden. See appendix 5.

25. See Beisner, *Prospects for Growth*, 23–24.

26. As an aside, it is interesting to note, in contrast to the emerging biocentric ethic among many environmentalists, which insists that every species of life is of equal value, that Scripture recognizes a clear hierarchy of earthly life: man first, then animate life, and finally inanimate life. The gulf between animate and inanimate life is so great that in this passage God speaks as if plant life were not life at all. The gulf between human and animal life is equally great, so that just as man may kill and eat vegetables, so also he may kill and eat animals (Gen. 9:3), but "Whoever sheds the blood of man by man shall his blood be shed; for in the image of God has God made man" (Gen. 9:6).

27. Calvin, *Psalms*, 4(2):104–5.

28. Athanasius, *Letters*, 60.4, to Bishop Adelphius, in *A Select Library of the Nicene and Post–Nicene Fathers of the Christian Church*, second series, fourteen volumes, edited by Philip Schaff and Henry Wace, Volume IV, *St. Athanasius: Select Works and Letters*, translated by John Henry Cardinal Newman, edited by Archibald Robertson (Grand Rapids: Eerdmans, [1891] 1975), 576, emphases added.

29. Loren Wilkinson, ed., *Earthkeeping in the Nineties: Stewardship of Creation*, rev. ed. (Grand Rapids: Eerdmans, 1991), 108.

30. According to David B. Barrett, a statistician of missions, the number of professing Christians in the year 2000 will be nearly 2 billion—an increase of nearly 270 percent since 1900, while total world population will have increased by about 287 percent, for a net decline of professing Christians as a proportion of world population from 32.8 percent in 1900 to 31.4 percent in 2000. (Data calculated from statistics in David B. Barrett, "Statistics, Global," in *Dictionary of Pentecostal and Charismatic Movements*, edited by Stanley M. Burgess, Gary B. McGee, and Patrick H. Alexander (Grand Rapids: Zondervan, 1988), 812–13.) The decline of professing Christians *as a proportion of world population* over the century, however, masks a much sharper opposite trend during the last fifteen years of the century—from a low of 29.8 percent in 1985. If Barrett's historical statistics and projections are right, the proportion declined by 3 percentage points in eighty-five years but will have regained 1.6 percentage points—over half—in just fifteen years. Major increases in mission activity probably explain part of the reversal, but it is likely that long-term demographic trends also play an important role. The largely evangelized nations of Europe and North America experienced high rates of population growth, consequent to falling death rates caused by improved living standards, principally during the nineteenth century. The largely unevangelized nations of Asia and Africa, and to some extent Latin America, experienced high rates of population growth for the same reasons from about 1950 to 1980. The effect would be a temporary decline in the proportion of professing Christians—most of whom, at the turn of the century, were Europeans, North Americans, and Latin Americans—during the third quarter of the twentieth century. After that, declining population growth rates in Asia and Africa would contribute, with increased missions, to a reversal of the trend.

The anemic condition of much of Western Christianity discourages many Christians. They could be encouraged by the news from the rest of the world. In Latin America, the number of Protestants will have grown from about fifty thousand in 1900 to about 20 million in the year 2000—a stunning annual growth rate of 7.5 percent (far higher than the population growth rate); in Africa, it is likely that the number of Christians will have grown from under 10 million in 1900 to nearly 400 million in the year 2000 (John Jefferson Davis, *Christ's Victorious Kingdom: Postmillennialism Reconsidered* [Grand Rapids: Baker, 1986], 81). Similar rapid growth is occurring in Asia, with some missiologists predicting that South Korea will be the world's most Christianized nation within a decade or two, and the newsletter of Asian Outreach predicting that by the middle of the next century China will be the world's leading missionary sending nation.

For general discussion of the long-term impact of the growth of Christianity in the world, see Davis, *Christ's Victorious Kingdom*; Kenneth L. Gentry, *The Greatness of the Great Commission: The Christian Enterprise in a Fallen World* (Tyler, TX: Institute for Christian Economics, 1990); Peter J. Leithart, *The Kingdom and the Power: Rediscovering the Centrality of the Church* (Phillipsburg,

NJ: Presbyterian & Reformed, 1993); and four very helpful books by the Roman Catholic historian and sociologist of religion Christopher Dawson: *Religion and the Rise of Western Culture*, Gifford Lectures, 1948–1949 (London: Sheed & Ward, 1950); *Progress and Religion: An Historical Enquiry* (London: Sheed & Ward, 1938); *The Judgment of the Nations* (New York: Sheed & Ward, 1942); and *Dynamics of World History*, edited by John J. Mulloy (original edition, New York: Sheed & Ward, 1958; Mulloy edition, La Salle, IL: Sherwood Sugden & Company, 1978).

31. Some writers have argued that the clause "be fruitful and multiply and fill up the earth" is not a command. For example, Bratton writes, "Although set in the imperative, 'be fruitful and increase' is actually, as the Genesis texts clearly indicate, a blessing. . . . God's blessing is therefore not an ethical imperative. . . ." (*Six Billion & More*, 43). But the verbs are in the imperative, and her argument commits a fallacy of false choice. Command and blessing are not exclusive (as we see in the fact that the Fourth Commandment's prohibition of working on the sabbath translates into the blessing of rest). God blessed mankind by giving us the command to be fruitful and multiply, and we in turn are blessed when we obey the command: "Behold, children are a heritage from the LORD, the fruit of the womb is a reward. Like arrows in the hand of a warrior, so are the children of one's youth. Happy [blessed] is the man who has his quiver full of them" (Ps. 127:3–5); "Blessed is every one who fears the LORD, who walks in His ways. . . . Your wife shall be like a fruitful vine in the very heart of your house, your children like olive plants all around your table. Behold, thus shall the man be blessed who fears the LORD. The LORD bless you out of Zion, and may you see the good of Jerusalem all the days of your life. Yes, may you see your children's children" (Ps. 128:1, 3–6).

32. Some writers argue that the blessing/command for humans to multiply and fill up the earth is balanced and limited by the command for other creatures to do so, too. Calvin DeWitt writes, in his foreword to Bratton's *Six Billion & More*:

> If we read the Bible with ourselves in mind, we naturally see this blessing as ours. And it is. But it is not ours exclusively. It was given before we came. It was first given thus: "And God created great whales, and every living creature that moveth . . . and every winged fowl after his kind: and God saw that it was good. And God blessed them, saying, Be fruitful, and multiply, and fill the waters in the seas, and let fowl multiply in the earth" (Gen. 1:21–22, KJV).
>
> That *other* creatures are so blessed, and blessed first, is not only humbling for us but also critically important. The populations of creatures—in their wondrous variety of kinds—are expected by their Creator to bear fruit through God-given means of reproduction; they are expected to develop biological and ecological interrelationships; they are expected to bring fulfillment of the Creator's intentions for the good creation.
>
> God's blessed expectation for the populations of *other* creatures helps put our human population into context. We, *and they*, are blessed. We, *and they*, are

to reproduce, develop our kinds, and fulfill the earth to its God–intended completeness.

. . . .

Our human species thus is provided meaningful context by the scriptures: (1) Our own population joins with the populations of the other creatures God has made, participating one with another in the blessed expectation of reproducing and increasing our kinds, biologically and ecologically developing our kinds, and fulfilling the earth to its God-intended completeness, and (2) our own human kind enjoys this blessed expectation not only ourselves but also for the populations of all God's creatures.

It is here that we come to our present profound difficulty. Increasingly we people are occupying the land to the exclusion and extinction of the *other* creatures. This leads us to ask, "Does our God-given blessing of stewardship of creation grant us license to deny creatures God's blessing of fruitfulness and fulfillment? May we take this blessing of reflective rule to negate God's blessing to the fish of the sea and the birds of the air?"

We have come to a time when the impact of humankind—our exploding number multiplied by the power each wields and the defilement each brings [note the negative view of mankind inherent in this language]—not only denies the creatures fruitfulness and fulfillment but also extinguishes increasing numbers of them from the face of earth. . . .

. . . .

. . . . We people might not want to look at our exploding number and the per capita consumption and destruction [note the focus here, opposite what the image of God leads us to expect] by which this number is multiplied. But it is by such growth and multiplication that we have begun to empty the earth of its creatures. [DeWitt, "Foreword," in Bratton, *Six Billion & More*, 9–11. See also Bratton's similar argument, 42–3.]

But this argument founders on at least three points: (1) There is a substantive difference between what God told Adam and what He told the fish and birds: He told Adam to be fruitful, multiply, and fill up the *earth*, i.e., the land or ground, not the sea or the sky. (2) The argument commits the fallacy of false choice, treating man's filling up the earth as if it were exclusive of other creatures' doing so, but that is not logically necessary, and it is an empirical question whether it is actually so. It is, indeed, at the very heart of the population debate. For (3) to assume, as DeWitt's argument does, that continued human population growth must result in more species extinctions, and then to argue on that basis that continued human population growth is therefore not consistent with God's blessing/ command for other creatures to multiply is to assume the conclusion to prove the conclusion—to argue in a circle. It is at least theoretically possible for continued human population growth to go hand in hand with continued multiplication of other species. The Biblical vision of the image of God in man and of wise and righteous dominion sketched above leads to precisely that conclusion. And history indicates that people can, when they set out to do so, not only preserve species from extinction but multiply their numbers far beyond what would occur

naturally—as happens with any animals humans choose to cultivate. No one wor-
ries, after all, about chickens going extinct, although Americans alone now slaughter over 6 billion of them annually, or about wheat going extinct, although
Americans alone now harvest over 73 million tons annually. (U.S. Department of
Commerce, Bureau of the Census, S*tatistical Abstract of the United States, 1993*
[Washington: Government Printing Office, 1993], tables 1144, 1131.) At the risk
of being accused of crass anthropocentrism, let me point out that the key to ensuring the survival and flourishing of other creatures is to give people an incentive to
cultivate them, i.e., to exercise one of the elements of the cultural mandate. For
when people cultivate things, their multiplication increases so much that extinction ceases to be a live option.

33. For statistical and historical analysis, see, e.g., Julian L. Simon and Herman
Kahn, edd., *The Resourceful Earth: A Response to 'Global 2000'* (New York and
Oxford: Basil Blackwell, 1984), chapters 2–9A, 11–14, 15B; Julian L. Simon,
The Ultimate Resource (Princeton: Princeton University Press, 1981), chapters
1–10, and *Population Matters: People, Resources, Environment & Immigration*
(New Brunswick, NJ, and London, UK: Transaction Publishers/Hudson Institute,
1990), chapters 4–13; Max Singer, *Passage to a Human World: The Dynamics of
Creating Global Wealth* (Indianapolis: Hudson Institute, 1987), chapters 5–10;
Beisner, *Prospects for Growth*, chapters 5–7; and Julian L. Simon, ed., *The State
of Humanity* (Oxford: Blackwell, 1995), chapters 27–34.

34. It is also true that the total amount of any given mineral in the earth is
enormous relative to annual consumption—in most cases, enough for millions of
years at present rates (see Beisner, *Prospects for Growth*, 118, table 7–2). But it is
also true that much of the total of each of these minerals is so diffuse that, with
present technology, extracting and refining it would be prohibitively expensive.
Precisely how much is or, with changing technology, ever will become economically useable is a question to which only a prophet—not a mere scientist or economist—should venture an answer. It helps to keep in mind, though, that it is now
economically profitable to mine copper ores that are less than one-tenth as pure as
the least pure ores minable profitably around the turn of the century. The result is
an effective multiplication of the useful quantity of copper in the earth's crust by
hundreds or even thousands of times. Similar changes will surely take place in
mining and refining technologies for other minerals.

35. Daniel J. Boorstin, "A Case of Hypochondria," *Newsweek*, July 6, 1970,
28; cited in Julian L. Simon, *The Economics of Population Growth* (Princeton:
Princeton University Press, 1977), 499.

36. Fernand Braudel, *Civilization & Capitalism 15th-18th Century*, 3 volumes, trans. Siân Reynolds (San Francisco: Harper & Row, 1981, 1982, 1984),
Volume 1, *The Structures of Everyday Life*, 78–90.

37. See Simon and Kahn, edd., *The Resourceful Earth*, chapters 16–17; Simon,
ed., *The State of Humanity*, chapters 43–53; Simon, *The Ultimate Resource*, chapter

9; Simon, *Population Matters*, chapters 1–2; Singer, *Passage to a Human World*, chapters 11–13; Beisner, *Prospects for Growth*, chapter 8.

38. To be a little more precise, a detailed land use study in 1974 yielded an estimate of approximately 1 percent. The percentage is likely to have grown little since then, because most of the world's population growth has been urban, not rural, meaning that population is concentrating, not spreading out. C. A. Doxiadis and G. Papaioannou, *Ecumenopolis, the Inevitable City of the Future* (New York: W. W. Norton, 1974), 179; cited in Jacqueline Kasun, *The War Against Population: The Economics and Ideology of World Population Control* (San Francisco: Ignatius Press, 1988), 37, and in Beisner, *Prospects for Growth*, 57.

Appendix 1: The Garden and the Wilderness

1. It was previously published in E. Calvin Beisner, *Man, Economy, and the Environment in Biblical Perspective*, The Staley Distinguished Christian Scholar Lecture Series, Covenant College, 1991 (Moscow, ID: Canon Press, 1994), 21–34.

2. I am indebted to James Jordan and David Chilton for calling attention to how the Tabernacle and the New Jerusalem are modeled after the Garden of Eden.

3. For the importance of the concept of *logos* to the Biblical doctrine of man and of man's relationship to the rest of creation, see Gordon H. Clark, *The Johannine Logos*, 2d ed. (Jefferson, MD: Trinity Foundation, 1989), and Clark, *A Christian View of Men and Things: An Introduction to Philosophy*, 2d ed. (Jefferson, MD: Trinity Foundation, 1991). The tremendous importance of *logos*—reason, logic, rationality—to the image of God in man makes it alarming to see the attack on *logos* (often coupled with an attack on science and technology) that has become increasingly common in feminist—including "Christian feminist"—literature. E.g., Catharina J. M. Halkes, *New Creation: Christian Feminism and the Renewal of the Earth*, trans. Catherine Romanik (1989; Louisville, KY: Westminster/John Knox Press, 1991), chapter 8; Charlene Spretnak and Fritjof Capra, *Green Politics: The Global Promise*, rev. ed. (Santa Fe, NM: Bear & Company, 1986), 117–19 and elsewhere.

4. David Chilton, *Paradise Restored: An Eschatology of Dominion* (Tyler, TX: Reconstruction Press, 1985), 39–40.

5. Dixy Lee Ray, with Lou Guzzo, *Trashing the Planet: How Science Can Help Us Deal with Acid Rain, Depletion of the Ozone, and Nuclear Waste (Among Other Things)* (Washington: Regnery Gateway, 1990), 171.

6. Elizabeth Pennisi, "Conservation's Ecocentrics: A Wild, Some Say Macho, Vision for Saving Species," *Science News* 144:11 (September 11, 1993), 168–71.

APPENDIX 2: A Christian Perspective on Biodiversity

1. By listing ozone protection and enhanced greenhouse reduction among opportunity costs, I do not mean to imply that I agree with prevailing claims about those problems. I have argued against them in my *Prospects for Growth: A Biblical View of Population, Resources, and the Future* (Westchester, IL: Crossway Books, 1990) and in various articles and lectures since then.

2. Citations below from White's article are taken from a reprint as an appendix in Francis A. Schaeffer's *Pollution and the Death of Man* (Wheaton, IL: Tyndale House, 1970; reprint edition, Wheaton: Crossway Books, 1992), 121–44.

3. White, "Historical Roots," 133.

4. White, 124. White's assertion that modern science and technology have their roots in the late Renaissance and the Enlightenment, particularly in the works of Francis Bacon and René Descartes, perpetuates a common misunderstanding of the history of science—one prompted by the secularist notion that science and (especially Christian) religion are antithetical. Bacon was by no means the originator of inductive empirical method in the sciences and was, in fact, much more wedded to deductive method than is commonly thought. Further, inductive, empirical investigation leading to technological innovations had a long and fruitful history in the Middle Ages and was, in fact, precipitated by Biblical revelation and Christian doctrines founded on it. See Morris R. Cohen, "The Myth About Bacon and the Inductive Method," *Scientific Monthly* 23 (1926), 504–8, and Stanley L. Jaki, "Science and Censorship: Hélène Duhem and the Publication of the 'Système du monde'," *Intercollegiate Review* XXI (Winter 1985–1986), 41–49, who writes:

> In volumes 6 and 7 [of the *Système du monde*, the French historian and philosopher of science Pierre] Duhem presents a vastly documented tudy of the work of Buridan and Oresme. These two luminaries of fourteenth-century Sorbonne arrived at such scientific breakthroughs as the formulation of what later became known as Newton's first law of motion without which his second and third laws and the entire system of classical physics are inconceivable. . . . Most important, in those posthumous volumes Duhem stated most emphatically that Buridan and Oresme broke with the debilitating Aristotelian physics of motion by reflecting on what was demanded by the Christian dogma of creation in time and out of nothing. . . . What Duhem unearthed among other things from long-buried manuscripts was that supernatural revelation played a crucial liberating role in putting scientific speculation on the right track. But then the claim, so pivotal for the secularist anti-Christian interpretation of Western cultural history—that science and religion are in irreconcilable conflict—could only be deprived of its prima facie credibility. It is in this terrifying prospect for secular humanism, for which science is the redeemer of mankind, that lies the explanation of that grim and secretive censorship which has worked against Duhem (and his few allies) by two principal means: One is the prevention of major scholarly evidence in favor of Duhem's perspective to appear in print or at least to be printed by

"prominent" publishing houses. The other is selective indignation in scholarly societies and their journals—allegedly devoted to universal truth regardless of race, religion, and politics. [p. 48]

5. "Especially in its Western form, Christianity is the most anthropocentric religion the world has seen." White, 134.

6. White, 135.

7. White, 135.

8. White, 140.

9. White, 139.

10. White, 139.

11. White, 144; see also pages 141–43.

12. White, 134.

13. White, 134.

14. See, for example, Steven Rosen, "Ahimsa: Animals and the East," *The Animals' Agenda* (October 1990), 21–25.

15. Robert James Bidinotto, "Environmentalism: Freedom's Foe for the '90s," *The Freeman*, 40:11 (November 1990), 409–420, 410; citing Lindsy Van Gelder, "It's Not Nice to Mess with Mother Nature," *Ms.* (January/February 1989), 60.

16. Arne Naess, "The Shallow and the Deep, Long-range Ecology Movements: A Summary," *Inquiry* 16:95–100.

17. David Rothenberg, "Introduction: Ecosophy T: from intuition to system," in Arne Naess, *Ecology, Community and Lifestyle: Outline of an Ecosophy*, trans. and rev. David Rothenberg (Cambridge and New York: Cambridge University Press, 1989), 2.

18. Rothenberg, "Introduction," in Naess, 1.

19. Kim Bartlett, "Of Meat and Men: A Conversation with Carol Adams," *The Animals' Agenda* (October 1990), 13).

20. Rothenberg, "Introduction," 8, 9.

21. Naess, *Ecology, Community and Lifestyle*, 28.

22. Naess, 28.

23. Bidinotto, 414.

24. Harris, Godlovitch, and Godlovitch, *Animals, Men and Morals*; cited in Bidinotto, 412.

25. Naess, 28.

26. David Patrice Greanville, "Holocaust at the Animal Shelter," *The Animals' Agenda* (January/February 1990), 44.

27. Peter Singer, *Animal Liberation: A New Ethics for Our Treatment of Animals* (New York: Random House/New York Review Book, 1975), 7.

28. Patrick Corbett, "Postscript," in *Animals, Men and Morals*, by John Harris, Stanley Godlovitch, and Roslind Godlovitch (Taplinger Publishing, 1972), cited in Bidinotto, 412.

29. Raymond F. Surburg, "The Influence of Darwinism," in *Darwin, Evolution, and Creation*, ed. Paul A. Zimmerman (St. Louis: Concordia, 1959), 196. Furthermore, "Darwin and Nietzsche were the two philosophers studied by the National Socialists [Nazis] in working out the philosophy set forth in Hitler's *Mein Kampf.* In this work Hitler asserted that men rose from animals by fighting. It was the contention of the Fuehrer that this struggle, where one being feeds on another and the blood of the weaker is the life of the stronger, has continued from time immemorable and must continue until the most highly advanced branch of humanity dominates the whole earth." Surburg, 196.

30. Cited in David Noebel, *Understanding the Times: The Story of the Marxist/Leninist, Secular Humanist, and Biblical Christian Worldviews* (Manitou Springs, CO: Summit Press, 1991), 831; citing George C. Roche, *A World Without Heroes* (Hillsdale, MI: Hillsdale College Press, 1987), 248.

31. Bidinotto, 415.

32. *Baron's*, March 5, 1990, cited in Bidinotto, 412. See John G. Hubbell, "The 'Animal Rights' War on Medicine," *Reader's Digest* (June 1990), 70–76.

33. Desmond Morris, *The Animal Contract: Sharing the Planet* (London: Virgin Books, 1990), 169.

34. Jean L. McKechnie, et al., eds., *Webster's New Twentieth Century Dictionary of the English Language, Unabridged*, 2d ed. (USA: Collins-World, 1977), 234.

35. Bidinotto, 412.

36. Kingsley Davis, "The Climax of Population Growth," *California Medicine* 113 (November 1970), 33–39.

37. Kingsley Davis, "Population Policy and the Theory of Reproductive Motivation," *Economic Development and Cultural Change* 25 (Supplement, 1977), 176.

38. Sydney Singer, "The Neediest of All Animals," *The Animals' Agenda* (June 1990), 50–51.

39. Emphasis added; cited in the Regnery Gateway Fall/Winter 1993 book catalogue, p. 2, in advertisement for Kathleen Marquardt, with Herbert M. Levine and Mark LaRochelle, *Animalscam: The Beastly Abuse of Human Rights* (Washington: Regnery Gateway, 1993). Newkirk's equating the killing of Jews in the Holocaust with the killing of chickens for food echoes an increasingly common—and frightening—theme in environmental literature: likening ecological problems (which typically are unintentional and do not involve murder) with the Nazi Holocaust (which was intentional and murderous). See Charles T. Rubin, *The Green Crusade: Rethinking the Roots of Environmentalism* (New York: Macmillan/Free Press, 1994), 189–90.

40. Cited in Dixy Lee Ray, with Lou Guzzo, *Trashing the Planet: How Science Can Help Us Deal with Acid Rain, Depletion of the Ozone, and Nuclear Waste (Among Other Things)* (Washington: Regnery Gateway, 1990), 169.

41. Michael W. Fox, *Returning to Eden* (New York: Viking, 1980); cited in Bidinotto, "Environmentalism: Freedom's Foe for the '90s," 412.

42. David Brower, cited in Rael Jean Isaac and Erich Isaac, *The Coercive Utopians* (Washington: Regnery Gateway, 1985); also in Ray, *Trashing the Planet*, 169.

43. Cited in Ray, 168.

44. *New Age Journal* (September/October 1991), reprinted in *Reader's Digest* (April 1992), 147.

45. Cited in Evan Eisenberg, "The Call of the Wild," *New Republic* (April 30, 1990) p. 31. Naess apparently thinks so little of human beings that he cares little whether there are a hundred million or a billion of them, since elsewhere he suggests an ideal population of a billion; see Petr Borrelli, "The Ecophilosophers," *The Amicus Journal* (Spring 1988) 32–33.

46. Cited in Virginia I. Postrel, "The Green Road to Serfdom," *Reason* (April 1990) 24.

47. Cited in *Access to Energy* 17:4 (December 1989).

48. See Paul R. Ehrlich, *The Population Bomb*, rev. ed. (original edition 1968; New York: Ballantine, 1986); Paul R. Ehrlich and Anne H. Ehrlich, *The Population Explosion* (New York: Simon and Schuster, 1990); Kingsley Davis, "The Climax of Population Growth," *California Medicine* 113 (November 1970), 33–39; Jacqueline Kasun, *The War Against Population: The Economics and Ideology of Population Control* (San Francisco: Ignatius, 1988), 196; David Brower, cited in Rael Jean Isaac and Erich Isaac, *The Coercive Utopians* (Washington: Regnery Gateway, 1985); also in Ray, *Trashing the Planet*, 169. For a more thorough discussion of the anti-human attitudes that dominate much of the environmentalist movement, see E. Calvin Beisner, "Imago Dei and Population Concerns," lecture 1 of The Staley Distinguished Christian Scholar Lectures, Covenant College, October 29–31, 1991 (Moscow, ID: Canon Press, 1994).

49. For theoretical explanation and historical data proving decreasing resource scarcity, See Beisner, *Prospects for Growth*, 105–130.

50. T. C. Whitmore and J. A. Sayer, ed., *Tropical Deforestation and Species Extinction* (London and New York: Chapman & Hall, 1992).

51. See Julian L. Simon and Aaron Wildavsky, "On Species Loss, the Absence of Data, and Risks to Humanity," in *The Resourceful Earth: A Response to 'Global 2000'*, edited by Julian L. Simon and Herman Kahn (Oxford and New York: Basil Blackwell, 1984), 171–83. Simon and Wildavsky renew the charges, after reviewing the literature since their first article, in "Species Loss Revisited," in *The State of Humanity*, edited by Julian L. Simon (Oxford: Blackwell, 1995).

52. Notice an important thing Heywood and Stuart are *not* saying here, as well as what they really *are* saying. They are *not* saying that the loss of some 20 percent of the tropical forests would have led us to expect "very large numbers of species [to] have been lost [entirely to the world]," but only that the deforestation

would have led us to expect "very large numbers of species [to] have been lost *in some areas.*" And then what they *are* saying is that even this seemingly intuitively sensible expectation has turned out to be unconfirmed by the data: "Yet surprisingly there is no clear-cut evidence for this. . ."!

53. Norman Myers, *The Sinking Ark* (New York: Pergamon, 1979).

54. Norman Myers, "A Major Extinction Spasm: Predictable and Inevitable?" in *Conservation for the Twenty-first Century,* edited by David Western and Maryc C. Pearl (New York and Oxford: Oxford University Press, 1989).

55. Citing Ariel E. Lugo, ed., "Diversity of Tropical Species," in *Biology International,* special issue, 1989.

56. Simon and Wildavsky, "Species Loss Revisited," in *The State of Humanity.*

57. I have argued in *Prosperity and Poverty: The Compassionate Use of Resources in a World of Scarcity* (Westchester, IL: Crossway Books, 1988) that the Bible supports a free market economy, and have pointed out that this does not equate with a licentious market. There is no more role for false advertising or the sale, without adequate warning, of inherently unsafe products in the free market than there is for "Murder, Inc." or "Madam Molly's Marvelous Maids."

APPENDIX 3: Anomalies, the Good News, and the Debate over Population and Development

1. See Bruce F. Gardner and Theodore W. Schultz, "Trends in Soil Erosion and Farmland Quality," in *The State of Humanity,* edited by Julian L. Simon (Oxford: Blackwell, 1995).

2. See chapters 27–34 of *The State of Humanity,* ed. Simon.

3. See chapters 43–53 of *The State of Humanity,* ed. Simon.

4. See Roger A. Sedjo and Marion Clawson, "Global Forests Revisited," and Julian L. Simon and Aaron Wildavsky, "Species Loss Revisited," in *The State of Humanity,* ed. Simon. Even proponents of the theory of mass species extinction admit that "Known extinction rates are very low," that "the number of recorded extinctions for both plants and animals is very small" (V. H. Heywood and S. N. Stuart, "Species Extinctions in Tropical Forests," in *Tropical Deforestation and Species Extinction,* ed. T. C. Whitmore and J. A Sayer [New York: Chapman and Hall, 1992], 94, 93), and that "Closer examination of the existing data . . . supports the affirmation that little or no species extinction has yet occurred" (K. S. Brown and G. G. Brown, "Habitat Alteration and Species Loss in Brazilian Forests," in ibid., 128). No hard data exist to support claims of rapid extinction, and field studies have cast grave doubts on island biogeography theories on which high extinction rate hypotheses were based.

5. In reality, the human contribution to ozone-depleting chemicals is minute compared with nature's contribution—probably less than a tenth of a percent per

year—and there is no evidence of significant long-term trends in stratospheric ozone concentrations. See Dixy Lee Ray, with Lou Guzzo, *Environmental Overkill: Whatever Happened to Common Sense?* (Washington: Regnery Gateway, 1993), chapters 3–4, and S. Fred Singer, "Stratospheric Ozone: Science and Policy," in *The State of Humanity*, ed. Simon.

6. See J. Laurence Kulp, "Acid Rain," in *The State of Humanity*, ed. Simon, and Edward C. Krug, "Acid Rain: An Example of Environmental Epistemology," *Mining Engineering*, vol. 44, no. 12 (December 1992), 1431–34.

7. See Robert C. Balling, Jr., *The Heated Debate: Greenhouse Predictions versus Climate Reality* (San Francisco: Pacific Research Institute for Public Policy, 1992); Patrick Michaels, *Sound and Fury: The Science and Politics of Global Warming* (Washington: Cato Institute, 1992), and Michaels, "The Greenhouse Effect and Global Change: Review and Reappraisal," in *The State of Humanity*, ed. Simon; Sherwood B. Idso, *Carbon Dioxide and Global Change: Earth in Transition* (Tempe, AZ: Institute for Biospheric Research/IBR Press, 1989). Balling and Michaels, both climatologists who have focused extensive research on global warming theory and published heavily on it in refereed journals, argue that warming projections are vastly exaggerated and that the correlation between CO_2 increase and warming is neither simple nor strong. Idso, a research physicist specializing in the impact of CO_2 on plant health and soil ecology, argues that the beneficial effects of enhanced atmospheric CO_2 far outweigh the deleterious effects.

8. This qualifier would, in my view, almost never be met in the real world.

9. *The New York Times*, April 25, 1993; cited in *The Howard Phillips Issues and Strategy Bulletin*, May 31, 1993.

10. The World Bank, *World Development Report 1992: Development and the Environment* (New York: Oxford University Press, 1992), 273.

11. See Kenneth Hill, "The Decline of Childhood Mortality," and Samuel Preston, "Human Mortality Throughout History and Pre-History," in *The State of Humanity*, ed. Simon.

12. *World Development Report 1992*, 272.

13. See Robert W. Fogel, "The Contribution of Improved Nutrition to the Decline in Mortality Rates in Europe and America," in *The State of Humanity*, ed. Simon; Fogel, "Nutrition and the Decline in Mortality Since 1700: Some Additional Preliminary Findings," in *Long Term Factors in American Economic Growth*, edited by Stanley L. Engerman and Robert E. Gallman, Conference in Research in Income and Wealth, vol. 41 (Chicago: University of Chicago Press [for National Bureau for Economic Research], 1986); Fogel, "Second Thoughts on the European Escape from Hunger: Famines, Chronic Malnutrition, and Mortality Rates," in *Nutrition and Poverty*, edited by S. R. Osmani (Oxford: Clarendon Press, 1992); and Fogel, "Biomedical Approaches to the Estimation and Interpretation of Secular Trends in Labor Productivity, Equity, Morbidity, and Mortality

in Western Europe and America, 1780–1980," typescript, University of Chicago.

14. It should go without saying that where a long and intense civil war is taking place—as in Angola and Ethiopia—any alleged connection between poor economic performance and population growth is going to be untestable.

15. *World Development Report 1992*, 225.

16. The countries are: Angola, Benin, Botswana, Burkina Faso, Burundi, Cameroon, Central African Republic, Chad, Congo, Ethiopia, Gabon, Gambia, Ghana, Guinea, Guinea Bissau, Ivory Coast, Kenya, Liberia, Madagascar, Malawi, Mali, Mauritania, Mozambique, Namibia, Niger, Nigeria, Rwanda, Senegal, Sierra Leone, Somalia, Sudan, Tanzania, Togo, Uganda, Zaire, Zambia, and Zimbabwe.

17. The sources are *World Development Report 1992* and *Social Indicators of Development on 1991–92, Data on Diskette* (Washington: The World Bank, 1992 and annually).

18. *World Development Report 1992*, 273. Importing food does not mean people suffer from food shortages or general poverty, as illustrated by the fact that in 1990 Japan imported about 480 pounds of cereal per capita while Nigeria imported only about 10.

19. See, among many studies that indicate this, Maurice Schiff and Alberto Valdés, *The Plundering of Agriculture in Developing Countries* (Washington: The World Bank). For a poignant account of one such policy, see the chapter "Ethiopia: The Communist Uses of Famine," in Arch Puddington, *Failed Utopias: Methods of Coercion in Communist Regimes* (San Francisco: Institute for Contemporary Studies Press, 1988).

20. *World Development Report 1992*, 272–73.

21. U.S. Department of Commerce, Bureau of the Census, *Historical Statistics of the United States: Colonial Times to 1970*, (Washington: U.S. Government Printing Office, 1975), vol. 1, p. 57, Series B 136–147.

22. Max Singer, *Passage to a Human World: The Dynamics of Creating Global Wealth* (Indianapolis: Hudson Institute, 1987), 5–6.

23. Singer, *Passage to a Human World*, 36.

24. I discuss this at length in *Prospects for Growth: A Biblical View of Population, Resources, and the Future* (Westchester, IL: Crossway Books, 1990), chapters 6–7, and in *Man, Economy, and the Environment in Biblical Perspective*, The Staley Lectures, Covenant College, 1991 (Moscow, ID: Canon Press, 1994).

25. See Beisner, *Prospects for Growth*, 96–103.

26. I argued against an entitlement/distributivist definition of justice on Biblical grounds in "Justice and Poverty: Two Views Contrasted," *Transformation*, vol. 10, no. 1 (January/April 1993), 16–22, reprinted in expanded form in *Christianity and Economics in the Post-Cold War Era: The Oxford Declaration and Beyond*, edited by Herbert Schlossberg, Vinay Samuel, and Ronald J. Sider (Grand Rapids: Eerdmans, 1994), 57–80. See also my *Prosperity and Poverty: The Com-*

passionate Use of Resources in a World of Scarcity (Westchester, IL: Crossway Books, 1988), chapters 4–5. For an excellent (although largely secular) critique of an entitlement theory of justice, see Walter Block, "Private Property, Ethics, and Wealth Creation," in *The Capitalist Spirit: Toward a Religious Ethic of Wealth Creation*, edited by Peter L. Berger (San Francisco: Institute for Contemporary Studies, 1990).

27. A classic discussion of the strengths and weaknesses of democracy is Alexis de Tocqueville's *Democracy in America*, of which there are many editions. For more specific critiques of democracy in principle, see Lord Percy of Newcastle, *The Heresy of Democracy* (Chicago: Henry Regnery, 1955); Erik von Kuehnelt-Leddihn, *Liberty or Equality: The Challenge of Our Time*, rev. ed. (Front Royal, VA: Christendom Press, 1993); Kuehnelt-Leddihn, *Leftism Revisited: From de Sade and Marx to Hitler and Pol Pot*, rev. ed. (Washington: Regnery Gateway, 1990).

APPENDIX 4: A Critique of the Evangelical Declaration on the Care of Creation

1. The magazine's editors here deleted Gore's specifics: about 8,000 per year now, projected to increase to 100,000 per year by the turn of the century (p. 24, graph), or perhaps about 1,000 per century (10 per year) now (p. 24, text, implied), or about 36,000 per year now (p. 28), or simply "thousands per year" (pp. 121, 143).

2. Here I may have been mistaken. The figure common in the literature is four per century. But solid empirical evidence for this and almost all other figures regarding species extinction rates is almost entirely lacking.

APPENDIX 5: Issues and Evidence, Not *Ad Hominem*, Should Characterize Environmental Debate; A Response to Richard Wright

1. *Perspectives on Science and Christian Faith* 47:2 (June 1995), 80–91.

2. On which see Robert C. Balling (Ph.D., geography; director of the Office of Climatology and associate professor of geography at Arizona State University; author of over fifty papers on global warming in journals of climatology), *The Heated Debate: Greenhouse Predictions Versus Climate Reality* (San Francisco: Pacific Research Institute for Public Policy, 1992); Sherwood B. Idso (Ph.D., soil science; former adjunct professor in geology, geography, botany, and microbiology, Arizona State University; author of more than 400 articles in refereed journals, including some 70 on the effects of increased atmospheric CO_2), *Carbon Dioxide and Global Change: Earth in Transition* (Tempe, AZ: Institute for Biospheric Research/IBR Press, 1989); Patrick J. Michaels (Ph.D., climatology; associate professor of environmental sciences, University of Virginia; author of

many articles in refereed journals of climatology, forestry, and meteorology), *Sound and Fury: The Science and Politics of Global Warming* (Washington: Cato Institute, 1992); Frederick Seitz, Robert Jastrow, and William A. Nierenberg (all with Ph.D.s in fields relevant to global warming, and all having published on the subject in refereed journals), *Scientific Perspectives on the Greenhouse Problem* (Washington: George C. Marshall Institute, n.d.). (I include authors' credentials here and in the next two notes simply to head off *ad hominem* argument.)

3. On which see Edward C. Krug (Ph.D., soil chemistry; field scientist with the National Acid Precipitation Assessment Program, author of more than thirty articles in refereed journals), "The Great Acid Rain Flimflam," *Policy Review*, Spring 1990, 44–48; John J. McKetta (Ph.D., chemical engineering; author of more than 400 articles in refereed journals and of ten professional books, professor and chair of chemical engineering at the University of Texas, Austin), "Acid Rain—The Whole Story to Date," National Council for Environmental Balance, 1988; and J. Laurence Kulp (Ph.D., engineering; director of the National Acid Precipitation Assessment Program under the EPA; affiliate professor of civil engineering, University of Washington; author of many articles in refereed journals), "Acid Rain," in *The State of Humanity*, edited by Julian L. Simon (Oxford: Blackwell, 1995 [forthcoming]); and most importantly, National Acid Precipitation Assessment Program, *1990 Integrated Assessment Report* (Washington: NAPAP, 1991).

4. On which see Hugh W. Elsaesser (Ph.D. in dynamic meteorology, participating guest scientist at Lawrence Livermore National Laboratory, author of over 100 articles in refereed journals), "An Atmosphere of Paradox: From Acid Rain to Ozone," in *Rational Readings on Environmental Concerns*, edited by Jay H. Lehr (New York: Van Nostrand Reinhold, 1992); S. Fred Singer (Ph.D., physics; former professor of environmental sciences, University of Virginia; former chief scientist, U.S. Department of Transportation; former director, National Weather Satellite Center; presently director, Science and Environmental Policy Project; author of more than 400 articles in refereed journals), "My Adventures in the Ozone Layer," *National Review*, June 30, 1989, 34–38, and "Stratospheric Ozone: Science and Policy," in *The State of Humanity*, ed. Simon.

5. On which see T. C. Whitmore and J. A. Sayer, edd. (for the International Union for the Conservation of Nature), *Tropical Deforestation and Species Extinction* (London and New York: Chapman & Hall, 1992). This fascinating book took shape as an attempt to respond to various essays by Julian L. Simon and Aaron Wildavsky (e.g., Simon, "Disappearing Species, Deforestation and Data," *New Scientist*, May 15, 1986, and Simon and Wildavsky, "On Species Loss, the Absence of Data, and Risks to Humanity," in *The Resourceful Earth: A Response to 'Global 2000'*, edited by Julian L. Simon and Herman Kahn [Oxford: Blackwell, 1984]) charging that no sound empirical evidence existed for claimed rapid rates of species extinction. Despite this, the book's editors sum up the findings of the

many studies that led to the book as follows: "Many people have asked IUCN to comment on the numerous conflicting estimates of species extinction and some would like us to come up with a firm and definitive figure for the number of species which are being lost in a given period of time. The data available would not enable this to be done with any reasonable degree of scientific credibility and we have not attempted to do so in this book" (xi), and acknowledgment that expected rapid species loss as a result of habitat disruption has been disconfirmed appears in chapter after chapter.

6. Indur M. Goklany, "Richer Is Cleaner: Long-Term Trends in Global Air Quality," in *The True State of the Planet*, edited by Ronald Bailey (New York: Free Press, 1995), 339–77; The World Bank, *World Development Report, 1992* (Oxford and New York: Oxford University Press, 1992); G. Grossman and A. Krueger, *Environmental Impacts of a North American Free Trade Agreement*, Discussion Paper 158 (Princeton, NJ: Woodrow Wilson School, Princeton University, November 1991); N. Shafik and S. Bandyopadhyay, *Economic Growth and Environmental Quality: Time Series and Cross-Country Evidence*, Policy Research Working Papers (Washington: World Bank, June 1992); N. Shafik, *Economic Development and Patterns of Change*, Oxford Economic Papers (forthcoming). See also Mikhail Bernstam, "The Wealth of Nations and the Environment," Institute of Economic Affairs, 1991; cited in Gregg Easterbrook, *A Moment On the Earth: The Coming Age of Environmental Optimism* (New York: Viking, 1995), 330–31. Easterbrook also cites the work of Princeton University economists Gene Grossman and Alan Krueger showing "that countries increase pollution output as GNP climbs toward the level of about $5,000 per person in constant dollars. Then, as knowledge accumulates and affluence makes possible investments in emission controls, pollution begins to decline" (331).

7. Calculated from raw data for over 180 countries in The World Bank, *Social Indicators of Development on Diskette, 1994* (Washington: The World Bank, 1994).

8. Gregg Easterbrook, *A Moment on the Earth: The Coming Age of Environmental Optimism* (New York: Viking, 1995), 561.

9. Among his many books are *The Economics of Population Growth* (Princeton: Princeton University Press, 1977); *Basic Research Methods in Social Science*, 2d ed. (New York: McGraw, 1985); *The Economic Consequences of Immigration* (Oxford and New York: Blackwell, 1989); *Population and Development in Poor Countries* (Princeton University Press, 1992); *Population Matters: People, Resources, Environment, and Immigration* (New Brunswick, NJ: Transaction, 1989); *The Ultimate Resource* (Princeton University Press, 1982); (ed.) *Research in Population Economics*, 4 volumes (Greenwich, CT: Jai Press, 1978, 1980, 1981, 1981); (ed. with Herman Kahn) *The Resourceful Earth: A Response to 'Global 2000'* (Blackwell, 1984).

10. Among his books are *On Escalation: Metaphors and Scenarios* (Westport,

CT: Greenwood Press, 1965); *On Thermonuclear War* (Greenwood, [1961] 1978); *Thinking About the Unthinkable in the Nineteen Eighties* (New York: Simon & Schuster, 1985); (et al.) *The Next Two Hundred Years*, rev. ed. (New York: William Morrow, 1976); (ed. with Julian L. Simon) *The Resourceful Earth.*

11. Among his many books are (ed. for the AAAS) *Global Effects of Environmental Pollution: Proceedings of the American Association for the Advancement of Science Symposium, 1968* (Norwell, MA: Kluwer Academic, 1970); (ed.) *The Changing Global Environment* (Kluwer, 1975); (intro.) *Global Climate Change: Human and Natural Influences* (New York: Paragon House, 1989); *The Ocean in Human Affairs* (Paragon House, 1989); (ed.) *Physics of the Moon*, Science and Technology Series, Volume 13 (San Diego: American Astronautical Society/Univelt, 1967); (ed.) *Voyage to the Planets: Proceedings of the Goddard Memorial Symposium, 5th, 1967*, Science and Technology Series, Volume 16 (AAS/Univelt, 1968).

12. Among her books are (ed.) *Marine Boring and Fouling Organisms* (Seattle: University of Washington Press, 1959); (with Lou Guzzo) *Trashing the Planet: How Science Can Help Us Deal with Acid Rain, Depletion of the Ozone, and Nuclear Waste (Among Other Things)* (Washington: Regnery Gateway, 1990); (with Lou Guzzo) *Environmental Overkill: Whatever Happened to Common Sense?* (Washington: Regnery Gateway, 1993).

13. "In each of the last three decades [Lester Brown] proclaimed that world food production had peaked and food per capita would henceforth decline, leading to inevitable widespread famines.

"In 1967 . . . he asserted, 'The trend in grain stocks indicates clearly that 1961 marked a worldwide turning point . . . food consumption moved ahead of production.' . . .

"Again, in 1974, Brown predicted . . . that the end was nigh after world food stocks were drawn down following bad harvests in 1972 and 1974. Brown again saw the transition to the end . . . in 1984: 'If we go back to 1950 and look at the economic, agricultural, and social trends, we can see a clear breaking point somewhere around 1973.'

"In 1989, Brown once again keyed into reductions in the world's grain stocks and declared that global food shortages were at last at hand. His record remains unbroken; he has been wrong every time—world food supplies continue to grow while prices steadily decline." Ronald Bailey, *Eco-Scam: The False Prophets of Ecological Apocalypse* (New York: St. Martin's Press, 1993), 46, citing Lester Brown, "The World Outlook for Conventional Agriculture," *Science*, 158:604–611 (Nov. 3, 1967), 604; Lester Brown, *On the Fate of the Earth: Peace on and with the Earth for All Its Children* (San Francisco: Earth Island Institute, 1984), 141; and Lester Brown, *State of the World 1989* (New York: Norton/Worldwatch, 1989), 41.

PARTIAL BIBLIOGRAPHY

THE FOLLOWING LISTS THE MOST IMPORTANT BOOKS, ARTICLES, AND papers used in writing this book. Many other sources—some cited in footnotes—also were consulted.

Ackerman, Diane, et al. "Declaration of the 'Mission to Washington': The Joint Appeal by Religion and Science for the Environment," in *A Directory of Environmental Activities and Resources in the North American Religious Community*, 162–65. New York: Joint Appeal by Religion and Science for the Environment, 1992.

Adams, Lawrence E. "Green Visions for Green Christians." Unpublished paper on file.

Adler, Jonathan H. "Little Green Lies: The Environmental Miseducation of America's Children." *Policy Review*, Summer 1992, 18–26.

Aeschliman, Gordon. "Somebody got shot in the head: Creation after the fall." *Prism* 1:2 (December/January 1994), 7.

—————. "Editorial: Welcome to the Inaugural Issue of Green Cross." *Green Cross* 1:1 (Fall 1994), 5.

Anderson, Terry L., ed. *Multiple Conflicts Over Multiple Uses*. Bozeman, MT: Political Economy Research Center, 1994.

Anderson, Terry L., and Donald R. Leal. *Free Market Environmentalism*. San Francisco: Pacific Research Institute, 1991.

Anderson, Vinton R. "Statement by Religious Leaders at the Summit on Environment," June 1991, in *A Directory of Environmental Activities and Resources in the North American Religious Community*, 160–61. New

York: Joint Appeal by Religion and Science for the Environment, 1992.

Arnold, Ron, and Alan Gottlieb. *Trashing the Economy: How Runaway Environmentalism Is Wrecking America*. Bellevue, WA: Free Enterprise Press, 1993.

Au Sable Institute. *Official Bulletin, 1995*. Mancelona, MI: Au Sable Institute, 1995.

Bailey, Ronald. *Eco-Scam: The False Prophets of Ecological Apocalypse*. New York: St. Martin's Press, 1993.

Bailey, Ronald. "Raining in Their Hearts." *National Review* 42:23 (December 3, 1990), 32–36.

Bailey, Ronald, ed., *The True State of the Planet*. New York: Free Press, 1995.

Balling, Robert C. *The Heated Debate: Greenhouse Predictions Versus Climate Reality*. San Francisco: Pacific Research Institute for Public Policy, 1992.

Bandow, Doug. "Ecology as Religion: Faith in Place of Fact." Washington: Competitive Enterprise Institute, January 1993.

Barney, Gerald O., with Jane Blewett and Kristen R. Barney. Arlington, VA: Millennium Institute, 1993.

Basney, Lionel. *An Earth-Careful Way of Life: Christian Stewardship and the Environmental Crisis*. Downers Grove, IL: InterVarsity, 1994.

Bast, Joseph L., Peter J. Hill, and Richard C. Rue. *Eco-sanity: A Commonsense Guide to Environmentalism*. Lanham, MD: Madison Books/The Heartland Institute, 1994.

Beisner, E. Calvin. "Anomalies, the Good News, and the Debate over Population and Development." Review of *Six Billion and More: Human Population Regulation & Christian Ethics*, by Susan Power Bratton. *Stewardship Journal* 3:3 (Summer 1993), 44–53.

—————. "Are God's Resources Finite? A group of Christian leaders claim they are, but does the claim square with the evidence?" *World* 8:27 (November 27, 1993), 10–13.

—————. "A Christian Perspective on Biodiversity: Anthropocentric, Biocentric, and Theocentric Approaches to Bio-Stewardship." Address to the South Carolina Division of the Society of American Foresters, Annual Meeting, June 1–3, 1994, "Maintaining Biodiversity in a Free Society."

—————. "Clearing the Smog of Environmental Issues." *World* 5:22 (October 27, 1990), 7.

—————. "Deforestation of the truth—Eco/illogic: Taking issue with the claims of the Green Cross society." *World* 10:5 (April 22, 1995), 24–25.

——————. "The Double-Edged Sword of Multiculturalism." *Occasional Paper of the National Association of Evangelicals*, September 1994, abridged reprint of "The Double-edged Sword of Multiculturalism." *The Freeman*, 44:3 (March 1994), 104–12.

——————. "Environmental Concern: Is It Justified? Is There a Crisis?" Address to Reformed University Fellowship, University of Arkansas, Fayetteville, Arkansas, March 24, 1992.

——————. "Environmentalism or Stewardship? What Is the Christian's Responsibility?" in *Proceedings from the Seminar on Ecology and Religion* April 30–May 1, 1993. Washington: Competitive Enterprise Institute, 1993.

——————. "The Greening of the Cross." *The Freeman* 45:7 (July 1995), 429–32.

——————. "*Imago Dei* and the Population Debate." Address to the Christianity Today Institute on Population and Global Stewardship, Lisle, Illinois, April 21–23, 1994.

——————. "Issues and Evidence, Not *Ad Hominem*, Should Characterize Environmental Debate; A Response to Richard Wright." Prepublication draft submitted to *Perspectives on Science and Christian Faith*, scheduled for publication in December 1995.

——————. "It Cuts Both Ways: There Are Two Extremes in the Environmental Debate." *World* 7:34 (February 6, 1993), 16.

——————. "Justice and Poverty: Two Views Contrasted," in *Christianity and Economics in the Post-Cold War Era: The Oxford Declaration and Beyond*, edited by Herbert Schlossberg, Vinay Samuel, and Ronald J. Sider. Grand Rapids: Eerdmans, 1994.

——————. "Life As a Slug: A Perspective on Deep Ecology." *Crosswinds: The Reformation Digest* 3:1 (Summer 1995), 6–9.

——————. *Man, Economy and the Environment in Biblical Perspective.* The Staley Lectures, Covenant College, 1991. Revised edition, Moscow, ID: Canon Press, 1994.

——————. "Managing the Resources of the Earth." Address to the New Agenda For Justice Conference, Christian Public Policy Council, Falls Church, Virginia, January 27, 1989.

——————. "Out of Balance" (a review of Al Gore's *Earth in the Balance*), in *Where Do We Go From Here? An Agenda for Conservatives During Cultural Captivity*, edited by George Grant. Franklin, TN: Legacy Communications, 1993.

——————. "People Pollution." *Christian Renewal* 8:18 (June 18, 1990), 1,

15.

——————. "Population Growth As Blessing or Blight?" *Antithesis: A Review of Contemporary Christian Thought and Culture* 1:4 (July/August 1990), 14–21.

——————. *Prospects for Growth: A Biblical View of Population, Resources, and the Future*. Westchester, IL: Crossway Books, 1990 (out of print, available from the author).

——————. "Putting Environmental Myths into Perspective." Address to the Education Policy Conference of the Constitutional Coalition, St. Louis, Missouri, January 28, 1994.

——————. Rejoinder to "Another View: ESA's Sider takes issue with *World* critique." *World* 8:30 (January 8, 1994), 24.

——————. Review of *Earth in the Balance: Ecology and the Human Spirit*, by Albert Gore. *Principles in Politics* (Center for Public Policy, Covenant College), October/November 1992, 3-4.

——————. Review of *The Environment and the Christian: What Can We Learn from the New Testament?* ed. Calvin B. DeWitt. *World* 6:35 (February 15, 1992), 14–15.

——————. "Stewardship in a Free Market," in *The Christian Vision: Morality and the Marketplace*. Hillsdale, MI: Hillsdale College Press, 1994.

Bolch Ben, and Harold Lyons. *Apocalypse Not: Science, Economics, and Environmentalism*. Washington: Cato Institute, 1993.

Bratton, Susan Power. "A Fierce Green Fire Dying: Christian Land Ethics and Wild Nature." Au Sable Forum Papers, 1987: A Christian Land Ethic. Mancelona, MI: Au Sable Institute.

——————. "Christian Care for Creation: Across the Continents . . . Through the Centuries." *Green Cross* 1:2 (Winter 1995), 6–11.

——————. *Six Billion and More: Human Population Regulation and Christian Ethics*. Louisville, KY: Westminster/John Knox Press, 1992.

——————. "Six Billion Neighbors to Love: The Bible and Human Population Growth." *Prism* 2:2 (January 1995), 20–23.

——————. "The Worth of Every Child: Human population growth and reverence for life." *Sojourners* 23:7 (August 1994), 24–26.

Bray, Anna J. "The Ice Age Cometh: Remembering the Scare of Global Cooling." *Policy Review* 58 (Fall 1991), 82–84.

Campolo, Tony, and Gordon Aeschliman. *50 Ways You Can Help Save the Planet*. Downers Grove, IL: InterVarsity Press, 1992.

Carson, Rachel. *Silent Spring*. Boston: Houghton Mifflin, 1962.

Case, Debbie Pontynen. "Healing the Land: Floresta Plants Trees and Hope in

The Dominican Republic." *Green Cross* 1:1 (Fall 1994), 11.

Coffman, Michael S. *The Philosophy, Politics and Science of Biological Diversity*. Bangor, ME: Environmental Perspectives, 1994.

Coffman, Michael S. *Saviors of the Earth? The Politics and Religion of the Environmental Movement*. Chicago: Northfield, 1994.

Cole, H. S. D., et al., eds. *Models of Doom: A Critique of The Limits to Growth*. New York: Universe Books, 1973.

Council on Environmental Quality and Department of State. *The Global 2000 Report to the President*, volume 1. New York: Penguin Books, 1982.

Cromartie, Michael, ed. *The Nine Lives of Population Control*. Grand Rapids: Eerdmans/Washington: Ethics and Public Policy Center, 1995.

Culotta, Elizabeth. "Will Plants Profit From High CO_2?" *Science* 268 (May 5, 1995), 654–56.

Daley, Herman E. "Land and Resources: Nature's Forgotten Contribution." Au Sable Forum Papers, 1987: A Christian Land Ethic. Mancelona, MI: Au Sable Institute.

De Muer, D., and H. De Backer. "Revision of 20 Years of Dobson Total Ozone Data at Uccle (Belgium): Fictitious Dobson Total Ozone Trends Induced by Sulfur Dioxide Trends." *Journal of Geophysical Research* 97:D5 (April 20, 1992), 5921–37.

Derr, Thomas Sieger. "The Challenge of Biocentrism." November 1994. Paper presented to the Ethics and Public Policy Center Conference on the Environment, Washington, D.C., Spring 1995.

DeWitt, Calvin B. "Christian Environmental Stewardship: Preparing the Way for Action." *Perspectives on Science and Christian Faith* 46:2 (June 1994), 80–89.

—————. *Earth-Wise: A Biblical Response to Environmental Issues*. Grand Rapids: CRC Publications, 1994.

—————. "God's Love for the World and Creation's Environmental Challenge to Evangelical Christianity," *Evangelical Review of Theology* 17:2 (April 1993), 134–50.

—————. "Rekindling the Fierce Green Fire: Preface to a Christian Land Ethic." Au Sable Forum Papers, 1987: A Christian Land Ethic. Mancelona, MI: Au Sable Institute.

—————. "Seven Degradations of Creation," *Perspectives*, February, 1989, 4–8.

—————. "The Status of Creation: Scientific Evaluation and Biblical Response." Presentation to the Christianity Today Institute, The Environment and Christian Witness, Carol Stream, IL: October 28, 1993.

_____. "Take Good Care: It's God's Earth." *Prism* 1:2 (December/January 1994), 8–11.

DeWitt, Calvin B., ed., *The Environment and the Christian: What Can We Learn from the New Testament?* Grand Rapids: Baker, 1991.

DeWitt, Calvin B., and Ghillean T. Prance, eds., *Missionary Earthkeeping.* Macon, GA: Mercer University Press, 1992.

Drake, Susan. "The Global Forest: God's Provision for Life." *Green Cross* 1:1 (Fall 1994), 8–10, 12–15.

Durning, Alan Thein. "Consumption: The neglected variable in the population and environment equation." *Sojourners* 23:7 (August 1994), 20–23.

_____. "Deforestation: The Big Picture." *Green Cross* 1:1 (Fall 1994), 14.

Earth Works Group. *50 Simple Things You Can Do to Save the Earth.* Berkeley: EarthWorks Press, 1989.

Easterbrook, Gregg. "A House of Cards: Bitter and confusing, the debate over the greenhouse sheds more heat than light." *Newsweek*, June 1, 1992, 24, 29–33.

_____. *A Moment On the Earth: The Coming Age of Environmental Optimism.* New York: Viking, 1995.

Edwards, Denis. *Jesus the Wisdom of God: An Ecological Theology.* Maryknoll, NY: Orbis Books, 1995.

Ehrlich, Paul, and Anne Ehrlich. *Extinction: The Causes and Consequences of the Disappearance of Species.* New York: Random House, 1981.

_____. *Healing the Planet: Strategies for Resolving the Environmental Crisis.* Reading, PA: Addison-Wesley, 1991.

_____. *The Population Explosion: From Global Warming to Rain Forest Destruction, Famine, and Air and Water Pollution—Why Overpopulation is Our #1 Environmental Problem.* New York: Simon & Schuster, 1990.

Evangelical Environmental Network. *An Evangelical Declaration on the Care of Creation.* Philadelphia: EEN, 1993. Published, among other places in *Prism* 1:2 (December/January 1994), 12-14.

_____. *Let the Earth Be Glad: A Starter Kit for Evangelical Churches to Care for God's Creation.* Monrovia, CA: World Vision, 1994.

Finger, Thomas. "Modern Alienation and Trinitarian Creation," *Evangelical Review of Theology* 17:2 (April 1993), 190–208.

Foreman, Dave. *Confessions of an Eco-Warrior.* New York: Harmony Books, 1991.

Foundation for Economic Education. *Man and Nature.* Irvington-on-Hudson,

NY: FEE, 1993.

Fuller, Robert C. *Ecology of Care: An Interdisciplinary Analysis of the Self and Moral Obligation.* Louisville, KY: Westminster/John Knox Press, 1992.

Fumento, Michael. "The Prophets of Doom: How to Achieve Fame and Fortune by Being Spectacularly Wrong." *Crisis,* February 1991, 14–18.

——————. *Science Under Siege: Balancing Technology and the Environment.* New York: William Morrow, 1993.

Gehris, Kathy. *Stewardship of Creation: Guide for Older Children.* Resources for Outdoor Ministry. Philadelphia: Westminster Press, 1984.

Gelderloos, Orin. *Eco-Theology: The Judeo-Christian Tradition and the Politics of Ecological Decision Making.* Glasgow: Wild Goose Publications, 1992.

George, Ivy. "The Propaganda of Prosperity: The Human Cost of Maldevelopment." *Sojourners* 23:7 (August 1994), 15–18.

Gore, Al. *Earth in the Balance: Ecology and the Human Spirit.* New York: Houghton Mifflin, 1992.

Granberg-Michaelson, Wesley. *Ecology and Life: Accepting Our Environmental Responsibility.* Issues of Christian Conscience Series, ed. Vernon Grounds. Waco, TX: Word Books, 1988.

——————, ed. *Tending the Garden: Essays on the Gospel and the Earth.* Grand Rapids: Eerdmans, 1987.

Grizzle, Raymond E., and Michael G. Cogdill. "Subduing the Earth While Tending the Garden: A Proposal for a More Balanced Environmental Ethic," *Faculty Dialogue* 20 (Winter 1993–94), 73-81.

Halkes, Catharina J. M. *New Creation: Christian Feminism and the Renewal of the Earth,* trans. Catherine Romanik. 1989; Louisville, KY: Westminster/John Knox Press, 1991.

Hardin, Garrett. *Exploring New Ethics for Survival: The Voyage of Spaceship Beagle.* New York: Viking, 1972.

——————. *Filters Against Folly: How to Survive Despite Economists, Ecologists, and the Merely Eloquent.* New York: Viking, 1985.

Heyne, Paul. "Are Christians Called to be 'Stewards' of Creation?" *Stewardship Journal* 3:1 (Winter 1993), 17–22.

Hill, P. J. "Can Markets or Government Do More for the Environment?" Paper presented to the Ethics and Public Policy Center Conference on the Environment, Washington, D.C., Spring 1995.

——————. "Environmental Theology: A Judaic-Christian Defense." Unpublished paper presented to the Pacific Research Institute Colloquium

"The Ethics of a Free Economy." San Francisco, November 5-6, 1993.

——————. "Markets and the Environment: Friend of Foe?" Paper presented to the Ethics and Public Policy Center conference "Creation at Risk? Religion, Science, and Environmentalism," Washington, D.C., November 17–18, 1994.

Hodgson, Richard G. "The Earth: Our Lifeboat or Our Death-boat?" *Pro Rege* 22:3 (March 1994), 1–7.

Idso, Keith E., and Sherwood B. Idso. "Plant responses to atmospheric CO_2 enrichment in the face of environmental constraints: a review of the past 10 years' research." *Agricultural and Forest Meteorology* 69 (1994), 153–203.

Idso, Sherwood B. *Carbon Dioxide: Friend or Foe? An Inquiry into the Climatic and Agricultural Consequences of the Rapidly Rising CO_2 Content of Earth's Atmosphere*. Tempe, AZ: Institute for Biospheric Research/IBR Press, 1982.

——————. *Carbon Dioxide and Global Change: Earth in Transition*. Tempe, AZ: Institute for Biospheric Research/IBR Press, 1989.

Idso, Sherwood B., and Bruce A. Kimball. "Tree Growth in Carbon Dioxide Enriched Air and Its Implications for Global Carbon Cycling and Maximum Levels of Atmospheric CO_2." *Global Biogeochemical Cycles* 7:3 (September 1993), 537–55.

Intergovernmental Panel on Climate Change. *Climate Change: The IPCC Scientific Assessment*. Ed. J. T. Houghton, G. J. Jenkins, and J. J. Ephraums. Cambridge: Cambridge University Press, 1990.

——————. *Climate Change 1992: The Supplementary Report to the IPCC Scientific Assessment, Combined with Supporting Scientific Material*. Ed. J. T. Houghton, B. A. Callander, and S. K. Varney. Cambridge: Cambridge University Press, 1992.

Joint Appeal by Religion and Science for the Environment. *A Directory of Environmental Activities and Resources in the North American Religious Community*. New York: Joint Appeal by Religion and Science for the Environment, 1992.

Jordan, James B. *Through New Eyes: Developing a Biblical View of the World*. Brentwood, TN: Wolgemuth & Hyatt, 1988.

Kapur, Praveen (Sunil). "Let There Be Life: Theological Foundations for the Care and Keeping of Creation," *Evangelical Review of Theology* 17:2 (April 1993), 168–75.

Kasun, Jacqueline. *The War Against Population: The Economics and Ideology of Population Control*. San Francisco: Ignatius, 1988.

Kerr, Richard A. "A Fickle Sun Could Be Altering Earth's Climate After All." *Science* 269 (August 4, 1995), 633.

Kiessling, Kerstin-Lindahl, and Hans Landberg, eds. *Population, Economic Development, and the Environment*. Oxford: Oxford University Press, 1994.

Kitschelt, Herbert. *The Logics of Party Formation: Ecological Politics in Belgium and West Germany*. Ithaca, NY: Cornell University Press, 1989.

Kloosterman, Nelson D. "Environment as Religion: Matthew Fox's Creation Spirituality as a Paradigm for Environmental Ethics." Paper submitted for The Willard Environmental Ethics Symposium, April 15, 1993.

Kok, John H. "Contemporary Environmental Ethics: A Tempest in a Teapot," *Pro Rege* 22:3 (March 1994), 8–14.

Krueger, Fred. "Why Ecology Is a Christian Issue: A Historical Review of the Ecological Path Not Taken." *Green Cross* 1:2 (Winter 1995), 16–18.

Krug, Edward C. "Acid Rain: An Example of Environmental Epistemology." *Mining Engineering* 44:12 (December 1992), 1431–4.

—————. "'Environmentally Incorrect' Federal Employee Fired: Gore's Office Instrumental in Ouster." *Human Events*, May 22, 1993, 15.

—————. "Environmentalism: Abuse of a Just Cause." *Chronicles: A Magazine of American Culture*, June 1993, 44–46.

—————. "The Great Acid Rain Flimflam." *Policy Review* 52 (Spring 1990), 44–48.

Lamb, Henry, and Michael S. Coffman. *Global Biodiversity Assessment Section 9: Human Influences on Biodiversity: A Summary*. Bangor, ME: Environmental Perspectives, and Hollow Rock, TN: Environmental Conservation Organization, draft, October 5, 1994.

—————. *Global Biodiversity Assessment Section 10: Measures for Conservation of Biodiversity and Sustainable Use of its Components: A Summary*. Bangor, ME: Environmental Perspectives, and Hollow Rock, TN: Environmental Conservation Organization, draft, September 2, 1994.

Lehr, Jay H. ed. *Rational Readings on Environmental Concerns*. New York: Van Nostrand Reinhold, 1992.

Leithart, Peter J. "Snakes in the Garden: Sanctuaries, Sanctuary Pollution, and the Global Environment." Paper presented to an Ethics and Public Policy Center conference on Religion and Environmentalism, Spring 1993.

Leopold, Aldo. *A Sand County Almanac, with Essays on Conservation from Round River*. New York: Ballantine Books, 1966.

Livingstone, David N., et al. "Eco-Myths: Don't believe everything you hear about the church and the environmental crisis." *Christianity Today*, April

4, 1994: 22–33.

Longman, Karen. "Equipping Students with a Christian Land Ethic: The Role of Christian Colleges." Au Sable Forum Papers, 1987: A Christian Land Ethic. Mancelona, MI: Au Sable Institute.

Lovelock, James. *The Ages of Gaia: A Biography of Our Living Earth*, rev. ed.. New York: W. W. Norton, 1995.

Macaulay, Hugh. "Is Environmental Pollution the Principal Environmental Problem?" *The Freeman* 45:7 (July 1995), 426–28.

Makower, Joel. *The E-Factor: The Bottom-Line Approach to Environmentally Responsible Business*. New York: Plume/Penguin, 1994.

Manes, Christopher. *Green Rage: Radical Environmentalism and the Unmaking of Civilization*. Boston: Little, Brown, 1990.

Mann, Charles C., and Mark L. Plummer. "The High Cost of Biodiversity: A controversial plan to protect North American biodiversity calls for nothing less than resettling the entire continent. That may be too much to ask of the people who already live there." *Science* 260 (June 25, 1993), 1868–71.

Mastra, Wayan. "Environment and the Christian Faith: A Holistic Approach from Bali," *Evangelical Review of Theology* 17:2 (April 1993), 259–68.

Mazur, Laurie Ann, ed. *Beyond the Numbers: A Reader on Population, Consumption, and the Environment*. Washington: Island Press, 1994.

McDaniel, Jay B. *With Roots and Wings: Christianity in an Age of Ecology and Dialogue*. Maryknoll: Orbis Books, 1995.

McKibben, Bill. *The Comforting Whirlwind: God, Job, and the Scale of Creation*. Grand Rapids: Eerdmans, 1994.

Meeks, Catherine. "Subduing Nature . . . and People of Color: Race, class, and the theology of dominion." *Sojourners* 23:7 (August 1994), 29–30.

Menken, Jane. *World Population and U.S. Policy: The Choices Ahead*. New York and London: W. W. Norton, 1986.

Michaels, Patrick J. "Climate Change and Public Policy: Reaping the Whirlwind of Federal Monopoly." Unpublished paper, Department of Environmental Sciences, University of Virginia, Charlottesville, VA, n.d.

——————. "The Climate-Change Debacle: The Perils of Politicizing Science." Paper presented to the Ethics and Public Policy Center Conference on the Environment, Washington, D.C., Spring 1995.

——————. *Sound and Fury: The Science and Politics of Global Warming*. Washington: Cato Institute, 1992.

Miller, Janice. *This Blue Planet: Finding God in the Wonders of Nature*. Chicago: Moody Press, 1994.

Miller, Tracy C. "Environmental Policy: The Role of Property Rights and Markets," *Pro Rege* 22:3 (March 1994), 15–23.

Monastersky, Richard. "The Deforestation Debate: Estimates vary widely over the extent of forest loss." *Science News* 144:2 (July 10, 1993), 26–27.

Monsma, Stephen V., ed. *Responsible Technology: A Christian Perspective*. Grand Rapids: Eerdmans, 1986.

Morris, Desmond. *The Animal Contract: Sharing the Planet*. London: Virgin Books, 1990.

Mpanya, Mutombo. "African Land Ethics: Contribution to a Christian Perspective on Land." Au Sable Forum Papers, 1987: A Christian Land Ethic. Mancelona, MI: Au Sable Institute.

Nelson, Robert H. "Environmental and Scientific Values: A Conflict of Two Theological Traditions." Paper presented to a Conference on Business and the Environment: Applying Science to Environmental Policy in Canada and the United States. Big Sky, Montana, June 3–6, 1989.

——————. "Unoriginal Sin: The Judeo-Christian Roots of Ecotheology." *Policy Review* 53 (Summer 1990), 52–59.

Ngie, Modou. "Shaped By the Powerless: 'A new way of seeing' population, consumption, and the environment." *Sojourners* 23:7 (August 1994), 28–30.

Nicholls, Bruce J. "Responding Biblically to Creation: A Creator-Centered Response to the Earth," *Evangelical Review of Theology* 17:2 (April 1993), 209–22.

North, Gary. *Is the World Running Down? Crisis in the Christian Worldview*. Tyler, TX: Institute for Christian Economics/Dominion Press, 1988.

Olson, Edwin A. "A Response to Richard Wright's 'Tearing Down the Green'." Prepublication draft submitted to *Perspectives on Science and Christian Faith*.

——————. "Environmental PC—It Ain't Necessarily So." Paper presented to the annual meeting of the American Scientific Affiliation, Seattle, Washington, 1993.

Pauling, Sharon. "Too Many People?" *Sojourners* 23:7 (August 1994), 8–10.

Prance, Ghillean T. "The Contribution of the Indigenous Peoples of South America and of Christian Missions toward a Christian Land Ethic." Au Sable Forum Papers, 1987: A Christian Land Ethic. Mancelona, MI: Au Sable Institute.

Pratney, Winkey. *Healing the Land: A Supernatural View of Ecology*. Grand Rapids: Baker Book House/Chosen Books, 1993.

Ray, Dixy Lee, with Lou Guzzo. *Trashing the Planet: How Science Can Help*

Us Deal with Acid Rain, Depletion of the Ozone, and Nuclear Waste (Among Other Things). Washington: Regnery Gateway, 1990.

—————. *Environmental Overkill: Whatever Happened to Common Sense?* Washington: Regnery Gateway, 1993.

Redekop, Calvin, and Wilmar Stahl. "The Impact on the Environment of the Evangelization of the Native Tribes in the Paraguayan Chaco," *Evangelical Review of Theology* 17:2 (April 1993), 269–83.

Roberts, Leslie. "Academy Panel Split on Greenhouse Adaptation." *Science* 253 (September 13, 1991), 1206.

Rockefeller, Steven C., and John C. Elder. *Spirit and Nature: Why the Environment Is a Religious Issue*. Boston: Beacon Press, 1992.

Rubin, Charles T. *The Green Crusade: Rethinking the Roots of Environmentalism*. New York: Macmillan/Free Press, 1994.

—————. "Managing the Planet: The Politics of 'The Environment'." Paper presented to the Ethics and Public Policy Center Conference on the Environment, Washington, D.C., Spring 1994.

—————. "Who Says You Can't Have It All? The Politics of 'The Environment'." Paper presented to the Ethics and Public Policy Center conference "Creation at Risk? Religion, Science and the Environment," Washington, D.C., November 17–18, 1994.

Rubin, Edward S. *Global Warming Research: Learning from NAPAP's Mistakes*. Contemporary Issues Series 53. St. Louis: Washington University, Center for the Study of American Business, July 1992.

Ruether, Rosemary Radford. *Gaia & God: An Ecofeminist Theology of Earth Healing*. San Francisco: HarperCollins, [1992] 1994.

Sagan, Carl, et al. "An Open Letter to the Religious Community," January 1990, in *A Directory of Environmental Activities and Resources in the North American Religious Community*, 158–59. New York: Joint Appeal by Religion and Science for the Environment, 1992.

Schaeffer, Francis A., and Udo Middelman. *Pollution and the Death of Man*, rev. ed. Wheaton, IL: Crossway Books, 1992.

Schwarz, Hans. "A Critique of Christendom's Relation to Land with Direction Towards a Christian Land Ethic." Au Sable Forum Papers, 1987: A Christian Land Ethic. Mancelona, MI: Au Sable Institute.

Seaton, Chris. "Environment and Youth," *Evangelical Review of Theology* 17:2 (April 1993), 284–86.

—————. *Whose Earth?* Cambridge: Crossway Books, 1992.

Seitz, Frederick, Robert Jastrow, and William A. Nierenberg, *Scientific Perspectives on the Greenhouse Problem*. Washington: George C. Marshall

Institute, n.d.

Seitz, Russell. "A War Against Fire: The Uses of 'Global Warming.' *The National Interest* 20 (Summer 1990), 54–62.

Shaw, Vera C. *Thorns in the Garden: Meditations on the Creator's Care.* Nashville: Thomas Nelson, 1993.

Sheaffer, John R., and Raymond H. Brand. *Whatever Happened to Eden?* Wheaton: Tyndale House, 1980.

Sider, Ronald J. *One-Sided Christianity? Uniting the Church to Heal a Lost and Broken World.* Grand Rapids: Zondervan, and San Francisco: HarperCollins, 1993.

——————. "Redeeming the Environmentalists." *Christianity Today*, June 21, 1993, 26–29.

Simon, Julian L. "The Environmental Crisis That Isn't: A Reply to Arthur Waskow." *Moment*, June 1992, 48–49, 52, 61.

——————. *Population Matters: People, Resources, Environment, and Immigration.* New Brunswick, NJ: Transaction: 1990.

——————. *The Ultimate Resource.* Princeton: Princeton University Press, 1981; rev. ed. forthcoming.

Simon, Julian L., and Aaron Wildavsky. "Assessing the Empirical Basis of the 'Biodiversity Crisis'." Washington: Competitive Enterprise Institute, May 1993.

Simon, Julian L., and Herman Kahn, eds. *The Resourceful Earth: A Response to 'Global 2000'.* Oxford and New York: Blackwell, 1994.

Simon, Julian L., ed. *The State of Humanity.* Oxford and New York: Blackwell, 1995.

Singer, Max. *Passage to a Human World: The Dynamics of Creating Global Wealth.* Indianapolis: Hudson Institute, 1977.

Singer, S. Fred. *Free Market Energy: The Way to Benefit Consumers.* New York: Universe, 1984.

——————. "Stratospheric Ozone: Politically Correct and Other Views." *Economic Directions* 5:3 (April 1995), 1–6. (Center for Economic and Policy Education, Saint Vincent College, Latrobe, PA.)

——————. "Warming Theories Need Warning Label. The debate over global warming has been more hype than fact." *The Bulletin of the Atomic Scientists*, June 1992, 34–39.

Skole, David, and Compton Tucker. "Tropical Deforestation and Habitat Fragmentation in the Amazon: Satellite Data from 1978 to 1988." *Science* 260 (June 25, 1993), 1905–10.

Spretnak, Charlene, and Fritjof Capra. *Green Politics: The Global Promise,* rev. ed. Santa Fe, NM: Bear & Company, 1986.

Stewart, Ruth Goring. *Environmental Stewardship: 6 Studies for Individuals or Groups*. Global Issues Bible Studies, edited by Stephen Hayner and Gordon Aeschliman. Downers Grove, IL: InterVarsity Press, 1990.

Sugden, Chris. "Guest Editorial: Evangelicals and Environment in Process," *Evangelical Review of Theology* 17:2 (April 1993), 119–21.

Summerton, Neil W. "Principles for Environmental Policy," *Evangelical Review of Theology* 17:2 (April 1993), 225–40.

Thompson, Paul. "Thinking Beyond the Numbers: Population Issues and Global Stewardship." *Prism* 2:2 (January 1995), 10–19.

United Nations Environmental Programme. *Only One Earth*. New York: UNEP, 1989.

Van Dyke, Fred. "Beyond Sand County: A Biblical Perspective on Environmental Ethics." *Journal of the American Scientific Affiliation*, March 1985, 40–48.

——————. "Ethics and Management on U.S. Public Lands: Connections, Conflicts and Crises," *Evangelical Review of Theology* 17:2 (April 1993), 241–56.

——————. "Planetary Economies and Ecologies: The Christian World View and Recent Literature." *Perspectives on Science and Christian Faith* 40:2 (June 1988), 66–71.

Vander Zee, Delmar. "The Environmental Pulse in Academia," *Pro Rege* 22:3 (March 1994), 24–30.

Walsh, Brian J., and J. Richard Middleton. *The Transforming Vision: Shaping a Christian World View*. Downers Grove, IL: InterVarsity Press, 1984.

Whaley, R. S. "The World's Forests: A Brief Overview." *Green Cross* 1:1 (Fall 1994), 12.

Whitmore, T. C., and J. A. Sayer, eds. *Tropical Deforestation and Species Extinction*. London and New York: Chapman & Hall, 1992.

Wilkinson, Loren. "Gaia Spirituality: A Christian Critique," *Evangelical Review of Theology* 17:2 (April 1993), 176–89.

——————. "The Stewardship of Creation: Why Christians Ought to Be Environmentalists and Environmentalists Ought to Be Christians." *Green Cross* 1:1 (Fall 1994), 16–21.

Wilkinson, Loren, ed. *Earthkeeping in the Nineties: Stewardship of Creation*, rev. ed. Grand Rapids: Eerdmans, 1991.

Wise, David S. "Discovering the Importance of Christ in a Christian Land Ethic." Au Sable Forum Papers, 1987: A Christian Land Ethic. Mancelona, MI: Au Sable Institute.

Wolters, Albert M. *Creation Regained: Biblical Basics for a Reformational Worldview*. Grand Rapids: Eerdmans, 1985.

World Evangelical Fellowship Theological Commission and Au Sable Institute Forum. "Evangelical Christianity and the Environment," August 26–31, 1992, *Evangelical Review of Theology* 17:2 (April 1993), 122–33.

World Resources Institute. *The 1992 Information Please Environmental Almanac*. New York: Houghton Mifflin, 1992.

Wright, Chris. "Biblical Reflections on Land," *Evangelical Review of Theology* 17:2 (April 1993), 153–67.

Wright, Richard T. "Tearing Down the Green: Environmental Backlash in the Evangelical Sub-Culture." *Perspectives on Science and Christian Faith* 47:2 (June 1995), 80–91.

Young, John M. L. "Theology of Missions, Covenant-centered." *Christianity Today*, November 22, 1968, 10–11, 13.

Young, Richard A. *Healing the Earth: A Theocentric Perspective on Environmental Problems and Their Solutions*. Nashville: Broadman & Holman, 1994.

INDEX OF SCRIPTURE REFERENCES

INDEX OF SUBJECTS

INDEX OF PERSONS